THE RIGHTEOUS OF SWITZERLAND:

HEROES OF THE HOLOCAUST

THE RIGHTEOUS OF SWITZERLAND:

HEROES OF THE HOLOCAUST

by

Meir Wagner

edited by
Andreas C. Fischer
and
Graham Buik

Ktav Publishing House, Inc.

Library of Congress Cataloging-in-Publication Data

Wagner, Meir..
    The righteous of Switzerland : heroes of the Holocaust / by Meir Wagner. edited by
Andreas C. Fischer, Graham Buik.
    p. cm.
ISBN 0-88125-698-6
    1. Righteous Gentiles in the Holocaust-- Switzerland --Biography. 2. World War,
1939-1945--Jews--rescue--Switzerland. 3. Holocaust, Jewish (1939-1945)--Personal
narratives. I. Fischer, Andreas C., Buik, Graham II. Title.

D804.65 W34 2000
940.53'18--dc21

                                                                        00-046487

Distributed by
Ktav Publishing House, Inc.
900 Jefferson Street
Hoboken, NJ 07030
201-963-9524 FAX 201-963-0102
Email ktav@compuserve.com

Dedicated to the people of Switzerland

Table of Contents

Introduction

The original reason for writing this book was to document the humanitarian acts of Swiss citizens who helped to save Jewish lives during World War II and whose efforts have been recognized by the awarding of the Yad Vashem "Righteous Among the Nations" medal.

In terms of its original purpose, this book is now complete. The stories of the thirty-seven Swiss men and women honored as "Righteous Among the Nations" between 1964 and 1999 are all contained within its compass, and they form the heart of the book. But that is not "the end of the story". Indeed, two more Swiss citizens have recently been nominated by Yad Vashem.

Meanwhile, in the course of researching this book, the humanitarian deeds of other individuals have also come to light. These often unassuming heroes did not seek publicity, but their stories, too, deserve to be told. Accordingly, it was decided to extend the scope of this book to include some other lesser-known accounts of Swiss citizens who helped save Jewish lives during the war. Some of them are being published here for the first time.

A word about the structure of the book would be appropriate here. Each chapter is built around the actions of one or more individuals and their particular part in the events they lived through. To this end, eyewitness accounts and testimonials have been used extensively. Thus, while each chapter is a story in itself, it does not purport to give a comprehensive history of the events it describes—or, indeed, full details of the involvement of other individuals. In some cases, the people, places and events overlap, and certain chapters (particularly concerning the children at La Hille castle) naturally complement each other with additional insights and details.

The people honored in this book were not afraid to think for themselves. In this book, they also speak for themselves—and sometimes they are very outspoken indeed. They touch on issues that are of considerable interest and importance in the context of twentieth-century history. Much work still remains to be done in addressing some of these issues systematically.

Here, suffice it to say that, in conversations on both sides of the Atlantic, the author and editors have been struck repeatedly by the fact that two factors often seem to be overlooked concerning Switzerland and World War II. For the record, we mention them here:

1) During the war itself, some 21,000 Jewish refugees did ultimately find refuge and safety in Switzerland. A further 20,000 Jews of Swiss nationality also lived safely in Switzerland during the war.

2) By virtue of its political neutrality, Switzerland was able to represent the diplomatic interests of 43 nations during World War II, including the United States and Britain. One subsidiary effect of this was that it helped make possible the rescue work of Swiss diplomats (such as Carl Lutz and Harald Feller in Budapest), and facilitated the humanitarian activities of the Swiss Red Cross, several of whose delegates are profiled in this book.

But back to the stories themselves. The rescue efforts were often a matter of teamwork. Thus, the names of some "Righteous Among the Nations" of other countries also appear in these pages—including some well-known names like Raoul Wallenberg of Sweden (see "The Courageous Consul in Besieged Budapest") as well as Pastor André Trocmé and the inhabitants of Le Chambon-sur-Lignon (see "Rallying a Town to Stand Up to the Oppressor").

Other "Righteous" of French nationality to whom particular tribute is paid in these pages include Ernest Brouze and Germaine Brouze (see "The Good Samaritan's Summerhouse Refuge"), Germaine Hommel, Léon Balland and Marthe Bouvard (see "Masterminding the Escape"), and Jean Deffaugt (see "Triumphs and Tragedies in the Life of a 'Schlepper'")— while Marianne Cohn, a heroine of the Jewish Resistance, is also mentioned in the same chapter.

If we have omitted any names or failed to acknowledge the role of other individuals in any instance, this was emphatically not our intention. Readers are invited to share additional experiences and memories, for possible inclusion in later editions, while any corrections or clarifications would be gratefully welcomed.

Any copyright holders who have not been acknowledged or identified in respect of material reproduced herein are also requested to contact the publisher so that appropriate rectification can be made.

This book is offered as a contribution to the ongoing endeavors of historical documentation, as a source book, and as a starting point for further research and study. The positive examples it contains deserve to be celebrated. They also challenge each reader to ponder some searching questions that deserve to be answered. How willing would we have been to stand up for justice and humanity in circumstances similar to those recounted here? How willing are we to do so today?

Future generations need to hear the stories of these brave men and women—and others like them. Their testimony is unanimous and unequivocal: regardless of the circumstances, regardless of the political system under which one has to operate, evil and injustice must be resisted, not ignored. In the face of these examples, no excuses will pass muster. For those who follow the voice of their conscience, there will always be a way.

Acknowledgements

I would like to thank personally all those who have contributed in so many different ways to making this book possible:

Federal Councilor and former President of the Swiss Confederation Flavio Cotti, and National Councilor François Loeb. Winterthur Insurance (Winterthur); Novartis International AG (Basle); Nestlé SA (Vevey); the Coordination Commission for the Presence of Switzerland Abroad of the Ministry of Foreign Affairs (Berne); Mr Adi Gast, Zurich; Mr Mark Hager, ALM International Corp., New York; and the Foundation of the UBS, Zurich.

Moshe Meisels for his initial research and compiling material for the first German version of the book; Andreas C. Fischer for his translation of the German version into English as well as contributing considerable additional research and new material; Graham Buik and his sister Shirley McLean for their excellent editing, verification and proofreading work; Else Ruth Wagner, Gene H. Hogberg, Roger Schärer and Richard O. Marsh for their valuable input and editorial help.

Cornelio Sommaruga, the former President of the International Committee of the Red Cross, and Martin Morger at the ICRC library in Geneva.

Faith Whittlesey, the former US Ambassador to Switzerland, who has seen the value of this publication as a contribution to better understanding between the USA and Switzerland.

Particular thanks are also due to some of those whose names are mentioned in the pages of this book: Harald Feller, Marcel Pasche, Federal Court Judge Dr. Vera Rottenberg-Liatowitsch, Eva Koralnik-Rottenberg, Renée Leder-Wittels, Françoise Reymond, René Bouvet, and especially Anne-Marie Im Hof-Piguet and Herbert Herz, who provided many helpful suggestions and valuable additional material.

Ákos Kerényi helped us a lot by expertly guiding us through Budapest—the Lutz and Born sites—and by his hospitality.

Dr. Uriel Gast and Jonas Arnold contributed considerably by providing us with essential pictorial material of great historic value from the Archiv für Zeitgeschichte at the ETH University of Zurich. The help of Brigitte Thomas and the Alliance Amicale du Vernet is also gratefully acknowledged.

Last but not least, Bernard Scharfstein and his team at Ktav Publishing House, Inc. for their part in making this book a reality.

A great deal of effort has gone into the preparation and verification of the material contained in this book. Notification of any possible errors or omissions would, however, be appreciated.

Meir Wagner
Basle, October 2000

Unsung Heroes of the Holocaust

This book tells the little-known stories of brave Swiss citizens who saved Jewish lives during World War II. While their government pursued an official policy of neutrality, these courageous men and women listened only to the voice of their conscience. They risked opposition, hardship, danger and death to help fellow human beings in need. As a result of their determined efforts, multiple thousands of lives were saved.

These unassuming heroes have too long remained in obscurity. Most of them avoid publicity—their only concern was to do what they could to help. But justice and historical accuracy demand that their stories be told.

Drawing extensively on the testimonials of eyewitnesses and those whose lives were saved, Meir Wagner presents accessible accounts of the actions of these courageous men and women—and the convictions which motivated them. Their ranks include diplomats, Red Cross delegates and volunteers, clergymen, nuns, as well as "ordinary" citizens quietly going about their daily lives, resourceful and resolute in their unrelenting struggle to rescue the innocent. Their testament to humanity is unanimous and unequivocal. These are individuals who refused to compromise in the face of evil. They did not shrink from disobeying orders and instructions where these conflicted with the dictates of their conscience.

Many of them have been recognized by the Yad Vashem Holocaust Memorial in Jerusalem and honored with the "Righteous Among the Nations" medal; the deeds of others are only now coming to light. Their stories constitute a witness to future generations that, in the face of overwhelming darkness and despair, the flame of humanity was kept alight.

In a world that is quick to forget, to relativize, this book is a timely reminder that some things are, indeed, sacred. Moral character, true humanity—these are values that must never be allowed to go out of fashion. Here are role models worth emulating. Here are positive examples that deserve to be celebrated. These are stories to read and re-read. This is a book to keep and to treasure—but also, above all, a book to be shared. The author and publisher hope that every reader will find inspiration and encouragement from its contents—and realize the urgency of sharing this precious heritage with the next generation.

Foreword

by Federal Councilor Joseph Deiss,
Head of the Swiss Federal Department of Foreign Affairs

History is a patchwork of light and shadow, the skeins inextricably tangled. And the way we read history is never fixed. The debate on the role of Switzerland in World War II is a case in point.

This debate began very early, in fact during the War itself. It has intensified since the 1960s. From the start, it was a variegated tapestry, often unknown abroad: translations of books on Swiss history are few and far between.

New studies and new testimonies are constantly enriching our analysis of Switzerland's behavior during World War II. This work marks an important step in this direction.

This volume traces the fate and deeds of courage that have too often and too long gone unrecognized. It also reproduces the moving testimony of people whose lives were saved. These accounts demand our fullest and undivided attention.

Let us pay heed to this great lesson of humanity that all these Righteous teach us.

Let us pay heed so that we do not ever forget.

Joseph Deiss

National Councilor François Loeb

For someone from a later generation, writing a preface about the "Righteous" of Switzerland is no easy task.

No easy task because I experienced the appalling cruelty of National Socialism subconsciously as a haunting, crippling angst gripping our country and me with it.

No easy task because every realization, each change from subconscious to conscious, requires us to look unsparingly into the mirror.

No easy task because experiencing this consciousness also brings into question how we act today and how we will act in the future.

As someone from a later generation, writing a preface about the "Righteous" of Switzerland fills me with gratitude.

Gratitude that, even in Europe's darkest hours, there were human beings who acted with humanity.

Gratitude that people of our nation stood out like beacons to show the way.

Gratitude that the "Righteous" are even yet showing us the way of humanity for the present and the future, challenging us to take a stand against injustice, whatever form it takes.

Gratitude that I, in contrast to those who were persecuted, should live to learn from the example of the "Righteous".

François Loeb

Statement by Herbert Herz
Delegate of Yad Vashem

In those evil times, the Jews were considered fair game. First in Germany, then in the countries occupied in the rapid-fire triumphs of the German Wehrmacht. The Nazi barbarians and their henchmen raged mercilessly against those human beings whose only crime was to have been born Jewish. Some men and women revolted against the injustice and extended a helping hand.

These women and men followed only their conscience. They showed human solidarity and opened their homes to those persecuted souls. Or they helped them in other ways, going against the laws of the land in spite of all the risks that that involved. Yad Vashem calls them "Righteous," those saviors, no matter whether it was one Jew or hundreds of Jews that they saved by their selfless actions and at risk to their own lives. On the medal is engraved a proverb from the Talmud: "Whoever saves one soul has saved the whole universe."

Of the seventeen thousand "Righteous Among the Nations" recognized by Yad Vashem, thirty-seven of Swiss nationality are registered. That is honorable for a country that was spared from Nazi occupation. It is time to bring these "Righteous" out of the forgotten shadows and into the light of day, as a credit to their country and an example for the younger generation.

If you ask the "Righteous" what motivated them, they will say with one accord that they were impelled by an inner strength. They could not have acted differently—it would have been unthinkable for them to stand by as spectators to the misery around them and not get involved.

Besides the acknowledged "Righteous," there are also a sizable number of other Swiss citizens who would have merited recognition. We know of many cases, but we lack the testimonial statements of those whom they saved. After more than fifty years, that is hardly surprising. The commission for recognition of the "Righteous" in Israel is very meticulous about testimonial statements and evidence. The list of the honored of Switzerland is not a closed list. We are continuing our research. For us it is a matter of justice.

In the name of Yad Vashem and all the survivors of the Shoah, the Jewish people express their everlasting appreciation to the "Righteous Among the Nations" recorded in this book. Their thanks also applies to all of those nameless Swiss men and women who helped Jews to escape from the Nazi henchmen.

The lessons of the past are only of value if they serve the present and help to shape the future. The epic of the "Righteous," true heroes of whom their homeland can be proud, teaches us: There is a duty to disobey orders if those orders are inhumane or offend against the conscience.

Herbert Herz
Geneva, September 2000

The Chairman of the International Committee of Yad Vashem

It was my fortune to live the first year of World War II in Switzerland, so I do remember the anguish of this neutral, internationally respected country. Then I had the fortune in the summer of 1940 to return to Jerusalem via Mozambique and Cairo.

There was a crescendo of hatred and depression that threw its shadow over all of Europe in those dark, cruel days.

Righteous Swiss citizens kept the candle of humanity alight in this time of cruel darkness. Those righteous men and women gave us the will to continue and gave us faith in G-d and man.

As Chairman of the International Committee of Yad Vashem, I welcome the initiative to publish a book dedicated to the memory of people that lived a life of values in the awful period of destruction.

Dr. Josef Burg

Speech given by Yitzhak Mayer, Ambassador of Israel, on September 6, 1999, at the Amtshaus in Berne

Ceremony to Honor the "Righteous Among the Nations" Award of the Medals of Yad Vashem

"You who are about to be honored are the letter of indictment against the silent masses"

The "Righteous Among the Nations" medal, for having shown the courage of one's convictions in the past, is an act of consolidation, an act of healing for the future.

Coming generations will be overwhelmed by hopelessness for mankind when they critically look at the history of the present century. What else could be their feeling when they faced the depth of the abyss in which man had obviously fallen? It would be impossible for them to reconcile the verse in the book of Genesis according to which we are all created in God's likeness with the horrific images of men and women, young and old, robbed of their dignity, packed into cattle wagons, sent to the gas chambers and herded together at the edge of common graves by their own kind. By itself it is a tragedy of hitherto unparalleled dimensions, because it has shaken the foundations of faith itself.

The feeling of hopelessness must increase when one gains the knowledge that the Holocaust was the result of the demoniac ruling class who openly and shamelessly committed their hideous crimes and the silent masses brought into line. Silence perhaps is a misleading expression because in fact their quiet was approving, consenting. It reached from a hysterical "Yes!" to self-conditioned participation. Millions of upright citizens of villages and towns all over Europe, who had been taught to live according to God's laws and to love their neighbor, got up every morning to fulfill their eight-hour Shoah working day.

They were punctual and efficient. They attached great value to doing excellent work so that they would merit the respect of their superiors and friends. They worked hard, for days and weeks and months, to perfect themselves in the basics of their duties. They never ever stopped to realize in horror that they were engaging in the most massive genocide history had ever seen. They were the crushing weight of the giant guillotine set in motion over the world by the executioners of Berlin. The question of the Holocaust, then, is not so much what happened but, first and foremost, how it was possible that it could happen. The answer can only be hopelessness.

We are gathered here today to honor men who stood up from the blind and dazzled masses, who thought of the value of their own humanness and who at the risk of their own life saved lives of people they had never seen before, to whom they did not owe a favor, except perhaps their own decision to resist bestiality. These humans did not expect thanks, but they saved the honor of humankind. The commemoration of their deeds builds up hope again and is testimony to the truth of the Bible verse that man was created in God's own image.

These men must give the undeniable testimonial to coming generations that there is hope for the future because there were men and women like them in the past.

The courage to stand up for one's convictions is perhaps the highest of virtues. It includes all other virtues. When the inner gauge for justice gets under pressure, this courage is awakened. When a fellow human being, completely encircled, cries out for help, then his pleas must call for sympathy and immediate action because this courage will respond. When streets and squares, cities and countries bow as if hypnotized to the omnipresent evil, and not a single voice shouts "Stop it!", and when the one who dares to has been brutally quieted and lynched, then this courage is awakened.

Read aloud the stories of the heroes who are honored today. Read the stories of the ones who left us before we became aware of what they had done so that we could not thank them—for we owe them eternal gratitude. Let us rejoice for those who are still among us and to whom we can give thanks while they are alive. This is an anthology of the courage to stand up for one's convictions. Tell the stories in the classrooms, on the radio, in your television studios. Weave them into your literature and stage plays, your scripts and novels. Spread the optimism and trust in the human capacity to rise to unimaginable heights of moral perfection. These are the heroes—Swiss heroes because they are Swiss—universal heroes because they are humans.

The debate has shaken again most recently the positions which did not dare to articulate at that time. While deep convictions have been freed from the self-imposed silence, they are now showing clearly the syndrome of persecutors against the persecuted.

This corresponds to a famous Midrash interpretation of the Semitic word "Ivri", Hebrew, which means "on the other side of a borderline." The Jew would be on one side of an imaginary river and the whole world on the other side. The words, however, maybe instinctively chosen but today universally accepted to describe the planned extermination of the Jews during the Second World War, have nothing to do with this interpretation. The Greek word *Holocaust* sees an altar in the cremating chamber where the killed Jews are brought as a sacrifice and consumed entirely by the fire. This view nears the religious and means resignation; it sees it as a cosmic drama in which God has given the exact roles to the slaughterer and the one to be slaughtered.

The Hebrew word *Shoah*—catastrophe—sees a tragedy in the mass execution of the Jewish people, a tragedy in which nature has unleashed and deployed its horrifying power, like an earthquake, a flood, or a hurricane. There is no finger of accusation—neither in the word *Holocaust* nor in *Shoah*. There is no "What have you done to us all?", no separation between the persecutor and the victim. Holocaust and Shoah have become words in history which have grown out of their original etymology and taken an autonomous meaning. Holocaust and Shoah should signify what no other word can express, but certainly not the whole world on the one side and the Jewish people on the other.

We have come together to honor men who crossed the river. This commemoration sees in the attack on the Jews an attack on all of mankind. The Shoah is an attempt to extinguish the lives of specific members of a certain family and company, and therefore it is regarded as the attempt to eradicate the life of human society itself.

The material recompense, be it global or individual, is a judicial obligation which is binding for the victim as well as for the perpetrator. It is an imperative. But even so, this kind of justice is unsatisfactory for both sides as it concerns only the "what" and not the "why." The Shoah was possible because men and women, all too many in Europe, permitted and condoned it. They were not humans like the ones we can honor today. You, dear honored ones, you are the letter of accusation against the masses who did not stand up. Maybe you do not feel that way. Of course, you did not risk your life because of a feeling but because this belongs to the fabric of your being. If there had been more, many more like you, the Shoah would not have been possible. The rise of evil is only another manifestation of the decline of virtues lying in the nature of man.

In this sense we Jews, the children of the Shoah generation, have an obligation to do everything to see that the unfathomable evil will not be forgotten. But we are also obliged to name the good, which might be disparagingly small in comparison to the evil, but yet is of immense moral stature. We must make a universal effort at education, which has not yet begun, in order to trade onward the heritage of those few Righteous who stood up against the man-made horror. There is no universal recompense, there will be none. Man has globally failed; a global lesson from this failure man must learn.

Yitzhak Mayer
Ambassador of the State of Israel

Speech given by André von Moos, Member of the
International Committee of the Red Cross on
September 6, 1999, at the Amtshaus in Berne

Honorable Federal Councillor, Your Excellencies, Mr. President, honored representative of Yad Vashem, Ladies and Gentlemen.

Today I have the great honor of representing the ICRC at this ceremony during which Harald Feller, Jean-Edouard Friedrich and, posthumously, Dr. Imre Haynal, Ernest Wittwer, and Dr. Peter Zürcher will be awarded the Yad Vashem "Righteous Among the Nations" medal.

In the name of the ICRC and its president, Cornelio Sommaruga, I would like to express to those about to be honored and their relatives our greatest respect and admiration.

There are many decorations for outstanding services and deeds, but I believe that the "Righteous Among the Nations" medal is unique because it underlines the extraordinary moral attitude of the one who receives the medal and witnesses the recognition of an entire people.

The decoration, which was created in 1963 by the Knesset, Israel's parliament, honors all those who at the risk of their own life saved Jewish victims from the National Socialist regime. To date, about 16,500 men and women have been awarded the "Righteous Among the Nations" medal. This number might seem large but, in view of the millions of victims of the Shoah, it is in fact very modest.

Resistance against a dictatorship—whatever the nature of such a regime—demands extraordinary qualities and a high respect for human beings. Facing Nazism—the worst of all dictatorships—it demanded courage in order to refuse the violence and the acceptance of subjugation and extermination of millions of innocent victims. It required a strong will to defend the values of freedom, of dignity, and of tolerance, regardless of the price that might be exacted, even if this meant the loss of one's own life.

Among the decorated are former employees of the Swiss Red Cross, men and women who helped to save Jewish children during the Second World War under the auspices of the Children's Support Program. Some of these heroes are present among us today, and I take the opportunity to express to them my great admiration for what they have done. Their deeds have all too long gone unrecognized, but now, after research by the Swiss Red Cross and the media, have gained the attention they deserve.

The ICRC takes the task of recollection very seriously. In my opinion, the years 1987 and 1988 were a turning point in this respect. In 1987 Friedrich Born, ICRC delegate during the Second World War in Hungary, was awarded the "Righteous Among the Nations" medal posthumously, and the ceremony was held at Yad Vashem in Jerusalem, honoring him for his actions in favor of the Jews in Budapest. A year later, Professor Jean-Claude Favez published his work entitled *The International Red Cross and the Third Reich: Could the Holocaust Have Been Halted?* It analyzed the strong points and weaknesses of the ICRC in relation to the persecution by the Nazi regime of the civilian population. The ICRC regrets deeply not having been able to protect the victims in a better way.

Today, Jean-Edouard Friedrich, who is present among us and who was the delegate of the ICRC in Berlin in 1942 and 1943, will be honored. Like Friedrich Born and other members of other humanitarian organizations who have been honored for their actions, Jean-Edouard Friedrich did more than was expected of him.

Jean-Edouard Friedrich was not yet thirty when he was confronted with the persecution of the Jews in Germany and Holland, and during a mission in May 1943, he was filled with a deep feeling of revulsion. He set out to do everything in his power to help men, women, and children in the Third Reich who were being persecuted because of the race they belonged to.

A revolt can be effective if it represents the power of humanity, and it is no coincidence that, beside the first plaques inscribed with the names of those decorated with the "Righteous Among the Nations" medal, there is also a tree planted as a symbol of recognition for each of them. This dedication to humanity finds its expression in the foundation of humaneness—the most important building block of our movement which was proclaimed at the 1965 International Conference of the Red Cross. It reads as follows:

> The International Red Cross and Red Crescent movement was born of the desire to bring help to the wounded on the battlefields, regardless of their origin. It endeavors nationally and internationally to prevent human suffering. Its intention is to protect life and health and to respect the dignity of man. It promotes mutual understanding, friendship, cooperation and lasting peace among all peoples.

This principle goes above and beyond the framework of the Red Cross. It is universal. During the Second World War—twenty years before the fundamental principles were formulated—about sixteen thousand individuals spontaneously lived it, among them also those being honored today. Each one of them is an example for coming generations, and especially for those who visit the garden of the Righteous Among the Nations at Yad Vashem in Jerusalem. All of those reading the names at this memorial will be able to say, these men and women give us hope.

Speech given by Federal Councilor Joseph Deiss, Head of the Swiss Federal Department of Foreign Affairs, on September 6, 1999 at the Amtshaus in Berne

I am deeply moved to be taking part in this ceremony to bestow the title of "Righteous Among the Nations" on fellow citizens who shone out on account of their humanitarian deeds during World War II. When Europe was sunk in darkness and barbarity, these people, obedient only to conscience, gave us a lesson in humanity which we must never forget. Their example shows that a tragedy—even a tragedy on the scale of World War II—is never inevitable, and that each individual is able, by his behavior, to resist the horror and help to maintain the noblest values of humanity.

We are especially proud, as Swiss citizens, to see how our centuries-old humanitarian tradition is so admirably embodied in the individual acts of the heroes we honor today, and indeed of others—I am thinking of the more than 30 Swiss citizens who have already been honored by Yad Vashem. May their courage always inspire our individual and collective behavior, and help us to keep alive the democratic and humanitarian ideas that are fundamental to the life of this country.

Whether they were delegates of the ICRC or acted in a purely private capacity, these fellow citizens of ours did not hesitate to risk their lives to come to the help of victims of Nazi persecution. As Minister of Foreign Affairs, I am of course also very pleased to be able to thank those who distinguished themselves in performing their functions as members of the Swiss diplomatic corps. To all of them, on behalf of the Federal Council, I would like to express our heartfelt gratitude and our sincerest thanks for the example they give us.

Ladies and gentlemen, the German philosopher Jürgen Habermas wrote that the century now ending has produced more victims, more soldiers fallen in battle, more murdered civilians, more deported minorities, more people starved or tortured, more political prisoners and more refugees than anyone could ever have imagined. Sadly, we have to admit that he was right. At the dawn of the new millennium, there lies before us—as is clearly evident from the daily news—the immense task of doing all we can to promote ever greater respect for human dignity, human and minority rights, and peace between peoples. By their example, the people we are honoring today show us the way. Let us hope that the coming century will produce more heroes and defenders of human rights than we could ever have imagined.

Preface

by Dr. Herb London
President of the Hudson Institute

For years Americans have been told about the complicity of Swiss bankers with the Nazi war machine. In fact, this episode has even insinuated itself into recent American political activity. Yet it is only part of a story whose texture is far more complicated than this one dimensional tale suggests.

During World War II some Swiss families risked their lives in order to assist Jews trying to escape from the iron boot of Nazi oppression. Thousands were saved and today anonymous Swiss heroes are honored at the Yad Vashem Holocaust Memorial in Jerusalem.

Meir Wagner has performed an extraordinary public service in digging through historical archives and recording eyewitness accounts of courageous men and women who fought against these unspeakable crimes.

This book offers another view of history, a stirring and gripping tapestry of lives put at risk in order to save lives in jeopardy. It is a testimonial for the righteous who never lost a sense of our common human bond.

Let us never forget that in the darkest night of Nazi crimes there was a ray of light that served as a beacon for human solidarity. "Never again" is more than a plea; it is a pledge. But that pledge only has meaning when a human conscience recognizes the difference between good and evil.

Meir Wagner offers us evidence of that conscience at work. For that and for the compelling stories he presents we must be very grateful.

Herb London

The "Righteous Among the Nations" of Swiss Nationality

As of September 2000, a total of 39 men and women of Swiss nationality have been named as "Righteous Among the Nations" by Yad Vashem. Their names are listed below, together with the year of their nomination.

1964	Carl Lutz
1964	Gertrude Lutz
1966	Frieda Impekoven
1967	Hans Schaffert
1971	Paul Grüninger
1974	René Nodot
1976	Roland de Pury
1976	Jacqueline de Pury
1982	Ernest Prodolliet
1985	Maurice Dubois
1987	Friedrich Born
1987	Daniel Curtet
1989	Albert Gross
1989	Charles-Jean Bovet
1989	Rosa (Rösli) Naef
1990	Anne-Marie Im Hof-Piguet
1990	August Bohny
1990	Friedel Bohny-Reiter

1991	Marie Meienhofer (Sister Jeanne Berchmans)
1992	Marcel Pasche
1992	Renée Farny
1993	Martha Schmidt
1993	Sebastian Steiger
1996	Emile Barras
1996	Hildegard Gutzwiller
1997	Arthur Lavergnat
1997	Jeanne Lavergnat
1998	William Francken
1998	Laure Francken
1998	Fred Reymond
1998	Paul Calame-Rosset
1998	Ernest Wittwer
1999	Harald Feller
1999	Jean-Edouard Friedrich
1999	Peter Zürcher
1999	Arthur Schneeberger
1999	Anne Schneeberger
2000	Walter Giannini
2000	Emma Giannini

Marcel Pasche

Defenders of the Oppressed and Accomplices in Uniform

Born in Switzerland in 1912 in the German-speaking city of Berne, but raised in the French-speaking western part of the country, Marcel Pasche grew up fluent in both languages. In the small rural community of Vaumarcus in the canton of Neuchatel, his father was a leading figure in the Christian Union movement, and at a young age Marcel was privileged to meet leading personalities who were heavily involved in social and humanitarian work.

After finishing his schooling (with final examinations in German at the University of Lausanne, where the main language was French), Marcel entered the Swiss army in 1932. That was the year when social uprisings in Geneva were squashed by the government, which called in the army for help. Young recruits were ordered

1

to shoot into the protesting crowds, leaving 13 people dead on the streets of Geneva—an event which profoundly marked Marcel. The issues had been labor and social security.

Once his military service was over, Marcel became a student of theology. In 1934, after initial studies at the University of Lausanne, he transferred to the University of Basle, situated on the Rhine in the northwestern corner of Switzerland, bordering France and Germany.

This prestigious university (which was founded in 1459 by Pope Pius II) had a proud tradition of human and cultural values. While studying here, Marcel became acquainted with the famous professor of theology Karl Barth, who came to Basle after being expelled from Bonn in Germany because of his criticism of the National Socialist philosophy in 1937. Barth considered Nazism was a far greater danger to mankind than Communism. In Germany, the "nazification" of the churches was a gradual process, partly made possible through the expulsion and elimination of those who raised their voices in dissent, the most famous among them being Dietrich Bonhoeffer who was executed by the Nazi regime.

In Basle, young Marcel developed a strong personal antipathy towards the "brown" (Nazi) right-wing ideology in Germany. Karl Barth's theology became the pivotal point in his academic life, as it had been for many young students who escaped from Nazi Germany and came to Basle. In the meantime, Hitler's government was tightening its grip more and more over the German churches. It was the time when the "Confessing Church" ("Bekennende Kirche") was growing.

After his graduation, Marcel was initially assigned to a church in Lille in northern France, where he assisted the pastor, Pierre Bosc, who was Vice President of the Reformed Church of France at that time. Marcel married Mady Choffat, a young woman he had first met during the time his family had spent at Vaumarcus. The young couple were posted to Roubaix, close to the Belgian border. There they experienced the traumatic invasion by the German Wehrmacht on May 10, 1940.

THE FRENCH YEARS

The invasion of France was preceded by a literal human wave of Dutch and Belgian refugees, many of them Jews, following the blitz of their countries by the German troops in the spring of 1940. Marcel and his wife helped where they could, but by May 19, they themselves were on the road. The evacuation was extremely chaotic, under constant attack from German "stuka" ("Sturzkampfflieger" airplanes).

Crammed into a small Peugeot automobile, Marcel, Mady, four other women and two babies escaped by the skin of their teeth, aided mainly by a detailed Michelin Guide map. They found refuge at Pastor Bosc's summerhouse. That was where Marcel heard the radio broadcast by Marshal Pétain announcing the surrender of the French army and the armistice of May 8. He also heard General Charles de Gaulle's appeal of June 18, 1940, calling on the French to resist the invading German troops and to fight.

On August 1, the Pasche family returned to Roubaix, where they found their apartment intact but with three German bakers, soldiers of the Wehrmacht, living in it. In the fall of that year, they heard the nightly formations of German bombers setting off on their sorties to England. In spite of the fact that the Nazi occupying forces had forbidden it, they listened to the BBC broadcasts from England: "This is London. The French are speaking to the French."

The general chaos, the lack of food and the German offensive in the East in the summer of 1941 led many young French men and women to enter the Resistance (the French underground army). In August of that year, Marcel Pasche was ordained as a pastor of the Reformed Church in Roubaix. It was a time of great solidarity among practicing Christians, the church being a haven of refuge and relaxation for many of the locals and for the refugees.

The Protestant pastor of Swiss nationality now serving in Catholic France, and also speaking fluent German, soon became a vital link between the occupying forces and the French population. During this time of trials and hardship he became acquainted in particular with three Germans— Friedrich Günther, Friedrich Hahn and Carlo Schmid. The personal risk he took was enormous.

In a report he wrote in 1945, Marcel said: "It is important to note that these three men, with whom I had developed a relationship of complete trust, themselves held an independent attitude, opposing the Nazi regime as a consequence of their Christian faith. They knew that, based on the biblical teaching, they ought 'to obey God rather than men'. To put this principle into practice, however, was a clear proof of courage on their part."

What Marcel did not learn until long afterwards was that he was the only pastor in France to maintain regular contact with German soldiers who happened to be brothers in the faith, although wearing the Wehrmacht uniforms. These men not only became good friends; they were instrumental in alerting Marcel to the degree of pro-Nazi or anti-Nazi commitment of any superior, colleague or soldier of the SS, the Gestapo or the Wehrmacht he had to deal with as representative of the French population in the area of Lille and Roubaix.

THE MILITARY ADMINISTRATION

The northern part of France having just been overrun by the German troops, and the British army still battling around the area of Dunkirk, the occupying forces set up their "Oberfeldkommandatur 670" (OFK 670)—the military administration for the Nord and Pas-de-Calais regions. They requisitioned the Lille stock exchange building, "La Bourse". Total control of all aspects of public and commercial life ensued as administration was concentrated at this regional center: police, university, justice, textile factories, mining, transportation, church matters, everything...

Above the entrance to La Bourse, a large German flag displaying the swastika flapped in the wind, and armed sentinels were stationed on the imposing stairs leading to the upper floors. When Marcel Pasche came to the administration building for the first time in the fall of 1940, he showed his identification papers to the guard who, after examining them, surprised him by saying: "You are a pastor. So am I. My name is Friedrich Günther." This was the opening of a conversation which could have remained just a dialogue between two colleagues, but which soon developed into something far greater.

Friedrich Günther was no ordinary soldier. In fact, he was a member of the "Confessing Church" of Germany and was actively fighting against the nazification of the Christian churches. He acted as an interpreter, and due to his position of confidence, he was extremely valuable to a great many people.

Friedrich knew how to select his informants and where to pass on the information he picked up by accident. The concierge's quarters at the Lille stock exchange building had also become a gathering place for many pastor-soldiers who were passing through the city. The Wehrmacht uniform these clergymen wore protected them from the Gestapo, who would have arrested many of them without hesitation if they had been in civilian clothes. Many members of the Confessing Church kept in touch through Friedrich Günther. Pastor Marcel Pasche was instrumental not only in helping them on, but in spiritually supporting their Christian faith.

One day Marcel found himself in a very embarrassing situation: three young Frenchmen had fled clandestinely from their posts in the STO (Obligatory Labor Service) in Germany. But due to the fact that they were considered deserters, they could not be reintegrated into a family, a place of work, or even a food line. Friedrich Günther knew of a soldier who was in charge of the ammunition dumps at Saint-Armand-les-Eaux. This man was ready to take care of the three fugitives, giving them food ration cards and papers declaring them to be "heavy laborers". This ensured that they avoided investigation. Marcel later found out that plans of these ammunition dumps had been secretly passed on to London...

Friedrich Günther's help was particularly valuable in the case of raids on Jewish refugees in the area. When he learned that a raid was scheduled to take place early the next morning, he did not hesitate to inform the pastor. On discovering that the pastor was not at home, Friedrich took it upon himself to inform several people using the telephone he had at the concierge's booth, pretending he was a "high official of the Oberfeldkommandatur", a trick which he successfully repeated several times. Witnesses confirm that the life of a certain Mr. Rabinowitsch, who was living at rue Faidherbe 15 in Lille, was saved as a result.

Günther maintained close contact with Marcel Pasche and introduced him to many accomplices who could be trusted. His activities could not always be kept totally secret, of course. He had a number of enemies at OFK 670, among them some staunch Nazis. They managed to have Friedrich sent to the front. His unit was almost completely wiped out, but Friedrich returned.

THE SECRETARIAT OF JUDICIAL ASSISTANCE AT GERMAN TRIBUNALS

The following public notice appeared (in French) in two local newspapers, the *"Echo du Nord"* and the *"Journal de Roubaix"*, on November 23, 1942:

"Persons who desire to be assisted by a lawyer before the German tribunals, even though they may not have sufficient funds, may address themselves to this secretariat which is privately sponsored, every day from 9 to 12 o'clock, at rue Masurel 20, Lille."

Most of Europe had been overrun by Hitler's armed forces and was largely incapable of organizing social support. Pastor Marcel Pasche had the idea of setting up a service to help when he witnessed a 17-year-old girl being sentenced to 12 months in prison for "insolence". He intervened and succeeded in getting the sentence reduced to three months.

Marcel had discovered that another man, Henri Duprez, a Roubaix industrialist (who was a member of the Resistance) had also tried to set up such a legal assistance service, using his influence with the Catholic hierarchy. Duprez got to know a lawyer in Paris, Maître Michel Clément, whose services had been called upon by the wealthy Leignel family. Clément had succeeded in obtaining the release of Gustave Leignel, a former banker who had been imprisoned for possession of an old pistol.

Pasche and Duprez joined forces to set up a private organization, but they were determined that it should have "official" status. Marcel actively promoted the foundation of the "secretariat". Thanks to his excellent relationship with Dr. Carlo Schmid, an important man at OFK 670, permission was granted to run such a service.

Marcel recalls that it was a true bluff: the notice in the newspapers had actually been smuggled past the SS censors! Although there had never been any real official endorsement, it was sufficient to refer to this press release whenever any questions were asked about the legitimacy of the "secretariat".

The address of the "secretariat" was no accident, either. It was the business address of Gustave Leignel. Having regained his freedom, Gustave worked free of charge and helped families who found themselves in a similar situation. Local lawyers agreed to work together with the Parisian lawyer Michel Clément. Contributions from interested families helped others to be assisted at the German tribunals, which ranged from the "Sicherheitsdienst" (SD), to the "Feldgericht" (Field Tribunal), the Air Force Tribunal, and the "Oberfeldgericht", the supreme court of the armed forces.

There were several cases of "forgotten prisoners" they were able to help. These men, sentenced and imprisoned, had been neglected until representatives of the "secretariat" visited them.

Another valuable acquaintance was Friedrich (Fritz) Hahn, a German who helped the police ("Geheime Feld-Polizei"—GFP) because he spoke French. Fritz, like his friend Friedrich Günther, was a pastor and a member of the "Confessing Church".

In the middle of the war and under German occupation, the mission of Marcel Pasche and his accomplices was a delicate and hazardous undertaking. The links of the "secretariat" and its adepts to the Resistance could have been betrayed at any time, and tension was mounting. A report dated January 6, 1944 shows, however, that 430 families had so far gotten in touch with the "secretariat", and its intervention had been successful in 70 cases. Its activities continued right up until the liberation of France by the Allied forces.

CARLO SCHMID—A TRUE FRIEND

None of this would have been possible if Marcel Pasche had not been directed by Friedrich Günther, right on their first encounter at the concierge's booth in the fall of 1940, to get in touch with the legal advisor of the administration of the OFK 670, Dr. Carlo Schmid, an expert in international law.

Schmid was a man of imposing build. He worked in an office on the third floor of the "La Bourse" building, overlooking the main square of Lille, lending credence for any visitor to the importance of the function and office he held.

One chilly morning, Marcel, the young Swiss expatriate pastor not yet 30 years of age, met Dr. Schmid for the first time. He was very warmly received. An unusual experience indeed in those times.

Carlo's father—a native German—was a teacher at the University of Toulouse and had married a Frenchwoman. Carlo was born in southern France in 1896. His family moved to Germany before World War I broke out, which meant that Carlo had to join the German forces for the last part of the 1914–1918 war. After his discharge, he studied law and political sciences and became an expert at the International Court of Justice at the Hague.

In 1933 the Hitler regime prohibited any further promotion, and in 1940 Carlo Schmid was drafted as a legal adviser to the "Oberfeldkommandatur" (OFK) in Lille. There his mandate consisted of reviving the broken-down French legal system, overseeing the university, the museums, the religious institutions, etc.

Although the French (puppet) government at Vichy received its orders from the German military administration in Paris, OFK 670 in Lille came under the administration based in Brussels, Belgium. Carlo Schmid always tried to find a solution to any problem that would be in the best interests of the local population, particularly when he received conflicting orders from Paris and Brussels.

The relationship between Carlo Schmid and Marcel Pasche was marked right from the start by a high measure of confidence and real friendship. Although older than Marcel and much more learned, Carlo was always highly attentive to the suggestions of this pastor who was in direct contact with the people. Marcel, for his part, considered it an unparalleled privilege to meet this open and refined individual who, even in the middle of the war, maintained human dignity.

There was a lot of business to be done, so the two men met frequently. Whenever Marcel submitted the necessary forms in two languages, French and German, whether it was for permission to cross from occupied France to the "free" zone of Vichy, the transportation of coal or potatoes, a young people's get-together or for some charity, Dr. Schmid would approve the forms using a large rubber stamp with the swastika and the words "mit Befürwortung" ("with recommendation"). Documents marked in this manner carried no official authority; they looked official enough, though, to pass as authentic in most cases.

In 1942, Marcel Pasche was able to spend a few weeks of vacation in Switzerland. Prior to Marcel's departure from Lille,

Carlo Schmid had been helpful in issuing free passes for Mady and the children, but he could not find a way of issuing a pass for Marcel, since his profession was that of a pastor. Pastors were not allowed to travel freely. Marcel had to cross the border into his native country clandestinely.

Once in Switzerland, he found that there were a number of young theology students who were facing the prospect of joblessness because of the war situation. This gave Marcel an idea which, back in Lille, he shared with Carlo Schmid.

After much careful and secret planning, Marcel crossed the border into Switzerland once again in November that year. He met with a young pastor, Jacques Mottu, who volunteered to work as a churchman in the Lille area, undeterred by the hardship for which he would be trading an easier life in Switzerland despite the perilous times. With the help of Carlo Schmid, two more young Swiss pastors, François Grandchamp and Pierre Vallotton, were smuggled in and posted to Amiens and Reims. Schmid welcomed all of them and gave them papers that declared their stay legal and approved by the authorities.

Carlo Schmid was carefully screened by the Army Secret Police (GFP) after the attempt to assassinate Hitler on July 20, 1944. He was summoned to Brussels for questioning and nobody could predict what the outcome of the investigation would be. As a precaution, he had planned an escape in case the authorities decided to detain him. Fortunately, he did not have to make use of this contingency plan, as he was allowed to return to Lille, where he continued to work together with Marcel Pasche.

On August 28, 1944, OFK 670 was being dissolved. Feverish preparations for departure were taking place when one of the officers accused Friedrich Günther of desertion. After a scuffle, the Nazi officer shot him three times. Seriously wounded, Friedrich was taken to the hospital of La Calmette, where he died two days later.

Carlo Schmid and Marcel Pasche saw each other for the last time on September 1, 1945. On that occasion, Schmid cautioned Marcel to be extremely careful during the withdrawal of the Wehrmacht troops, since a single shot fired by a sniper—accidentally or not—would jeopardize the entire operation. It was a known fact that the worn out, weary troops were extremely "trigger-happy". Marcel therefore passed word on to the Resistance and was able to negotiate a 24-hour delay before the "Maquis" started their activities.

Dr. Carlo Schmid returned safely to Germany, where he became a high-ranking political advisor to the new government. He died in 1979.

HONORS

In 1992, the mayor of Roubaix offered Marcel Pasche the Medal of Honor of the City of Roubaix, to be presented to him on May 8, the anniversary of the armistice. Pastor Pasche accepted, on behalf of the Reformed Church that had played its part in Northern France during those difficult years.

Here are some excerpts from his speech given at the auditorium of the city hall of Roubaix:

"Honorable Mayor, Ladies and Gentlemen, dear friends,

"The distinction with which I am about to be honored causes me deep emotions, especially since it leaps back in history by about half a century. I have lived and experienced together with you and your parents the mobilization of 1939, Hitler's attack of May 10, 1940, the advancing and retreat of the British troops, the arrival of the Dutch and Belgian refugees, the sinister evacuation, the military defeat and the occupation of France by German troops.

"I understood what it was that Professor Karl Barth had declared to be 'the perverseness of Nazism' just five years prior to my coming to France. With the help of Pastor Friedrich Günther who was an active member of the Confessing Church,

I got to know Dr. Carlo Schmid, who played a considerable role in favor of the population suffering under the occupying forces. Friedrich Günther was assassinated by a Nazi officer. Dr. Schmid has become a high-ranking official in the German government. He is also responsible for the *rapprochement* of the peoples of France and Germany.

"During the four years of occupation, I was able to have recourse to a network of close and reliable Christian friends. Our notion of 'enemies' was wiped away. We became daring and audacious, even to the point where we helped young forced laborers in their camps in the Ardennes mountains; quite illegally, we 'imported' Swiss pastors to help the population in Northern France. We helped Jewish families and refugees and, last but not least, we operated the 'Secretariat of Judicial Assistance at German Tribunals in the department Nord and Pas-de-Calais' from 1942 to 1944. Numerous prisoners were freed and the lot of many remaining in prison was alleviated. The existence of such an organization astonished the Germans, and is considered unique in the lands occupied by the Nazis.

"All of this was possible through and with the help of trusted French friends ... and the assistance of my compatriot and friend, the Swiss consul Fred Huber who accompanied me on many of my missions.

"I would like to thank the population of Roubaix who, at the time of the liberation, did not suspect my numerous and manifold contacts with the occupying forces of being collaboration with the enemy. Perhaps the particular character of my relationship was understood all along? It was an expression of a continued Christian attitude. Thank you for giving me the opportunity to relive it today."

At the synagogue of Lille, on March 7, 1993, another ceremony took place. Marcel Pasche was presented with the Yad Vashem "Righteous Among the Nations" medal of honor together with his friends Pastor Henri Nick, Dr. Pierre-Elie and

Odile Nick, as well as, posthumously, Léon and Germaine Coghe.

Here are excerpts from Marcel Pasche's acceptance speech on that memorable occasion, which he began by reading some verses from Psalm 105:

" *O give thanks unto Adonai; call upon his name: make known his deeds among the people.*

Sing unto him, sing psalms unto him: talk ye of all his wondrous works.

Remember his marvelous works that he hath done; his wonders, and the judgements of his mouth;

O ye seed of Abraham his servant, ...

"All of us gathered here, officials and invited persons, Jews, Christians of diverse confessions, and Muslims, are the seed of Abraham, bearers of the Promise.

"The help to persecuted Jews has manifested a communion among this posterity of Abraham and a vision of the Promise.

"I acted with accomplices (accomplices they were because of the clandestine nature of the activities). First of all, my colleagues in the ministry. I still remember the doorbell ringing at the vicarage in the rue des Arts in Roubaix: 'Are you Pastor Pasche?' the visitor asked. 'Yes,' I replied. 'I have been sent here by Pastor Henri Nick. I am an Israelite!' When this visitor entered my office, we first had a look at his particular situation. And then we had recourse to other bearers of the Promise, more colleagues and friends near the Swiss border: Montbéliard, Institut Glay, Pontarlier... I find myself very honored to be associated with Pastor Henri Nick.

"Then there were accomplices in German uniforms, pastors of the Confessing Church, anti-Nazis, stationed in Lille. In his Memoirs, published in 1979, Carlo Schmid, the great man in the new government of the Federal Republic of Germany, writes, recalling the four years he spent in Lille: 'The Reformed Church has acquired great merit by saving the lives of Jews. The risks that some of its ministers took to help the Jews to escape will always be a chapter of glory in the history of the Reformed Church of France. She has shown herself worthy of the motto of the 'camisards' [insurgent Huguenots of the Cevennes after the edict of Nantes had been recalled, 1688] when their church was persecuted by the dragoons of the king of France: 'To know to resist...'

"More accomplices: I recall the names of the lady directors of the Ambroise-Paré clinic, Therese Matter and Eva Durrleman, then Léon Coghe and his wife, members of my congregation in Roubaix, and Miss Caudmont, bookkeeper at the Lyceum Fenelon in Lille who gave shelter to a Jewish pensioner without disclosing her identity to her superior.

"I had an accomplice who wore the habit of a nun: Sister Geneviève Gendron, of the Don Bosco order. Originally from Normandy, she was refined and maliciously intelligent at the same time, using her modest approach as a good sister to penetrate every stratum of society to find help from the most diverse personalities. After her talks with Jules Isaac, she founded the Jewish-Christian friendship group of Lille. She was commissioned by Cardinal Lienert to get in touch with the Protestant church. (To show her true ecumenism, Sister Geneviève attached a Star of David and a Huguenot cross to her crucifix, thus attracting the attention of many.) In Paris she met the papal envoy Angelo Roncalli. Later, during the discussion of Jewish matters at the Vatican II council, she traveled to Sotto il Monte near Bergamo in Italy, the home of Pope John XXIII, and established friendly contact with the family of the Pope. She sent to Rome by family courier her thoughts and suggestions, which were actually put on the agenda! I hold this sister in very high esteem, just like a mother. I wanted to give her honor right here, because her ministry was not understood by her colleagues at that time; she was expelled.

"I have mentioned only a few of my accomplices. But I keep with me the sentiment that I was encircled during the time of the occupation by a great many bearers of the Promise given to Abraham.

"I have witnessed with great joy the birth of the state of Israel in 1948. After the Shoah, it is a high-place of hope for mankind.

"In the communion of the descendents of Abraham who are partakers of the Promise, I salute you fraternally. Shalom le Israel!"

AFTER THE WAR

Five children were born to Marcel Pasche and his wife Mady; in 1950 the family returned to Switzerland, where a pastorate was vacant at Château-d'Oex. During the war, the father of another of Marcel's friends, Pastor Daniel Curtet, had been pastor there for a while.

It was in this tranquil mountain village that some of Daniel's remarkable Bible-coded letters written from war-torn central France had reached Pastor Curtet Senior. (See "The Bible-Coded Letters That Slipped Past the Censors.") The peaceful countryside was almost disconcertingly quiet for Marcel, though. He was soon looking for another, more challenging, assignment.

The late 1950s and early 1960s were marked by extensive construction of high dams in the Swiss Alps. Marcel and his family moved to Sion in the Valais where most of the building was going on. Hundreds if not thousands of foreigners of Italian, Spanish and other nationalities were brought in. Without them, the gigantic projects would not have been realized. Marcel Pasche became their pastor.

In this capacity, he was authorized to visit all areas of the huge construction sites at high altitudes to see the workers, but he did not leave unattended the families left down in the valleys, who were often in very dire circumstances. On several occasions he had to assist them when accidents happened, some of them with fatal consequences. Human failures or mechanical malfunctions could not be prevented in spite of strict safety measures and precautions. But nature, too, played its own dramatic role. Marcel was on duty when an avalanche broke loose from the glacier above the construction site of Mattmark in 1965, killing over eighty workers and engineers, burying them permanently under thousands of tons of ice.

In 1969 Marcel Pasche received a telephone call from Hans Schaffert. The two men had previously worked together when Marcel had invited Hans to come and assist him in his pastoral work in northern France at the end of the war. (See "The Protestant Pastor who Protected the 'Property of God'".)

Now, 25 years later, Hans had been appointed secretary of the Assistance Office of the Reformed Church of Switzerland (EPER) in Zurich. The massive needs of Christians in the eastern European countries under Communist control made physical and spiritual aid a necessity. Marcel was commissioned to travel to Romania and Hungary in the 1970s, bringing desperately-needed help to the suffering people there. A relief journey to Czechoslovakia in 1978 marked the itinerant pastor's final trip.

But Marcel Pasche maintained his contacts with Christians behind the Iron Curtain. The fall of the ominous Berlin Wall in 1989, when Marcel happened to be present in the still-divided city, brought back memories to him of 1945 when another totalitarian system had come to its ignominious end. At the ripe old age of almost 90, Marcel Pasche still enjoys reminiscing about his dramatic experiences, all written down in a booklet entitled *"Années de guerre et de fraternité"* (*"Years of war and brotherhood"*), and subtitled *"Sinister and luminous recollections of a pastor"*.

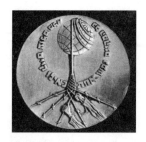

Frieda Impekoven

The Freedom-Giving Lady of Frankfurt

Frieda, the wife of the well-known playwright and actor Toni Impekoven, was startled by the shrill ringing of the doorbell of her apartment in Frankfurt, Germany.

When she opened the door, two men dressed in black leather coats were standing there. They introduced themselves as members of the Gestapo. One asked: "Are you Frau Impekoven?" When she replied in the affirmative, his companion ordered her brusquely: "Come with us!"

Frieda was taken to a tall building. The elevator took them to the top floor. There, in a small, sparsely lit room, two men were waiting to start the interrogation—even before Frieda could sit down. The man seated behind the desk immediately started firing a barrage of questions at her:

"Do you know Frau Wölffler? Is she your friend? Has she visited you at your apartment? Have you hidden Frau Wölffler at your apartment? Did you hide other Jews? Why did you visit her and bring her food? Do you do this regularly for other Jews? Do you always hide Jews?"

Frau Impekoven answered all these questions to the best of her knowledge. Suddenly, the second man, who was standing behind the desk, asked: "Are you related to Niddy Impekoven, the dancer?" When Frieda answered: "Yes, she is my daughter," the two men abruptly terminated the interrogation. "I regret having bothered you. I have been an admirer of your daughter for years, but unfortunately, I have never met her personally. She is a great dancer. I have seen many of her performances in Frankfurt and other cities. By the way," he added, "this incident is irrelevant. You may go." He accompanied Frieda to the elevator and shook hands with her.

How had this all started? Frau Wölffler had indeed telephoned the Impekovens, and admitted that she was an enthusiastic theatergoer. She was very fond of Toni Impekoven, the actor. During the conversation she mentioned that she felt very isolated as a lone Jewess left in Frankfurt. Her family had all fled. She had stayed behind because of her advanced age.

Frau Wölffler told the Impekovens how the authorities had taken away her apartment and moved her into a small furnished room. Frau Impekoven decided to pay her a visit. When she arrived at the guesthouse, she saw a sign outside the door: "Jews Only." She saw that Frau Wölffler did not have enough to eat, and on her second visit she brought some provisions.

After the two Gestapo interrogators let her go, she learned that Frau Wölffler had been arrested at the guesthouse and deported to the concentration camp of Theresienstadt.

GERMAN HUSBAND A SWORN ANTI-NAZI

Frau Frieda Impekoven, née Kobler, was born in Zurich in 1880. Her father was a well-to-do industrialist. Frieda married Toni Impekoven, a gifted actor and writer—one of the best-known in Frankfurt am Main—a producer and impresario. Many of his plays were successfully staged in the theater.

Toni was a sworn anti-Nazi. He hated Adolf Hitler and his whole regime. When Hitler came to power in 1933, Impekoven's plays were banned immediately. He was not allowed to direct or produce plays. He was forbidden to act and, after a short while, he was arrested. He was taken to a forced labor camp where he had to work on the state-owned farm of Rosenau at Spendingen.

Impekoven and even his wife were in constant danger of being interned at one of the many concentration camps, but Frieda continued to help Jewish refugees regardless. She provided them with food and hid people at her flat when the need arose.

One of the people she helped was Anton Müller from Kreuznach. "I am the son of Toni's oldest sister. She was married to a Jew, my father. I was raised according to the Jewish faith, and during the Nazi regime I was in jeopardy. My uncle Toni and his wife helped and assisted me where they could. When I had to flee, they hid me at their apartment in Frankfurt. They helped me make it to Switzerland."

Frieda Impekoven started to accommodate persecuted Jews at her home as early as 1939. One of them was Frau Knewitz. This lady wrote a letter of thanks to Frieda Impekoven on June 24, 1965. It read: "When I was in danger, you took me in, showing true friendship and hospitality. When you had heard of a Gestapo raid in our area, you offered me the shelter of your house although you knew that I was Jewish. I thank you from the bottom of my heart."

Richard Klein, editor of *Neue Presse*, a Frankfurt newspaper, confirmed that it was Toni Impekoven's stand against Hitler that had cost him his job in the theater. After the war, the Americans honored Toni for his bravery, fortitude and courage. They offered him a job as a theater manager, an offer that he gratefully accepted.

After the death of her husband, Frieda returned to her native Switzerland. In 1966 she was honored by Israel's ambassador to Switzerland, who presented her the Yad Vashem "Righteous Among the Nations" medal for her bravery against the Nazi regime and for having saved many Jewish lives.

Arthur and Anne Schneeberger

"Whoever Saves One Soul..."

Arthur Schneeberger was born in a village near Aarau in the German-speaking part of Switzerland. He studied textiles at Lille in France before setting up a hosiery business at Roanne in the Loire region in the early 1920s. He and his wife Anne became good friends and clients of a certain Mr Wolkowicz and his wife, a Jewish couple who also worked in the hosiery trade.

Mr Wolkowicz (born in 1899) had left his native Poland as a young man to earn his living away from the virulent anti-Semitism that had surrounded him there. After spending some time in Austria, he traveled to France in 1924 and settled in Roanne, where some Jews from his native town of Zdunskawola were already established. In due course, he set up his own hosiery business.

In 1940, the Wolkowicz family (father, mother, 7-year-old Benjamin and his baby brother Claude) were evacuated from their home following the German invasion of France. They spent the summer of 1940 in Haute Loire, returning to Roanne (then in the "free" zone) after the Armistice. But conditions went from bad to worse. The assets of Mr Wolkowicz' business were placed under the control of the Vichy government and Mr Wolkowicz himself (as a Jew and a foreigner) was taken to the

Le Vernet internment camp in the south of France, where he was held for one year.

In 1942, the "free" zone came under German occupation after the Allied landing in North Africa. Persecution of the Jews was intensified, and survival was the priority.

Claude, the younger son, just 3 years old, was still young enough to be safely placed with a nurse, who looked after him until 1945. Mr Wolkowicz and his wife began making plans to hide at a friend's house in a village near Roanne (later they would be forced to move on again to Varennes sur Allier). But taking proper care of Benjamin, now 9 years of age, was not going to be an easy task.

It was at this point that Mr Wolkowicz asked his good friend Arthur Schneeberger if he would be willing to take Benjamin into his home. Without the slightest hesitation, Arthur willingly agreed—fully aware of the enormous danger he was placing himself and his family in by giving accommodation to a Jewish child when he himself had the status of a foreigner and was thus already under suspicion and surveillance.

In his testimonial to Yad Vashem in 1998, Benjamin Wolkowicz recalls:

"So it was that I lived with this family from 1942 to 1945. They welcomed me as if I was their own son. These people had two daughters who were older than me and who were truly solicitous for my welfare. They were a Protestant family, which helps to explain why they behaved as they did. Meanwhile, I was attending a Catholic school.

"The Schneebergers' house at 77, Rue Albert Thomas was located about 100 meters away from the German soldiers' barracks. We saw the soldiers marching past every day: this represented a very real danger to my adopted family. Officially, as far as the neighbors were concerned, I was Mrs Schneeberger's nephew.

"When I was reunited with my parents in 1945, I remember that I shed a lot of tears. I have continued to maintain an excellent relationship with the Schneeberger family... I am eternally grateful to them: they put their own lives in peril and saved a Jewish child during a period of immense danger."

Arthur Schneeberger and his wife have been dead for several years now, but Benjamin Wolkowicz still regularly visits with their daughters, Anny Gilbert and Janine Hausermann, who now have children and grandchildren of their own. They love to reminisce about the experiences they shared during those troubled and dangerous years—including the summer vacations they spent at a house out in the countryside, and how the older girl (aged 15 in 1943) used to make young Benjamin hide in a barrel every time she heard an automobile approaching, in case it was a German vehicle.

In November 1999, at a ceremony at Roanne, Alfred Lazare, the Lyons representative of the French Committee of Yad Vashem, formally conferred the "Righteous Among the Nations" medal posthumously on Arthur and Anne Schneeberger, represented by their daughter, Madame Anny Gilbert-Schneeberger.

Ernest Prodolliet

Unrelenting Struggle to Rescue the Innocent

Ernest Prodolliet was born in Amriswil in 1905. He was a businessman before joining the consular corps of the Swiss Confederation. In 1938, Ernest Prodolliet was serving in the Swiss consulate in Bregenz, the capital of the county of Vorarlberg in western Austria. This beautiful medieval city is situated on the eastern shore of Lake Constance, also called the "Bodensee" or the "Swabian Sea".

Prodolliet was responsible for the passport and visa section at the consulate, and he made full use of his position to save hundreds of Jews desperately fleeing the Third Reich, by issuing Swiss transit visas to them.

In so doing, he flagrantly worked against the instructions of his superior, who was not particularly disposed to help persecuted Jews. Ernest Prodolliet, however, was well known in Jewish circles throughout Germany. His name was passed on from person to person.

Not a day passed without a number of refugees calling at the Swiss consular office at Bregenz. Their number increased after March 13, 1938, when Austria was annexed by Germany. The so-called "Anschluss" (annexation) reduced the former independent republic to an eastern province of the German Reich, "Ostmark". The consul decided to place a guard at the consulate's gates to ward off the influx of those seeking help. Ernest Prodolliet had to find new ways of operating.

One of those he saved was Elieser Lewin. Here is his account of Prodolliet's activities: "I was cantor and ritual (kosher) slaughterer at Rosenberg in Upper Silesia. When I faced deportation and internment at a concentration camp, my cousin from Zurich, Switzerland, suggested I should seek to obtain a forged visa for Shanghai. I could get it against payment. She would then travel to Bregenz, where two Swiss women—Gusty Bornstein and Hawa Sternbuch—could possibly help as they maintained good relations with the Swiss consulate.

"I traveled to Bregenz where I met Frau Sternbuch. I handed her my genuine German passport with the forged Shanghai visa, and she took it to the Swiss consulate. Forty Jews were already lined up at the gate that day, all wanting transit visas. Frau Sternbuch presented the passport and returned with a Swiss transit visa, good for a stay of 48 hours. We were all conscious of the fact that Prodolliet was aware of the forgery.

"Equipped with these papers, we traveled on to Switzerland. On the second day, Frau Sternbuch escorted me and other Jews to Italy. There we boarded a ship that took us to Palestine. Luckily, the British Navy did not intercept us on the high seas, and we landed at Ashdod. We entered the country illegally."

Ernest Prodolliet communicated with the government in Berne about the increasing number of Jewish refugees seeking help at the Swiss consular office. He included their personal reports about atrocities committed by Germans and Austrians. He emphasized that these were not just hateful words by vindictive people but matter-of-fact statements.

Gusty Bornstein helped Ernest Prodolliet in his endeavors to rescue the Jews. On July 7, 1982, she wrote about her experiences in a letter from Engelberg (a mountain resort near Lucerne): "When my brother was studying at Besançon,

France, he got to know Ernest Prodolliet, and I got acquainted with him and his wife, too. I also knew his daughter who died prematurely. All of them engaged in many missions to rescue persecuted Jews. I only want to mention Dr. Heinz Stanislaus and his bride (née Dreyfus) who were guests at the home of Ernest Prodolliet.

"Dr. Stanislaus was threatened with arrest and deportation by the Germans. He suggested that the furniture truck owned by Prodolliet's transportation company would be an ideal hiding place for him, and he could escape when it was driven from Germany to Switzerland. But Prodolliet strongly advised him against the idea. In spite of his warnings, two of Dr. Stanislaus's friends tried the method anyway using another truck. They did not make it. At the border they were caught by the Germans and shot dead on the spot. Dr. Stanislaus himself found refuge at the home of Ernest Prodolliet's family in Bregenz until he could move to a more convenient hiding place and finally to Switzerland. Thus, his life was saved."

Gusty Bornstein organized the illegal immigration of Jewish families throughout 1938. She recollects that Prodolliet issued many hundreds of transit visas which the refugees needed for their onward journey through Italy. They were headed for the Adriatic Sea, where they boarded a ship bound for Palestine.

INDIVIDUAL INCIDENTS OF BRAVERY

Mindel Schottenfeld was about 46 years of age when she met Prodolliet. On November 16, 1938, he issued 24-hours' leave to the middle-aged woman and her son Leo to visit Julius, her other son, who was sick and interned at the refugee camp at Diepoldsau. Of course, Frau Schottenfeld and her son never returned to the Reich. Similar leaves were also granted to other Jewish refugees, among them a Mrs. Rektor with her two young children.

On September 26, 1938, a Jewish physician by the name of Dr. Tauber tried to immigrate to Switzerland. At the checkpoint between Austria and Switzerland he was unable to present the necessary visa, but the Swiss border guards had already been informed by Ernest Prodolliet. He had asked them the let Dr. Tauber pass through. The same thing happened to his wife on October 1, 1938. Both actions were contrary to regulations.

As early as July of the same year, Ernest Prodolliet had made out a visa without being authorized to do so. It was for a man from Graz, Karl Schiffer. The Swiss consulate obviously had a reputation of being a safe haven for refugees, and was readily used by communists fleeing from all parts of Germany.

Ernest Prodolliet reconnoitered secret paths along the border in the Rhine valley. He even went so far as to drive refugees across the border in his own automobile. He smuggled Joseph Udelmann into Switzerland at Au, a small village situated on the shore of the upper Rhine.

The border guards on both sides had known Prodolliet well for a long time. Whenever he brought somebody with him they let them through. But on November 23, 1938, his luck seemed to have run out. The German border guards stopped him as he tried to cross the frontier with a refugee by the name of Max Wortsmann. Ernest Prodolliet claimed that his intention was only to "show" the man how and where to immigrate once he was in possession of valid immigration papers. He just wanted to help and assist Wortsmann at the checkpoint.

This incident served to speed up the end of this phase of Ernest Prodolliet's rescue activities. In mid-December 1938, he was summoned back from Bregenz, and once in Berne, disciplinary proceedings were opened against him. Questioned by the federal department of Justice and Police, Prodolliet admitted repeatedly having been in contact with Police Captain Paul Grüninger. Not only had he met him, he said, but they had actively worked together. The attempt to bring through Max Wortsmann, who had no valid identification papers and no visa, had been coordinated with Grüninger.

When the disciplinary proceedings came to a close, Ernest Prodolliet was accused of having issued and distributed Swiss entry visas and other legal documents to Jewish refugees. He was given a sharp verbal reprimand and transferred to the Swiss consulate in Amsterdam.

RESCUE CONTINUES IN OCCUPIED HOLLAND

The transfer to Amsterdam did not deter Ernest Prodolliet from further initiatives to rescue Jews. When Jews were being deported in 1942, in particular, he procured Swiss passports and distributed them to anxious would-be emigrants, saving the lives of many. It seems to have been his destiny.

Prodolliet's efforts to rescue Jewish people during his term of office in Amsterdam are well described in the book *"American Jewry and the Holocaust"* by Professor Yehuda Bauer, a noted Holocaust researcher at the Hebrew University in Jerusalem.

Gertrude van Tijn of the Jewish Council in Amsterdam was responsible for obtaining German exit visas. Jews who were persecuted or in danger of being deported had to go into hiding while they waited for visas. In order to obtain more money for her difficult task she got in touch with Ernest Prodolliet, at the very moment when the German authorities were closing down the Swiss consulate in Amsterdam in November 1942. Prodolliet handed her an address book with useful names and telephone numbers, together with 57,500 Swiss francs in cash for which she signed a receipt.

Gusty Bornstein had not lost contact with Ernest Prodolliet after his recall from Bregenz. She later described his time in Amsterdam: "When Ernest and his wife were transferred to Amsterdam at the beginning of World War II, they engaged, with great personal dedication, in a struggle to rescue the innocent. Their activities soon surpassed their official duties. In spite of the German occupation, they helped Jews in numerous ways.

"Unlike 1938 when the refugees were seeking asylum by clandestinely crossing the border between Austria and Switzerland, in Holland the Jews had to be saved from impending deportation and the latent threat to their lives. Ernest and his wife actively hid many Jews and, while Jews were waiting in their cache, the diplomat procured legal documents, some real and many of them expertly forged.

"Officially, it was forbidden to even let Jews enter the premises of the Swiss consulate. Ernest Prodolliet, however, had instructed the guard at the gate to let every Jew pass. Thus he helped many of them, literally at the last moment."

There were cases when Ernest Prodolliet went to the railway station to check the trains. Daringly, he showed the German officers expertly forged papers which they accepted. Thus he was able to lead many Jews away from a journey to certain death.

His rescue activities meant a constant battle, but they saved the lives of single people, couples and entire families. At least one hundred refugees succeeded in escaping via Italy thanks to Prodolliet's help.

HONORED BY GOVERNMENTS OF FRANCE, ISRAEL

After his transfer from Amsterdam, Ernest Prodolliet held various diplomatic posts, his last as consul at Besançon in eastern France. When he reached retirement age, he received a certificate, personally presented by French President General Charles de Gaulle, in recognition of his outstanding merits as a Swiss Consul in helping the refugees.

On November 18, 1983 the Ambassador of Israel to Switzerland, Jochanan Meroz, visited Ernest Prodolliet at the retirement home at Amriswil. There he decorated him with the Yad Vashem "Righteous Among the Nations" medal of honor.

In a short speech, Ambassador Meroz said: "Before and during World War II, Ernest Prodolliet helped many Jews without regard for his own life and safety. He is one of the good among men, a light and an anchor for many of his fellow human beings. During his terms of office in Austria and in Holland he did not hide behind paragraphs and rigid rules, but followed the road signs of his own conscience. He simply acted as a human being. He who saves but one Israelite saves the whole of mankind."

Ernest Prodolliet's nephew planted a tree in his honor at Yad Vashem. His true humanitarian acts during a barbarous time were well remembered on the occasion. For many he was the only hope in a time of hopelessness. His help and assistance were pure and altruistic and had always been supported by his wife Frieda.

Ernest Prodolliet was honored in many ways. He died at Amriswil in 1984.

Ernest Prodolliet in his old age, shown together with his wife and Gusty Bornstein who had helped him in his rescue work, aiding many refugees to escape the Nazi Reich and get across the border to Switzerland.

Gertrud Kurz

The Mother of the Refugees

In August 1942, Gertrud Kurz traveled, together with Basle banker Paul Dreyfus-de Günzburg, to visit Federal Councilor Eduard von Steiger at his holiday retreat. A few weeks earlier, the Swiss authorities had ordered the borders of Switzerland to be closed to civilian refugees, provoking a protest by thousands of Swiss citizens at the Parliament building in Berne. After a long discussion with Eduard von Steiger, Gertrud Kurz succeeded in securing his agreement to reopen the borders on a temporary basis.

Such was the measure of the influence of this courageous woman, who was already well known for her humanitarian work. Throughout Switzerland she became known as the "Mother of the Refugees". She helped Jewish refugees and any other refugees she encountered, because of her compassion for her fellow human beings.

In 1936, she was one of the founders of the Swiss Central Office for Aid to Refugees. She served as Secretary of the Kreuzritter movement (later known as the Christian Peace Corps), dedicated to reconciliation between peoples. She worked alongside Pastor Hans Schaffert (see "The Protestant Pastor who Protected the 'Property of God'"), whose colleague Marcel Pasche also spoke highly of her humanitarian work.

After the war, the fate of those who had perished under the Nazi regime while Switzerland's borders remained closed weighed heavily on her mind. Rather than putting the blame on the authorities, though, Gertrud Kurz blamed herself personally. In an interview, she once said: "Actually we should have sat down on the steps of the Parliament building and refused to go away until the asylum policy was made more humane."

Gertrud Kurz remained loyal to the authorities, while using her best efforts to influence them, both in her meeting in August 1942 and in the cases of individual Jewish and other refugees where she intervened to help. Her loyalty, coupled with her deep personal commitment to reconciliation and strong humanitarian convictions, made "Mother Kurz" a figure of distinctive moral authority and one of the best-loved Swiss celebrities of the twentieth century.

In 1962, she was officially nominated by the Swiss Federal Council for the Nobel Peace Prize. In 1965 she was awarded the Albert Schweizer Prize.

Gertrud Kurz, nee Hohl, was born at Lutzenburg on March 15, 1890. She married Albert Kurz and had three children. She died at Berne on June 26, 1972.

Twenty years after her death, she was honored as the first woman to be depicted on an official Swiss commemorative coin, minted in 1992.

Paul Grüninger

The Police Captain with a Conscience

April 3, 1939 was a black day for Paul Grüninger, the police captain at St. Gallen in northeastern Switzerland.

Early that morning he arrived for work as usual, but Anton Schneider, a police cadet who was responsible for the refugee files, blocked his way at the entrance to the central police station. Anton declared that the chief commander himself had ordered him not to let Captain Grüninger in.

Although the incident was unprecedented, Paul Grüninger was not surprised. He protested and feigned ignorance of the reason for this measure. However, he was aware of his "guilt", as he had helped refugees from Germany to cross the border into Switzerland and had given them residence permits. Such activities were clearly against Swiss federal regulations.

Paul Grüninger had been warned by a family friend who was working at the checkpoint near Bregenz, where the German and Swiss borders converged. (Austria had been annexed by the expanding German Reich a year earlier and no longer existed as a separate state.) He had been told that the Gestapo had his name on their wanted persons list and that he should stay away from German territory. But Paul Grüninger did not take the warning seriously and continued his illegal activities.

What Captain Grüninger did not know was that the Gestapo had gotten wind of his doings inadvertently through a Jewish woman he had helped. The woman had left her jewelry behind in a hotel in Bregenz, the German-Austrian border town. After her admission to Switzerland, she asked Captain Grüninger to help her recover her belongings. Grüninger got in touch with Ernest Prodolliet at the Swiss consulate in Bregenz, asking him to go to the hotel, get the jewelry and send it to him. He had worked with Prodolliet on several similar rescue missions in the past, so he knew he could be trusted.

In a letter to her relatives in Vienna, this woman wrote: "There is a wonderful police captain named Paul Grüninger. He promised to look after my jewelry and bring it to me from the hotel of our friend in Bregenz." The letter was intercepted by the German censors. The hotel owner was arrested by the Gestapo, the jewelry confiscated by the authorities, and the secret police (SD) decided to keep Grüninger under surveillance from then on.

After a while they informed the Swiss federal authorities in Berne about Grüninger's illegal activities. On April 3, 1939 a preliminary dismissal from office was ordered until legal proceedings could be formally opened against him.

Paul Grüninger was born in 1891, in the city of St. Gallen. He studied at the teachers' seminar at Rorschach. During World War I he served as a lieutenant in the Swiss army. After the war, he entered the police force of the canton of St. Gallen and was promoted to the rank of captain in 1925. Grüninger was also president of the Swiss police association and an active member of the board of the Swiss society for the protection of animals. He participated in international police congresses, and he had been responsible for security during several official state visits in St. Gallen.

"ANSCHLUSS" PRODUCES REFUGEE PANIC

On March 11, 1938 the German "Wehrmacht" (armed forces)

marched into Austria. In the notorious "Anschluss", the country was annexed by the Third Reich and renamed "Ostmark". With Nazi persecutions of the Jews pushed into the new province, many Jews tried to flee into neighboring countries.

One of these countries was Switzerland. Obtaining a visa was difficult, so Jewish refugees tried to enter illegally via the "green border" (unguarded field and forest paths) either alone or in groups. Many were picked up. In the northeastern region of Switzerland the refugees first came to the city of St. Gallen after they were caught by the police. There they were brought before Captain Grüninger.

Grüninger had been ordered not only to slow down the stream of refugees but to send them back. But he had seen with his own eyes how they arrived—cold, hungry, wounded, still in a state of shock and harrowed by the strain they had gone through during their flight. A battle was raging in his mind. Thoughts of sound judgment, sense of duty and his professional ethics were warring against his strong humanitarian feelings. He had to weigh the moral law of humanity against the cold letter of the law.

His instructions were clear—he had to refuse the fugitives entry to Switzerland. But he could not bring himself to act according to the regulations: "If I could not do anything for them, then these people who had just escaped would have to be separated from their relatives, sent back and they would be lost." That was what he was later to explain. But at the time, he knew that he was breaking the law and abusing his position by condoning illegal border crossings. He even encouraged border guards to show mercy when particularly pitiful refugees appeared.

In July 1938, the stream of refugees increased. The Nazi authorities themselves abetted the outflow, even bringing Jews to the German-Swiss boundary in the upper Rhine valley at St. Margrethen because they wanted to get rid of those they could not evict or eliminate otherwise. Soon the refugee procedures became systematized. With financial assistance from the Swiss

Association of Jewish Refugees, Grüninger set up a refugee camp at an old textile factory at nearby Diepoldsau.

By August 18, 1938, the situation had become critical. The Swiss authorities decided to close the borders to all those who could not produce a valid Swiss entry visa. The chief of the federal police in Berne, Heinrich Rothmund, officially declared that a small country like Switzerland was not capable of taking in uncounted numbers of refugees in an unrestricted manner. "The lifeboat is full" was the controversial motto.

But every day dozens of refugees from the refugee camp at Diepoldsau came to Captain Grüninger's office. Here, their fate was decided: either they were allowed to stay or they would have to be sent back. In most cases, it was the voice of the heart that spoke.

During this initial phase, Grüninger enjoyed the cooperation of his superior, councilor of state Valentin Keel, who himself had arranged the escape of high-ranking Social Democratic party officials from the former Austria. (As Social Democrats, they were in danger, too, under the Nazi regime.)

The Swiss Jews received donations of money from the United States for the support of the refugees. On December 18, 1938 the Swiss Association of Jewish Refugees met and declared that the problems of looking after the refugees would become critical if whole groups continued to be let in indiscriminately and illegally.

In particular, the situation was almost unmanageable for the Jewish community in St. Gallen According to a list compiled by Sidney Dreifuss, responsible for Jewish refugee support in St. Gallen, 360 illegal refugees had been admitted to the canton during the months of November and December 1938. The Association decided to address a letter to the Swiss authorities, drawing their attention to the mounting problems.

Again, Heinrich Rothmund, a senior official in the federal department of Justice and Police in Berne, decided to tighten border controls and to refuse entry to all refugees in order to stem the flow. This meant that all Jewish refugees without a visa would automatically be turned away and sent back to Germany.

It was at this point that Paul Grüninger decided to take matters into his own hands. He was not willing to compromise his conscience. He instructed the border guards to not refuse any Jewish refugees. Over 2,000 men, women and children were saved thanks to his magnanimous attitude.

When the borders were officially closed, Paul Grüninger started to personally escort refugees into Switzerland. He handed them temporary and permanent residence permits. He got in touch with the Swiss Association of Jewish Refugees and directed refugees from the camp at Diepoldsau to their offices in St. Gallen. In many cases refugees were helped to find a shelter in Switzerland where they could start a new life or emigrate. Grüninger was often seen at the camp, where he counted the refugees. He admitted later that he had tears in his eyes when he saw the misery and despair of those pitiful people.

WENT TO GREAT LENGTHS TO PROTECT LIVES, PROPERTY

Personal accounts of some of the refugees have described Paul Grüninger issued documents authorizing them to stay in Switzerland even though officially they were there illegally. Many of them remembered occasions when he reached into his own pocket to help financially. One day he bought a new pair of shoes for a little boy. Another time, Grüninger took a girl who was suffering from toothache to the dentist, paying the bill.

Grüninger not only let the refugees in; he also protected them and safeguarded their meager belongings. He knew that the Germans confiscated all valuables from the refugees they sent across the border. They were allowed to keep only 30 Reichsmarks per person—next to nothing. In order to circumvent that draconian measure, Paul Grüninger arranged for a secret depot at an inn in the western part of Austria. From the

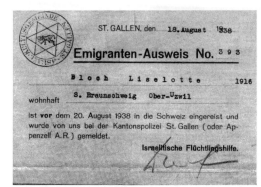

ST. GALLEN, den 18. August 1938

Emigranten-Ausweis No. 3 9 3

Bloch Liselotte 1916

wohnhaft S. Braunschweig Ober-Uzwil

ist **vor** dem 20. August 1938 in die Schweiz eingereist und wurde von uns bei der Kantonspolizei St. Gallen (oder Appenzell A.R.) gemeldet.

Israelitische Flüchtlingshilfe.

Emigranten-Ausweis No. 393, official identification document for Liselotte Bloch, "backdated" to August 18, 1938, stating that the bearer of this document had entered Switzerland before August 20, 1938 (deadline). It is signed by (Sidney) Dreifuss, Israelite Refugee Assistance in St. Gallen. (Source: Archiv für Zeitgeschichte, ETH-UNI Zurich)

Swiss consulate in Bregenz, Ernest Prodolliet regularly sent a diplomatic courier to the innkeeper, collecting the valuables and jewelry in order to bring them to Switzerland.

Paul Grüninger's family knew about his rescue mission. He had told them: "I'd rather break the rules than send these poor, miserable people back to Germany."

The Swiss Association of Jewish Refugees had to keep a record of the illegal immigrants that they sent regularly to the federal police department in Berne. The place and time of the illegal crossing had to be indicated and the refugee had to put his signature on the list. Grüninger helped to forge the dates for all those who had crossed after August 18 so that they would not be automatically refused entry.

Paul's wife Alice participated in and supported her husband's humanitarian activities. She relieved the refugees' needs wherever she could, especially when her husband brought home hungry, freezing children in torn clothes. She comforted the refugees at the camp at Diepoldsau, men and women who could not see any way out of their desperate situation.

When he was abruptly barred from entering his office that fateful day in April 1939, Grüninger knew that the entire rescue mission was in jeopardy. He remembered the detailed report that Berne had requested a few weeks earlier, according to which 259 refugees had been granted asylum after August 1938. That was when he had instructed the Swiss Association of Jewish Refugees to backdate the lists and questionnaires.

The Swiss Federal Council, the highest executive body in the country, consisting of seven members, discussed refugee-related matters and questions during a meeting held on January 20, 1939. According to the minutes of this meeting there were about 12,000 refugees in the country. As this number was considered to be the upper limit, the Federal Government decided to tighten the visa regulations for all foreigners seeking asylum in Switzerland. It was decreed that anyone not in possession of a visa should be refused entry on the spot.

Six days later, on January 26, Grüninger handed the requested report to his superior, Police Chief Valentin Keel. It contained the figures for the last five months. It stated truthfully that at that time there were 858 Jewish immigrants in the canton of St. Gallen, 262 of them having come in after the closing of the borders in August 1938. These refugees, however, had been allowed to immigrate with special permission from the St. Gallen authorities.

In his report Grüninger wrote: "We have been active mainly for humanitarian reasons. We could not force ourselves—we were not hard-hearted enough to send back any of the stream of refugees after November 10, 1938. It would have been shameful behavior on our part because these people had escaped an ill fate only under great hardship. We were led by the public opinion of the majority of the Swiss people, the media and the political parties.

"Whenever we did attempt to refuse someone entry to the country, there were heartrending scenes. The police staff and border guards declared that they would not go on doing service in such inhumane circumstances.

"We have heard that in the region of Basle hundreds of immigrants found refuge under similar conditions even after the month of August. Together with the Swiss Association of Jewish Refugees we are looking for possibilities of an onward journey for the refugees, and it appears that several hundred of them could soon leave Switzerland for Palestine. For this reason we have not seen any problem in granting them a limited residence permit."

In writing this report and streamlining the questionnaires, Grüninger hoped that matters would settle down a bit so that he could continue with his rescue work. Little did he know that his superior, Valentin Keel, had sent a totally different report to Heinrich Rothmund on January 28.

This report is on file. It reads as follows: "We have examined the administrative complaint of the High Command of the Border Guards and discovered that some officials of the cantonal police have not complied with the instructions to refuse illegal immigrants, mainly in cases where their health and life were in danger. Although we have to admit that this was an act of disrespect for the rules laid down by the authorities, we also have to say that complying with these rules is not easy for a person whose heart is touched by the misery. Maybe it is not easy to picture the real situation if you live far from the border.

"We have, however, given strict orders that absolutely no illegal crossings of the border must be allowed any longer. Nevertheless, Police Captain Grüninger has continued to allow people to get in. According to our information there are 859 immigrants in the canton of St. Gallen at the present time."

Heinrich Rothmund replied to Valentin Keel on February 11, 1939: "You have assured me that the responsibility for immigrant control will be taken away from Police Captain Grüninger. After thoroughly discussing with Captain Grüninger the matter of guarding the border at Diepoldsau after the withdrawal of the troops, I had given him clear instructions. Nevertheless, it appears that this civil servant and officer sanctioned or even provoked illegal immigrations off his own bat."

After receiving this official note, Valentin Keel immediately relieved Paul Grüninger of his responsibility for refugee matters. He did not want to dismiss him, though. He was aware of the fact that Grüninger knew about Keel's own actions in allowing Social Democrat party officials from the former Austria, as well as a number of Jewish refugees, to enter Switzerland illegally.

On February 28, 1939, the government of the canton of St. Gallen became involved. It had to examine the accusation brought forward against Paul Grüninger. At the same time, an official complaint was pending against Valentin Keel. The Swiss Patriotic Federation accused the Police Chief of having "smuggled in Social Democrats" from a foreign country. Keel countered this accusation by admitting that a few administrative mistakes had been made in the past, but that this concerned merely some eight persons.

"Everything I have done," said Keel, "was in accordance with the cantonal police rules and regulations. If I acted differently in some isolated tragic cases of human hardship, it was purely for humanitarian reasons and as a Christian. I take full responsibility for my actions."

In this way, Keel further incriminated Grüninger. He accused him of having allowed over 300 illegal border crossings on his own initiative. He advocated that Grüninger should be relieved of responsibility for refugee matters.

The steamroller against Grüninger had been set in motion, but he knew nothing of his fate. On March 13, Dr. Gustav Studer, another high-ranking officer in the St. Gallen police department, informed his boss, Valentin Keel, that one of the immigrants, Karl Adolf Werner, had made some severe accusations against Police Captain Grüninger. In particular, it had been proved that the date on which Werner had entered the country illegally was not the date stated in the list that the Swiss Association of Jewish Refugees had submitted to Berne. Furthermore, he claimed never to have been at the reception camp at Diepoldsau.

An investigation was opened, and the leader of Swiss Association of Jewish Refugees was questioned about Werner's statements. He admitted that sometimes he had not filled out the lists correctly. He conceded in particular that immigration dates did not correspond to the truth in several cases. He finally confessed that he had backdated at least fifty application forms at Grüninger's request.

The government authorities came to the conclusion that Paul Grüninger had either altered entries or forged forms. The police chief, Valentin Keel, further complicated the situation by stating that although no illegal immigrants should have been allowed to enter the country after August 1938, Paul Grüninger had made it impossible to say exactly how many had been allowed in because he had distorted the figures and issued permits without official control. This activity weighed particularly heavily, because Grüninger was not authorized to issue such documents. Valentin Keel effectively vindicated himself by accusing Paul Grüninger.

On March 5, 1939, Keel was re-elected cantonal councilor by a remarkable majority of the electorate's votes. Three weeks later, the government decided to question Paul Grüninger first before bringing charges against him or suspending him from office.

Just three days later, the interrogation report was submitted to the government. It was based on the statement of the leader of the Swiss Association of Jewish Refugees. According to him, between 135 and 170 questionnaires had been manipulated at the request of Paul Grüninger who wanted the details of immigration to be backdated. Apparently the accused captain had come to the office of the Swiss Association of Jewish Refugees about twice a day. He had spoken about this to an immigrant who was responsible for maintaining the files of new arrivals and departing refugees. This person saw no problem in doing as Grüninger asked, as he felt obligated to him for helping so many Jews escape the inferno of the Third Reich.

INTERROGATION DRAGS ON

The cantonal government then decided to proceed with Grüninger's interrogation. Grüninger claimed that he had always acted with the consent of the police department. He said that he had not concerned himself with the questionnaires except for ordering them to be corrected when information was lacking or wrong. He maintained that he had not received any order to change the immigrants' entry dates.

To make matters worse, the government got wind of an alleged attempt to influence one of the witnesses. Paul Grüninger had allegedly tried to coordinate his statement with that of the leader of the Swiss Association of Jewish Refugees. The committee of inquiry was informed that Grüninger had asked that person to accept responsibility for the forgery. The two men were confronted on April 3. Paul Grüninger maintained his version and admitted to a single case of changing a date. Had he not admitted that, the immigrant Karl Adolf Werner would have been exposed as a liar.

On April 5, two days after the interrogation, Paul Grüninger wrote his defense. In it he explained that changing the dates was irrelevant to the issue, since the number of refugees would have remained the same.

"I am going to explain why, in one single case, I offended against the instructions of the department," he wrote. "I acted as a human being and an officer out of commendable motives. One of the most valuable rights of sovereignty is the right of asylum. During our entire history we (the Swiss) have opened our doors in a liberal manner to political refugees, not because of sympathy for their person or their ideology, but on purely humanitarian grounds."

Before Grüninger's suspension, a discussion with far-reaching consequences took place between Heinrich Rothmund and Valentin Keel. Following the meeting, Keel brought a charge against his subordinate Paul Grüninger and urged the physician general to summon Grüninger for a psychiatric check-up, after which he could be interned in the mental asylum of Wil, near St. Gallen. When he learned of this scheme, Paul Grüninger immediately took steps to defend himself against the internment. He succeeded, but he could not prevent his dismissal without notice on May 12, 1939. He even lost all salary and pension rights, backdated to April 1939.

It is difficult to understand why Keel behaved as he did. As department head he had worked with Grüninger for many years. Was he unwilling to cover for the Captain because it would have meant facing charges and interrogation himself, as he had disregarded instructions in several cases? Or was he afraid of a possible German invasion of Switzerland, carrying with it consequences for "protectors of Jews"?

Paul Grüninger asked for the right to look at the files; he wanted to prove his statement that his superior knew what he was doing. Suddenly the files had disappeared. Not surprisingly, he was deeply disillusioned about his former superior and friend. He would have expected him to be honest and loyal.

TWO-YEAR ORDEAL

The proceedings against Captain Grüninger lasted two years altogether. Worse still, he could not find another job while the legal investigation continued. He had to move out of the police house by the end of June 1939, and had to ask his mother for financial support. Most of his former friends deserted him, but while he was socially stigmatized, his wife and his daughters stood by him.

The trial took place at the district court of St. Gallen. The court accused Paul Grüninger of forgery of official documents and of having misled his superior with false information about immigration dates. Extenuating circumstances included the fact that Paul Grüninger had not intended to achieve any personal gain from his actions. Objectively speaking, he had gone contrary to his instructions, but subjectively he had acted only on humanitarian grounds in allowing refugees to cross the borders and enter the country clandestinely. It was taken into account that Paul Grüninger had always thought he was acting in the sense and spirit of his superior, but that he failed to adhere to the rules and regulations of the law and to stay within the limits of his responsibilities. He had entangled himself step by step.

The judge sentenced Paul Grüninger for having "changed the date of a single document which remained formally correct but was altered in essence. By this, the refugee Martin Löffel was given the opportunity to travel through Switzerland and abroad, from where this person could organize refugee transport to Palestine."

All other offenses were considered obsolete and sufficiently expiated by the dismissal without notice as well as the financial consequences this had for Paul Grüninger. He was fined 300 Swiss francs and ordered to pay the costs of the investigation, amounting to 1,234.05 Swiss francs. The state absorbed 550 Swiss francs. Grüninger did not appeal against the verdict.

For a long time after his conviction, Paul Grüninger was unable to find a steady job, but he took every opportunity to make himself useful. He worked as a laborer on construction sites, as a fabric trader, carpet salesman, feed and wood merchant and commercial traveler. He became manager of a raincoat shop and worked as a driving instructor. His older daughter Ruth soon had to start working because the financial difficulties of the family were becoming increasingly acute.

It was several years after the end of World War II before Grüninger found decent employment again—as a teacher. He retired eventually to the small village of Au, situated on the eastern shore of Lake Constance.

The police had kept Paul Grüninger under surveillance throughout the legal proceedings in 1939. The attorney general had his mail controlled and his telephone bugged.

It was reported that Grüninger had contact with "schleppers" (smugglers of human beings) on several occasions. On

January 30, 1939 the chief of the Gestapo border commissariat, Josef Schreieder and his driver, Ernst May, traveled from Bregenz to St. Gallen. Grüninger's tail, or informant, duly reported that he had met the two gentlemen and sat in the station restaurant for 20 minutes. These two men, supposedly "schleppers", proceeded to the German consulate without Grüninger, and then left Switzerland after a stay of three hours. A Swiss traveler on the same train reported to the authorities that Schreieder and May had been discussing Swiss defense fortifications.

Grüninger was also suspected of being in touch with Mario Karzer, a notorious scrap dealer, and maybe even with Nazi sympathizer Carl Kappeler. Some observers voiced the suspicion that he was perhaps sympathizing with the NBS, a pro-Nazi movement, or that he was possibly even a member of the Frontist organization himself.

These reports led to further questioning by a judge from Zurich who was investigating illegal contacts with foreign powers. Grüninger assured him that Schreieder was an old acquaintance from his police force days. Perhaps he had been naive to assume that Schreieder's visit to Switzerland was for humanitarian reasons and that he, too, was trying to relieve the fate of the persecuted Jews, he told the judge.

Grüninger's frequent trips to Basle were a further object of speculation. It was some time before the tail discovered that he was working as the manager of a raincoat shop that belonged to a certain Elias Steinbuch, formerly of St. Gallen. He had offered Paul the job as a token of gratitude for his work as a police officer, helping refugees to escape.

In the end, all the observations failed to prove any suspicious activities, and after a while they were discontinued.

TESTIMONIALS FROM SURVIVORS

Frieda Prosner was nineteen years of age when she fled from Vienna. Today she lives in New York, under her married name of Prosner-Rosenberg. She remembers the events clearly: "When I heard that Switzerland had closed its borders, I traveled from Vienna to Bregenz. This was on August 18, 1938. For five long days and nights I hid in the dense forest on the eastern shore of the Rhine estuary into Lake Constance. I managed to escape in spite of all the patrols and crossed the border into Switzerland. There I was picked up and interned at the refugee camp at Diepoldsau on August 24. I risked being sent back to Germany by the Swiss authorities since I had crossed the border illegally and had no papers. After two days at the camp there was the visit of a police captain by the name of Paul Grüninger. He issued an official permit to me which allowed me to stay. He saved my life."

Berta Rothstein left her home in Burgenland (southeastern Austria) in August 1938. She headed for Italy, leaving behind her brother, his wife and their two children. When she asked at the Jewish relief center in Milan if they could do anything to help her relatives, she was given Paul Grüninger's name and telephone number. She was told that he had the means to bring Jewish refugees out of German "Ostmark" and into Switzerland.

Meanwhile, Berta's brother had been arrested by the Gestapo. This is Berta's story: "I received a message from my brother", she said, "who had managed to escape from prison, but was in great danger of being picked up again. He had to flee from German territory as quickly as possible. Therefore, I called Paul Grüninger and explained my brother's situation to him. Captain Grüninger gave me instructions to the effect that my brother and his family should travel to Feldkirch, near the Swiss border, and check into a certain hotel where they should wait. Someone would come by with further information about the way my brother and his family should go. It happened just as the man said. They walked at night, crossed the river into Switzerland and reached Appenzell. There, Paul Grüninger helped them to find shelter and refuge at the home of a Swiss family. Their whole flight took two months; finally, they were in safety."

A man by the name of Josef Berger, a trader from a small community in Vorarlberg (western Austria) recollects how he made his escape. "I jumped off a train headed for Dachau KZ, a concentration camp near Munich, Bavaria. I made it to the Swiss border. When I tried to cross, Swiss border guards picked me up. They took me to see a police captain in St. Gallen. He seemed to have been informed about my flight. The letter he held in his hands when I was in his office said that I was wanted by the German authorities in Vorarlberg for fraud and perjury. They requested my immediate extradition. Paul Grüninger read the letter to me and assured me that he believed me rather than the accusations. He considered them as a pretext for putting me under arrest in Germany.

"He also explained to me that he needed the help of the refugee support organization. He sent me to their office and promised that they would bring me to a place of safety somewhere in Switzerland. He would inform the German authorities that no refugee with my name was known to him. I was sent to Engelberg by the Swiss Association of Jewish Refugees. There I survived the war and the Holocaust."

Susi Mehl was 16 when she had to flee from Vienna towards the end of October 1938. She wanted to reach Switzerland, and she succeeded. On Friday, October 29, she met Police Captain Paul Grüninger. Susi recounts: "He was a man in whose company you did not have to tremble. He behaved like a father and a friend. During our conversation he explained, however, that he was under great pressure himself and that he would give me a permit as a last exception of all exceptions. A month later my parents wanted to emigrate too, but alas! they did not make it. Both were murdered at Auschwitz."

Moritz Weisz, a trader from Vienna, crossed the Rhine near Hohenems in September 1938 together with his wife Mathilde, his sister-in-law Hadassa Angelus, her 14-year-old daughter

Hanni and five other family members. After making their way to St. Gallen, all nine of them were hidden for a while by Recha Sternbuch.

Moritz soon found out that Recha had direct contact with Paul Grüninger, but nevertheless, they were all afraid of being picked up by the Swiss authorities as illegal immigrants. Recha went to see the leaders of the Swiss Association of Jewish Refugees. They contacted Paul Grüninger. "Soon afterwards we got documents allowing all of us to stay in Switzerland."

Another man, Karl Tennenbaum from Vienna, gave the following account: "My parents made it to the German–Swiss border but did not know how to go further. They were afraid to cross illegally. My wife was already in Switzerland. She contacted Captain Paul Grüninger. He advised her to encourage them to come to Switzerland and he would see to it that they would not be sent back. He kept his word."

Otto Ascher, another refugee from Vienna, reported that "I reached Diepoldsau together with my mother and my 14-year-old brother shortly after Christmas in 1938. We were taken to see Captain Grüninger. I explained to him that we were expecting an affidavit from the USA. But Grüninger was not naive and saw through my white lie. Nevertheless, he issued a permit so that we could stay in Switzerland."

Salomon Hocker tells his story: "My son Leon was a livestock trader and butcher at Kobersdorf in Burgenland. He took flight in the fall of 1938 and succeeded in escaping to Switzerland. He wrote to us to follow him. When crossing the border into the free country of Switzerland we should insist that a certain Captain Paul Grüninger had authorized our admittance. All we had to do was to sign a piece of paper at the checkpoint. Leon himself was arrested after two weeks and sent back to Germany via the border point of St. Margrethen."

Klara Hochberg from Vienna was 18 years old when she arrived at St. Margrethen. It was December 20, 1938. She was in possession of some sort of a free pass, issued by the police and signed by Paul Grüninger. Her relative, Silvain Braunschweig, had asked for this document and requested that it should be mailed to her. "I was let through without any difficulties by the Swiss border guards. When we met, I handed the letter to Paul Grüninger. He tore it up. All I could do was to thank him and promise not to tell anyone about it."

Another moving story is that of Hellmut Reiter. He fled alone when he was 13 years of age and had to leave his parents behind, both of whom were deaf mutes. He told Paul Grüninger about his family's plight. The Swiss police captain summoned the Reiters from Austria to be questioned in Switzerland for some official inquiry. Nobody suspected anything and they were able to pass through.

Another refugee from Graz, Hilde Weinreb, recalls that she was just a child at that time. "I had waited all day near the Swiss border together with my parents. We were all wet from the rain when finally it grew dark. We sneaked out of our hiding place and warily approached the border. The closer we got, the muddier the terrain became and we could not see the path any longer. There was deathly silence, except for the noise our feet made in the mud and the beating of our hearts.

"Suddenly, a man in a uniform appeared out of nowhere. He held a torch in his hand, shining the light into our faces. We must have looked ashen and were convinced that this was the end. But the man greeted us with a kind smile on his face. I looked at him as if hypnotized. He told us not to be afraid but to come with him to Switzerland and everything would be okay. It was as he said. Later on I learned the name of the man: it was Paul Grüninger, the police commander from St. Gallen himself."

Lotte Bloch was 22 when she fled from Vienna. She reached the Swiss frontier in September 1938. Her uncle, who lived in Switzerland, had telegraphed her a message saying that a visa was ready for her at the border. But shortly before reaching the checkpoint, Lotte was arrested by a gendarme still on German territory. However, the following day she escaped and made it to Switzerland where she was met by her uncle. Together they drove up to St. Gallen. On the way her uncle explained to her that the police commander himself, Paul Grüninger, was responsible for her entry permit. In St. Gallen they went to the Swiss Association of Jewish Refugees where she obtained a formal entry visa. It was backdated to August 18, 1938.

On October 27 the same year the Swiss Association of Jewish Refugees congratulated Paul Grüninger and sent him a note. It was his birthday. The note read:

"It is our ardent desire to thank you, honored Captain, and to wish you well in the name of all the members of our organization. We would like to express our deep gratitude for your humanitarian activities for all of us and especially for the pitiful refugees. Please do not regard it as a hackneyed phrase but be assured that these thanks come from the bottom of our hearts."

On August 26, 1946 Dr. Robert and Mrs. Elisabeth Bohensky from St. Gallen addressed the following stirring letter to Paul Grüninger who meanwhile had been demoted and lost his job:

"Eight years ago we were able to immigrate to Switzerland. Thanks to your magnanimity without red tape we have found refuge here in your beautiful country. In a few days we shall return to our home country.

"But now our hearts are filled with sadness when we look at your own fate. Here we were, rescued from the deepest distress and our savior gets into difficulties himself. It is totally incomprehensible that this your hard lot cannot be changed to a better one. You held up the humanitarian thought at a time when it was most difficult. The least we can do now is to take an interest in your fate. Maybe we refugees do not have the strength left, but somehow we know that any steps we could or should take would be to no avail.

"Perhaps when we are back in our home country we will be able to repay the immense debt we owe you. Please be assured that our souls are filled with this desire. May we say thank you and good-bye, forever deeply indebted to you."

THE STRUGGLE FOR REHABILITATION

In 1968 a cantonal councilor (member of the local parliament) Hans Breitenmoser from Gossau first asked the government for a review of the Grüninger affair. State councilor Willi Rohner (a member of the federal parliament) and his wife Gertrude started the ball rolling.

In October Rohner had written an article in "Der Rheinthaler", one of the local newspapers, entitled "Injustice should be put right". In this exposé he mentioned the new asylum policy of Switzerland, welcomed and praised by most Swiss, under which thousands of refugees were taken in from eastern European countries. He compared it to the beggarly attitude of the authorities thirty years earlier. He used Paul Grüninger as an example of former times. He described how the authorities had curtailed his responsibilities so that his rescue work was seriously hindered and even halted. He tried to throw a better light on Grüninger and his activities. He mentioned the help Grüninger gave to refugees who would have faced certain extermination without his intervention. He assured his readers that Paul Grüninger had acted out of deep moral conviction and had overstepped his responsibilities because of empathy for the victims.

Rohner asked whether perhaps the time had come to finally put right the gross injustices of the past. In a time of remembrance for the millions of victims who had been annihilated in the German extermination camps, should this not be a question of honor for the canton of St. Gallen? He challenged the general public to press for the rehabilitation of a man who had dared to disregard instructions in order to help and to rescue those who would otherwise have perished under a dark and barbarous regime. Grüninger had done what a true humanitarian spirit and his Christian heritage told him to do.

Yet, on December 16, 1968, the State Council decided that in the interests of all concerned it would not be wise to reopen the case. Willi Rohner's rousing and passionate appeal, however, was taken up by most major newspapers in Switzerland and echoed rapidly around the world. Paul Grüninger received letters from everywhere. Nevertheless, it took more efforts by his daughter, Ruth Roduner, friends and several well-known personalities to convince the government to take action to rehabilitate Paul Grüninger's reputation.

In early 1969 Ruth Roduner and Gertrude Rohner had an audience at the State Council of St. Gallen. They asked that a pension be granted to the former police officer. The request was turned down.

In the meantime, Grüninger had been honored by an association of Jewish War Veterans. Several other Jewish institutions decided to support Grüninger financially. The Jewish World Congress had once donated 500 Swiss francs to him in 1953. But in October 1969, the Jewish Community of Switzerland sent a letter of congratulations on the occasion of his 78th birthday together with a check for 1,000 Swiss francs.

A few months later, a cantonal councilor urged the government of St. Gallen to rehabilitate Paul Grüninger. Even the police department supported the plea. However, it was turned down once again.

Two daily newspapers, the "Nationalzeitung" of Basle and the "Badener Tagblatt" opened a bank account and collected money. They raised over 30,000 Swiss francs for Grüninger. In Constance, a German city adjoining Switzerland and situated on the shores of the lake, the story evoked great sympathy. Donation funds were collected there.

But it was only after the appointment of a new chief civic administrator, who re-examined the files, that the government of St. Gallen finally relented. In an official letter, Paul Grüninger was commended for his humanitarian ideals and resoluteness in those difficult times. However, not a word was said about financial compensation, let alone vindication.

In 1971 the Yad Vashem Memorial in Jerusalem awarded Paul Grüninger the "Righteous Among the Nations" medal of honor. On this memorable occasion, the aging former police captain thanked all those who had helped him during his own difficult times. He stressed how proud he was to have saved hundreds of lives even if it meant suffering himself. "My readiness to help is founded in my deep Christian conviction and world view. Although I found myself in need and dire straits many times, there was always a way out. I experienced God's help in a powerful and abundant manner."

The Minister of Justice of the German Federal Republic, Gustav Heinemann, who later became the President of West Germany, sent a magnificent bouquet of flowers to congratulate Paul Grüninger on the occasion of his 80th birthday.

A few months earlier, Swiss Television had aired a documentary by Felice Vitalis, "Captain Grüninger". It struck a chord around the world. An association called "Justice for Paul Grüninger" was founded. Its aim is to battle against racism and anti-Semitism in the sense and spirit of Paul Grüninger. The board members asked the government of St. Gallen to compensate Paul Grüninger for the wrong done to him and, as a gesture, to name a square near the police headquarters after him. The city council took heed, and today there is a square in the inner city bearing his name. His name is also engraved on a Jewish memorial plaque in Washington. Paul Grüninger was the first Swiss citizen to be honored in such a manner by the American government.

Paul Grüninger died on February 22, 1972 at 81 years of age.

The question of official rehabilitation was not yet resolved, though. In 1984, a well-researched report on Paul Grüninger, "the Rescuer of Refugees", appeared in one of Switzerland's major daily newspapers, the "Tages-Anzeiger". Although cantonal councilor Paul Rechsteiner requested vindication, the government declined, stating that there were no grounds in the canton's legal code for opening rehabilitation proceedings. The government's position was that, after 46 years, nobody could truly judge whether Paul Grüninger's actions and his dismissal had been right or wrong. The parliament adjourned the matter again.

In 1989 another cantonal councilor, Hans Fässler, advanced the cause once more. He left it open what form a possible rehabilitation might take. He suggested a research paper be written on the refugee policies of Switzerland during the war years along with a commemoration of Paul Grüninger on the occasion of the 50th anniversary of his dismissal. Again, the government refused to consider rehabilitation, the reasons remaining unchanged.

In the spring of 1991 the "Justice for Paul Grüninger" association sponsored an historical investigation, after the initiative taken by cantonal councilors Fässler and Rechsteiner. The distinguished historian Stefan Keller spent two years thoroughly researching the Paul Grüninger affair. He wrote a book, *"Grüningers Fall"* ("Grüninger's Case"). It found widespread publicity among magistrates, the Council of the Swiss Refugee Relief, the Jewish Community of Switzerland, historians, the "Jewish Children of the Holocaust" organization, and other influential figures including noted Nazi hunter Simon Wiesenthal. Finally, 2,500 people signed a petition addressed to the government of the canton of St. Gallen requesting the rehabilitation of Paul Grüninger.

In May 1991, a square in Ugriat Ono, Israel was named after Paul Grüninger.

Meanwhile, the "Jewish Children of the Holocaust" organization increased the pressure. "Forty-eight years after the end of the Second World War, in full knowledge of the hideous and murderous apparatus of National Socialism in Germany, the government of St. Gallen is apparently not willing or not in a position to place humanitarian reasons above legalism." The children and grandchildren of deported and murdered Jews were asking that full recognition be given to Paul Grüninger's humanitarian work.

On November 30, 1993, 54 years after Paul Grüninger's misdemeanor and 21 years after his death, recognition and respect were finally granted by the government. The speeches made by high-ranking officials were tantamount to full political rehabilitation. The cantonal government of St. Gallen, for example, recognized that the Captain had been guided solely by high ethical values which have since become the foundation of Swiss as well as international law. It was emphasized, however, that this was to be a political rehabilitation. It was made clear that today, strict conditions would be apply if anyone should claim reasons of conscience as justification for refusal of service.

In 1994 the Swiss Federal Council (the federal executive of the Swiss state) commented on Paul Grüninger's rehabilitation. It upheld the cantonal government's position and added that there was no way to rehabilitate Paul Grüninger legally at the federal level. Articles 77 to 81 of the penal code could not be applied. The deeds of Paul Grüninger and his dismissal could not be judged objectively by a federal jury after such a long time. The fact that canton law did not contain the legal instrument of vindication was further upheld. Swiss officialdom was going around in circles.

Nonetheless, the "Justice for Paul Grüninger" association welcomed the rehabilitation gestures made by the cantonal and federal governments. On June 24, 1994, a declaration was signed by cantonal councilors Paul Rechsteiner, now also a member of the federal parliament, and Hans Fässler, stating that the governmental authorities had finally admitted that the measures taken against Jewish refugees during the years prior to World War II were tantamount to racial discrimination.

Finally, in 1995, on the 50th anniversary of the end of World War II, the President of Switzerland, Kaspar Villiger, made a public apology for events in Switzerland during those years. He openly admitted that more could have been done for the Jews fleeing the Holocaust. It was further acknowledged that Police Captain Paul Grüninger had acted out of motives that were pure and righteous, and that he had rightfully refused to obey orders on moral grounds.

The legal rehabilitation of Paul Grüninger took place in 1995, when the sentences of the St. Gallen tribunal were reversed. Grüninger was acquitted posthumously. The verdict of 1940 was rendered null and void.

The film "Captain Grüninger", made during Paul Grüninger's lifetime, is being shown again and again in order to keep alive the memory of a courageous, upright and conscientious man who listened to the voice of his heart rather than the letter of the law.

Maurice and Eléonore Dubois

Standing Up to the Vichy Regime

In 1942 Maurice Dubois was the head of the Swiss Red Cross office, situated on the Rue du Taur near Capitole square at Toulouse in southern France. From a report by director Frank

Rue du Taur, Toulouse where the office of the Swiss Red Cross was situated before and during World War II. (Source: Andreas C. Fischer archives)

he had heard of the terrible conditions under which about one-hundred teenagers and also younger children, some from Spain and southern France but also many refugees from Germany and Austria, were existing in the small village of Seyre southeast of Toulouse.

When he visited the site, he saw

57

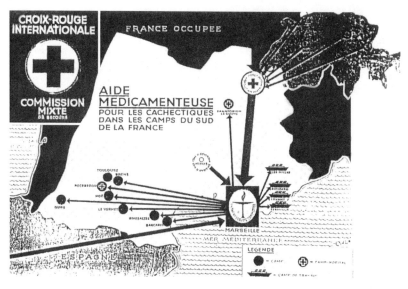

Map presented in the report to the commission of hygiene by the committee for the coordination of assistance to the camps, July 1, 1942. (Source: archives of CDJC, collection Joseph-Georges Cohen)

Receipts for aid parcels sent by Jewish relief workers to camp internees. (Source: archives of CDJC, collection Joseph-Georges Cohen)

the children suffering from jaundice, boils, scabies and other sicknesses. The buildings had few windows and conditions were inferior to those of cattle barns. He knew that help was needed, without delay. But he lacked the means. He contacted Berne and, after long and strenuous negotiations, the Swiss Red Cross started to look into the possibilities of how to take care of the poor children.

Maurice Dubois' wife, Eléonore, knew of a nearby uninhabited castle, Château La Hille, near Montégut-Plantaurel in the lovely valley of the Lèze river in the Ariège region. Although unused, it was being looked after by the caretaker of the stately castle at Foix. Eléonore Dubois succeeded in obtaining a lease on La Hille. About ninety children were taken to the castle and accommodated there.

Their situation improved considerably as a result of this transfer. They were divided into three groups according to their age. Dubois began actively to care for them. He visited the castle regularly to make sure that their living conditions were acceptable.

He could not, however, prevent the frequent visits by the French gendarmes. They were under orders from the German occupying forces to swoop on the castle every so often. But no arrests had been made. The Jewish children staying at La Hille thought they were safe.

Then, at dawn on August 26, 1942, "like lighting from the sky", a massive raid operation was mounted by the gendarmes on La Hille and other targets in the "free" zone.

One of the older children, Walter Kamlet, a refugee from Germany, wrote about his childhood experience: "On August 26, 1942, at four o'clock in the morning, the French gendarmes encircled the castle of La Hille. They entered by force, pistols in their hands, and stormed into the bedrooms. The middle and older children were scared out of their sleep. They sat on their beds and the girls started to cry. Some of them screamed and were really beside themselves. The gendarmes did not leave them much time to get dressed and to pack their belongings.

La Hille castle, seen from the east, as it is today. (Source: Andreas C. Fischer archives)

Outside Le Vernet memorial. (Source: Andreas C. Fischer archives)

(White) plaque commemorating the anti-fascist combatants—known and unknown—who died for the freedom of all peoples.

(Black) plaque commemorating the thousands of Jews, Gypsies and foreigners interned by the French Vichy regime before being deported to the Nazi camps where most of them were put to death: "We the generation of remembrance will never forget." (U.E.J.F. 1993)

Model of Le Vernet camp where people from 53 nations were interned. (Sources: Andreas C. Fischer archives, Museum of Le Vernet)

"After being lined up for a roll call outside the castle, 45 older children were marched off towards the small river Lèze. A truck was waiting on the country road on the other side of the bridge. The children were made to get on and were transported off to the camp of Le Vernet, situated about 15 miles to the north in the plains of the Ariège river. Le Vernet was a disciplinary camp that formed part of the system of exclusion and internment camps in the south of France. Conditions at Le Vernet were particularly hard.

"Before they were led away, the warden of La Hille, Rösli Naef, a Swiss woman living in France and working for the Red Cross, tried to negotiate with the gendarmes. They would not even listen to her but declared that within half an hour all of the arrested youths had to be ready for transportation. Warden Naef was very upset and ran up to Montégut, where she was able to call Maurice Dubois by telephone. He promised to do everything in his power to save the teenagers who were going to be confined behind the barbed wire fence of Vernet that same evening.

"Dubois traveled to Vichy without delay and contacted the Swiss Embassy. As he was not a diplomat himself, it was difficult to get them to do something, but after official intervention on their part, he was able to get in touch with the secretary general of the Ministry of the Interior of the Vichy regime. At the same time, Eléonore Dubois traveled to Berne, to obtain authorization from the federal government for the admission of the children to Switzerland.

"In Vichy, Maurice Dubois began by cautiously mentioning the 3,000 French children who were in Switzerland at that time recovering from the effects of the war. The Red Cross had not only invited them but was also looking after them during their recovery in Switzerland. This benevolence was acknowledged by the French government.

"Then Maurice Dubois mentioned the 45 children who apparently had been arrested in the small hours of the morning of August 26 at La Hille castle and transported to the Vernet camp. He openly described this pernicious action as an outrageous act of encroachment by the French gendarmerie. He emphasized that the Swiss Red Cross would not accept such interference and made it known that the situation of the French children in Switzerland was being seriously put in question.

"His daring words and his wife's intervention in Berne did not pass unheeded. The secretary general of the Vichy regime apologized for the incident. He explained that there must have been some sort of misunderstanding. He promised to arrange for the immediate release of the children from custody.

"Frau Naef was informed. She traveled to Le Vernet on her own initiative to tell the children. They were already standing with their bags packed at the forlorn train station, ready to be transported off. Official confirmation that they could return to the castle instead followed within a few hours on September 2, 1942. On the way back to La Hille, their temporary home, Frau Naef told them that they owed their lives to Maurice Dubois who had personally intervened with the authorities of the Vichy regime."

The intervention of Maurice Dubois also resulted in the release of three Jewish employees of the Swiss Red Cross who had been arrested in the raid at another home in Haute-Savoie. As director of all the Swiss Red Cross children's homes in southern France, he also protected the Jewish children at Le Chambon-sur-Lignon in Haute-Loire.

DID EVERYTHING TO MAKE LIFE BEARABLE

Another Swiss, Sebastian Steiger, who worked as a teacher at La Hille castle, reported that the work of Maurice Dubois and his wife did not stop there. Eléonore tried to consistently improve the children's lot at La Hille. She repeatedly contacted Berne and informed the Federal Council about the mortal danger the children were in, even after their return to the castle— because the gendarmes had menacingly promised that they would return. She asked the Swiss government to arrange things so that all Jewish children who were in jeopardy could

Le Vernet d'Ariège train station with cattle car (original) in which the internees were carried off to extermination camps. (Sources: Andreas C. Fischer archives)

receive a visa and seek refuge in Switzerland. Her plea fell on deaf ears.

Two young people, Ruth Tamir and Peter Salz, were among the refugee children at La Hille castle. Today they live in Israel. They remember that Maurice Dubois always had a heart for the children at the castle. In spite of the dire circumstances, he even helped to develop a good educational system at the home. Mostly they acted on their own initiative, seldom waiting for the go-ahead from their superiors in Berne. It was an open secret that Dubois had repeatedly lodged protests at Pierre Laval's office against the arrests and deportations of the youths. Laval was the head of the Vichy regime collaborating with the Nazis.

In an interview published in a Swiss newspaper in September 1988, Maurice Dubois declared that he knew that the deportation of the youths meant their certain death. He explained: "We had accommodated the refugee children at the shelter and wanted them to be at ease. But the French gen-darmes came again and again to make arrests. The authorities in Berne were not prepared to intervene. I approached the head of the visa and passport office of the Vichy regime and told him about my concern for the children. He assured me that if the Swiss government issued entry visas for the children, the Vichy regime would certainly give them the necessary exit visas, too. That would have created a precedent, of course, so I immedi-ately informed the head of the police department in Berne, Heinrich Rothmund. But he flatly refused to take any such action.

"As time went by, the young refugees at our shelter were in imminent and growing danger. Therefore, some tried to escape in small groups. Switzerland was the first choice, followed by Spain. Rösli Naef and I went to see the Swiss minister to Vichy France, Walter Stucki, and asked him to get in touch with Pierre Laval to inform him of the situation the children were in. Laval showed absolutely no interest in their fate. It seemed to me that the whole world was afraid of Germany. I therefore looked for other ways to get them out of France.

"By definition, the Red Cross should maintain its independence and neutrality. Its relations with governments and its tasks should be apolitical and impartial. But in my opinion the Red Cross did not always fulfil its moral duties during the Second World War. Was it fear of a possible German victory which sometimes caused it to leave the path of true neutrality?

"Of course, our task was paramount and had to be carried out under the most difficult of circumstances. Naturally, we did not want to arouse the suspicions of the government. But was the principle of impartiality so deeply anchored in our minds that some of us did not do everything in our power to save these children? This pussy-footing still weighs on my conscience.

"To this day, I have pangs of conscience about actions we should have taken but did not take. I still see the eyes of children on the deportation trains, I see mothers suckling their emaciated babies, I see human beings in striped prison clothes, I see the concentration camps...

"But I also see hope and courage. I remember the human warmth and strength and the dedication at our shelters in spite of the clear and real danger of death. I know that, during all the persecutions and deportations, the Swiss Refugee Assistance did a great work under the most difficult conditions imaginable. Who would ever be able to describe it all?"

WORK CONTINUED AFTER THE WAR; FINALLY THE HIGHEST HONOR

After the war, Maurice and Eléonore Dubois opened a home for concentration camp survivors at Adelboden in the Bernese Oberland. Later they also opened a home at Le Locle in western Switzerland for about 80 children suffering from social trauma.

Four survivors of La Hille castle now live in Israel: Alisa Domka from Haifa, Ruth Tamir from Ashkelon, Peter Salz from Lehawot Bashan and Dvorah Arel from Jerusalem. They arranged a meeting of the former La Hille children who had survived the war. The reunion took place on May 12, 1985 and Maurice Dubois was invited, too.

A few months later, Israel's ambassador Maurice Rivlin presented the Yad Vashem "Righteous Among the Nations" medal of honor to Maurice Dubois. He mentioned how Dubois had saved the lives of more than one hundred children by arranging their journeys from southern France and their entry into Switzerland. Two of the children who had survived the ominous attack by the gendarmes and survived the hazardous transit personally thanked Maurice Dubois at the ceremony.

Rösli Naef

The Loving Guardian of La Hille Castle

On March 16, 1943 a missive from Colonel Hugo Remund, chief medical adviser to the Geneva Headquarters of the Red Cross, reached Rösli Naef. She was the warden of the children's home at La Hille castle in southern France, run by the Swiss Red Cross. The message informed her of her immediate dismissal from her post and ordered her to return to Berne immediately. Rösli Naef protested.

She was accused of lack of discipline because she had repeatedly helped the children from La Hille castle to cross the border into Switzerland illegally. Several incidents, which had led to serious diplomatic tensions between Berne and Berlin, preceded her dismissal. For instance, during the night of January 3–4, 1943, four children were picked up by German border guards while attempting to cross the border between occupied France and Switzerland. The children were returned to occupied France and deported.

The German authorities at Lyons were informed, and the ICRC, fearful, decided to open an official inquiry. It revealed that Rösli Naef had encouraged the children to try to cross the border illegally. Apparently, she had sent more than 20 young children from La Hille castle to the border on various occasions, instructing them exactly where to go. Some of them

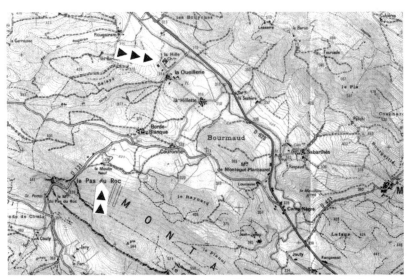

Section of map showing position of La Hille castle, west of Montégut-Plantaurel, and Moulin Neuf where the children could swim in the river Lèze. (Sources: Institut Géographique National, 1987, carte Série Bleue, feuille 2146 O)

La Hille castle viewed from the east. (Source: Andreas C. Fischer archives)

Israel Bravermann, one of the children who was taken away to the camp of Le Vernet awaiting deportation and whose life was saved by the intervention of Rösli Naef and Maurice Dubois. (Source: Sebastian Steiger)

spent the night at the Red Cross children's home at St.-Cergues-les-Voirons before crossing the Franco-Swiss frontier, southeast of Geneva. All was arranged and they had followed Rösli Naef's lead.

The Red Cross management in Geneva considered these actions to be a violation of Swiss neutrality and to have damaged the good relations between Berne and Berlin. The Red Cross feared that the Germans might stop the Swiss from giving any assistance at all to children suffering from war injuries. Because of these weighty considerations, it was decided to dismiss Rösli Naef immediately.

Rosa (Rösli) Naef was born in Glarus in central Switzerland. Even from her early youth, she wanted to help children. She studied nursing and then joined Dr. Albert Schweitzer in Africa at his jungle hospital in Lambarene. After a few years she returned to Switzerland and was appointed head of the Red Cross children's home at Seyre in southern France. The first director of this camp, M. Frank, together with his mother and his wife, had brought about one hundred refugee children from Germany and Austria to safety here after they had been separated from their parents.

The sanitary conditions at the Seyre shelter were unbearable. They led to sickness and epidemics. Naef complained about the situation to the director of the Swiss Juvenile Assistance of the Red Cross at Toulouse, Maurice Dubois. After learning of the untenable situation, he visited the shelter and decided to act. With the help of his wife Elen, he found and leased the uninhabited castle of La Hille, in the foothills of the Pyrenees, about

La Hille castle: main portal tower
and gate. (Source: Andreas C.
Fischer archives)

60 miles south of Toulouse. La
Hille was a real *château*;
although small, it had ramparts and walls, embrasures
and towers at the corners. The
children could be accommodated in much better conditions than at Seyre. The rooms
were spacious and comfort-
able.

Nevertheless, there was no
running water, no electricity,
no proper sewage system or
drainage, no clinic, no school.
That was where Rösli Naef's
organizational talents came
into play. She had the castle
repaired within a short time,
so that it provided acceptable
living quarters for the chil-
dren. Swiss and French volunteers organized a medical support service with doctors and nurses. The children could attend
a regular school according to their age. Frau Naef, not yet thirty years of age, looked after everything and everyone and,
despite her drive and occasionally brusque manner, the children loved her.

Two letters which have been preserved show appreciation
for Rösli Naef's self-sacrificing work at La Hille. Elias and Gitta
Sternbuch were actively involved in the rescue of Jewish
refugees in St. Gallen in north-eastern Switzerland.

Gitta wrote on October 24, 1942 in a letter to Rösli Naef:

*"First of all, I wanted to thank you from the bottom of my heart for
your outgoing concern for the sad lot of the persecuted Jews. At a time
when culture seems to have reached a terribly low level, I am touched
by having found a dear and noble human being who feels close to the
victims. I appreciate your readiness to give your utmost for those who*

are suffering. I admire you and congratulate you for the work and the sacrifice you are making. If you are only rewarded in this world by the children radiant with joy who embrace you as a mother, there will be a time, with God's help, when others will honor your great work. You may rest assured that your true reward is laid up for you in a better world.

"I am sending you the things we talked about. I have many shirts, dresses and coats which may be of use to the poor children who certainly need them. Thank you again for your readiness to take along these things for the children."

Many years later, on June 1, 1988, Elias Sternbuch—now living in Zurich—recalled:

"In all my contacts and negotiations with the Geneva office of the Red Cross, I heard about the activities of the Swiss Juvenile Assistance in southern France, and I personally saw Rösli Naef. Frau Naef had selflessly engaged in this Red Cross work. Together we tried to better the lot of the Jewish children who were staying at their temporary home at La Hille castle in France.

"Frau Naef had traveled to St. Gallen to fetch some clothing we had gotten ready for the young people. She also collected food such as cheese and dried vegetables for the hungry kids of La Hille. She has a lot of merit for helping and rescuing and saving these children."

Until August 26, 1942 it had been relatively calm at La Hille castle. The impact of the Vichy regime was not felt very much. The children thought they were safe. They diligently learned their lessons at school, they played and made some excursions in the area. They also developed their musical skills. There was real talent among these children.

But at dawn that summer day, the children were awakened by the noise of engines. Trucks were driving up. Loud voices were heard as the gendarmes talked and shouted. It was obvious that they were provoking an argument, but Rösli Naef stayed calm. Normally, not much caused her to lose her composure. Then she, too, raised her voice. Suddenly, it was deadly quiet at the castle. The children sensed that something nasty was about to happen.

Then they heard the heavy steps of six armed French gendarmes, led up the stairs by Warden Naef. They went from room to room. When they reached the room where the older children (above the age of 16 years) were, the gendarmes demanded their names and wrote them on their lists.

After the inspection, Naef asked the children to get dressed. She said something about an error or a misunderstanding and that there was only going to be a short trip to another camp. Nobody should be unnecessarily alarmed, as they would all return safely.

Frau Naef had arranged a quick breakfast for the children who were about to be marched off, and also gave them some bread and chocolate to take along. The children had to assemble in the courtyard. They were only allowed one small bag each. The gendarmes were pressing on.

Rösli Naef said goodbye to everyone and cheered them up. "I believe that we will see each other again soon," she reassured them. The gendarmes stepped in and separated her from the youngsters. Rösli and many of the children had tears in their eyes.

There was no time to lose. From Montégut where there was a telephone, she called Maurice Dubois in Toulouse and told him about the attack on the castle and the arrest of 45 children. She asked him to get in touch with the Vichy authorities without delay and to demand the liberation and return of the children to La Hille castle.

Rösli knew that the children had been taken to the camp of Le Vernet. She also knew that that was the first step towards deportation. She set off for Le Vernet by bicycle—but her bicycle punctured a tire! However, she managed to find a taxi. Arriving at the camp of Le Vernet in what was in those days a prestigious vehicle, she managed to gain admittance to the camp.

In his book *"Yovel"*, Jacques Roth from Paris, who was among the children, wrote about their feelings when Rösli Naef

Forlorn railway station of Le Vernet d'Ariège opposite Le Vernet internment camp. From here, hundreds of people were taken to Nazi extermination camps in eastern Europe in cattle cars like the one shown. (Source: Andreas C. Fischer archives)

arrived: "When we saw her, we all had hope again. Her presence had a very calming effect on us. She was our moral authority and a kind-hearted person. We had already been prepared for deportation, but Rösli Naef assured us that she would not leave us and that she would do everything she could to bring about our return to La Hille. She assured us that she was in contact with Maurice Dubois and that she expected good news from him at any moment.

PLANNING ESCAPES FOR CHILDREN FACED WITH DEPORTATION

"We were waiting to board the train to Poland, when, all of a sudden, Frau Naef came running up to the station, her face beaming with delight. She announced that we would be let free and could return to La Hille. Tears of joy were running down her cheeks."

After this serious incident, the children at La Hille enjoyed but a short time of tranquility. When German troops occupied the south of France in November 1942, new danger loomed.

Rösli Naef was convinced that raids by gendarmes or troops would ensue and that arrests of older children would follow. That was why she started a series of preparations to save the possible target group of children from arrest and deportation.

A guard duty was organized around the clock. The watchmen were to alert the residents of the castle before gendarmes or other armed men could reach the castle. A hideout was installed at the roomy attic above the chapel, to be used as a last resort. The place was called the "onion loft" because in former times they used to dry onions there. It had a secret entrance which was very difficult to find and known only to a chosen few. The password was *"shortcut"*.

For Rösli Naef, these preparations did not go far enough. She took all eventualities into account and decided to arrange for the most endangered children to escape to Switzerland.

Rösli Naef got in touch with the farmers in the area. She arranged with many of them that, if need be, she could hide some of the children on their farms. She also talked to Germaine Hommel, the headmistress of the Swiss children's home at St.-Cergues-les-Voirons—close to the Swiss border but still on French territory in Haute-Savoie. The two women agreed that this home would receive and give shelter to the exhausted refugee children before they crossed the border.

Back at La Hille castle there was bad news: the French gendarmes were starting their raids again, on the orders of the German occupying forces. Frau Naef took steps to ensure that they would not be caught by surprise again.

She called a meeting with the older children. Four of them, Peter Salz, Jacques Roth, Regina Rosenblatt and Margot Kern, were ready to attempt an escape to Switzerland. On December 22, 1942, provided with food for the journey, fresh underwear and Swiss francs, they started out toward the Swiss border some 350 miles to the north.

Dvorah Erel, née Margot Kern, now living in Jerusalem, described that journey: "Rösli Naef had personal papers prepared for us, a 'laissez-passer' (a free pass) with four French names. She also handed us some money, enough for the trip to the border. She had informed Germaine Hommel, the headmistress of the Swiss children's home situated on the slopes above St.-Cergues-les-Voirons, that we were coming. After a short rest, a young Frenchman led us across the border at night, under cover of darkness. I had been given the address of Rösli Naef's friend in Zurich. When I arrived there I was able to rest and recover for a few weeks.

"Later, Rösli Naef helped me and Regina Rosenblatt again. After being dismissed from office at La Hille, she returned to Geneva where she worked at the Henri-Dunant Refugee Children Center of the Red Cross. She procured jobs for Regina and me at the center as well. We were able to stay in Switzerland until the end of the war in 1945."

Following the success of the first attempt to escape to Switzerland, Rösli Naef continued to organize groups whom she sent on their way to this safe country. Between Christmas and New Year 1943, seven youths succeeded in crossing over without being picked up. Another three made it to Spain.

On the night of the 1st to the 2nd of January, however, there was a serious setback. Rösli Naef had sent another group of six youths to the border. They were Hans Garfunkel, Helga Klein, Betty Schütz, Lotte Nussbaum, Inge Joseph and Léon Lewin. They had spent one night at the children's home at St.- Cergues and were waiting for the right moment to cross into Switzerland.

While they were still in the dense border forest between France and Switzerland, they ran into a patrol. Five of them were caught and only one, Inge, escaped because a Swiss border guard felt sorry for her. She was allowed to go—but back to France. She kept trying, and on the third attempt she finally made it across the border. The others were placed under arrest and were sentenced on the spot to two weeks imprisonment for illegally crossing the border. They were taken to Annemasse, a French border town near Geneva.

When Warden Naef heard about the abortive trip, she knew what to expect at La Hille castle. She knew that the raids would start again and probably never cease. And indeed, the gendarmes encircled the premises on one of the following nights, searching for children. Rösli Naef, however, had taken precautions. The youngsters had been sent to the nearby farms and even the onion loft served as a hideout. None of the endangered children was arrested.

Jacques Roth, who was saved earlier, still remembers the love and outgoing concern Rösli Naef had for the refugees. "She never expected anything in return. Before she came to La Hille she had known nothing about Jews and their history. But once she was confronted with the hideous persecution of Jewish children, she wanted to find out more. She read books and asked questions. After the war Jacqueline Veuve made a movie about the life of Rösli Naef in which I also had a part." (The film *"La Filière"*—based on a book of the same name by Anne-Marie Im Hof-Piguet—was produced by Aquarius Films, Lausanne, in 1987.)

Rösli Naef was dismissed as warden of La Hille castle in May 1943 because of lack of discipline, which was considered to be a violation of Swiss neutrality. She was recalled to Berne. After the war, she was so disgusted with the way she had been treated and the official attitude of the Swiss authorities during the war, that she decided to leave Switzerland and settle in Denmark—a country that, she had heard, had saved almost all of its Jews.

When Rösli Naef was named by Yad Vashem as one of the "Righteous Among the Nations" in 1989, she modestly declined to accept the medal of honor. While attending a ceremony honoring, posthumously, Germaine Hommel and others at St.-Cergues-les-Voirons on October 4, 1992, she finally agreed to accept her award.

Rösli Naef died in her birthplace, Glarus in central Switzerland, in 1996.

Renée Farny

Masterminding the Escape

On December 17, 1941 the Swiss Red Cross took charge of "Les Feux Follets", a children's home at St.-Cergues-les-Voirons in the "free" territory of France in Haute-Savoie, a short distance from Geneva. (The building had previously housed the "Colonie de Vacances Italienne" set up by the Italian anti-fascists.) French children traumatized by the war could come to the Red Cross home to rest and recuperate for three months at a time. A Frenchwoman named Germaine Hommel was its warden, and her assistant was Swiss-born Renée Farny.

After the German troops had occupied southern France in November 1942, the number of Jewish refugee children arriving from Austria and Germany increased. Germaine Hommel and Renée Farny looked after them as if they were their own. Whenever a raid from the French gendarmes was imminent and the children were threatened with arrest and deportation, they courageously hid them, even if this meant risking their own lives.

When the gendarmes raided La Hille castle, also operated by the Swiss Red Cross, its warden Frau Rösli Naef contacted Germaine Hommel, asking whether she could accept endangered Jewish youths who were on the gendarme's search list.

The former Italian anti-fascist vacation home at St. Cergues-les-Voirons, Haute Savoie. Renamed "Les Feux Follets", it became a Swiss Red Cross children's home where French children came to recuperate from the trauma of war—and a stepping stone for refugee children from La Hille castle fleeing to safety in Switzerland. (Source: Herbert Herz archives, Yad Vashem, Geneva)

Madame Hommel readily consented and even offered assistance if any of them wanted to flee.

One of the children who used the escape route was Jacques Roth. He described how the French gendarmes had penetrated the castle on the night of December 20, 1942, arresting and abducting Jewish children aged over 16. Rösli Naef was well aware that this meant their deportation and certain death. For this reason, she decided to save the children's lives by helping them escape to Switzerland.

A group of four—Margot Kern, Regina Rosenblatt, Peter Salz and Jacques Roth—set out and Rösli Naef gave them some money for the journey. They wore the red insignia that identified French children traumatized by war who were recovering at the Swiss Red Cross homes. Frau Naef explained to the children how to get to "Les Feux Follets". Madame Hommel had been informed by Frau Naef about the arrival of the four young refugees.

Jacques Roth recalls: "We took the train to Toulouse and from there to Lyons. In the same compartment were soldiers of the German Wehrmacht (armed forces). Although at first we were afraid, we soon noticed that there were practically no controls. After Lyons we were on a train with two French gendarmes, and we reached our destination without any problems. The two house-mothers Hommel and Farny received us warmly and we were given a spacious room.

"Renée Farny introduced us to a young man, Léon Balland. He would later help us cross the Swiss border, she said. The next day, which happened to be December 23, our group went together with several children from the home to buy Christmas decorations for the tree. We soon reached a forest where we said goodbye to the other children and Renée Farny. Léon led us until we reached a barbed wire fence. Here he explained when the border patrols would be doing their rounds. We hid ourselves until the next patrol was past. Then Léon helped us across the border. Finally we were on Swiss soil and safe."

Today Jacques Roth lives in Paris.

Another child from La Hille castle, Lieselotte Nussbaum, recounted her flight after she had reached Haifa in Palestine right after the war. "In May 1942—I was nineteen at that time— Rösli Naef sent me to St.-Cergues-les-Voirons east of Geneva, where I was to assist Madame Germaine Hommel as group leader. Most of the children were not Jewish, whereas at La Hille the majority were. Some went to school in St.-Cergues-les-Voirons. After my arrival, I was given responsibility for a group of small children. Food and clothes were strictly rationed.

"On August 26, 1942, we were awakened during the night. Madame Hommel and Mademoiselle Farny both cried but they were powerless against the French gendarmes who claimed they had orders to take us away. A doctor at the home, Dr. Cohen from Berlin was arrested, too, together with his wife. First we were taken to a reception camp at Annemasse, then transferred to Annecy and finally to the deportation camp of Lyon-Vénissieux.

"We saw many of the prisoners being transported away. For some unknown reason, after a few days they released Dr. Cohen, his wife and me. They told us that the Red Cross [notably Maurice Dubois] had intervened on our behalf. When we reached St.-Cergues-les-Voirons again, Germaine Hommel and Renée Farny were overjoyed.

"But from then on we were in constant danger. Madame Hommel spoke to Léon Balland, the farmer's son who had volunteered to work at the home. On September 30, Léon led us by night safely across the Swiss border near Jussy. He happened to know of an old uninhabited farmhouse in no-man's-land where he wanted to hide us. But when we crossed the territory, we were stopped by a Swiss border patrol. We thought we were already at liberty, yet the Swiss sent us back to France. 'Orders are orders', they said.

"So we had no choice but to return to France. A young Swiss border guard, however, showed us a hiding place where we would not be discovered by the French or the Germans. In the small hours of the morning, we got back to the children's home at St.-Cergues-les-Voirons.

"We tried again. On October 4, Dr. Cohen, his wife and I set out again and, with the help of Léon Balland and Renée Farny, we went back again to the same spot near Jussy. Only this time we had a large group of children accompanying us, and while we were all walking along the border, the three of us just 'disappeared'. This time we made it across the border without any difficulties. Once in Switzerland, we were taken to a refugee camp in Geneva."

OTHER WITNESSES TESTIFY TO THE SKILFUL ESCAPE STRATEGIES

In a letter written by Peter Salz from Kibbutz Lehawot Habashan and addressed to Herbert Herz, the Yad Vashem representative in Geneva, many witnesses spoke of their personal experiences during the rescue of Jewish children at St.-Cergues-les-Voirons.

One of them wrote: "I was one of four children who were sent from St.- Cergues-les-Voirons to the Swiss border, accompanied by Léon Balland and Renée Farny who helped us cross illegally. We owe our lives to them. A few years later, we learned that Léon had apparently been caught by the Germans and killed. Fortunately, this turned out to be a false rumor."

The news of these successful escapes encouraged La Hille and St.-Cergues-les-Voirons to coordinate their efforts even more closely. Warden Rösli Naef sent more Jewish youths who were in jeopardy, and Madame Hommel helped them across the border to safety.

On December 31, however, two youths, Kurt Moser and Kurt Klein, were picked up by French border guards while attempting to cross. They were put in jail for two weeks, then released and sent back to La Hille.

A few days later, on January 2, 1943 five other youths, Inge Helft, Adele Hochberger, Inge Joseph, Walter Strauss and Manfred Vos attempted to flee to Switzerland after they had been led to the border by Renée Farny and Léon Balland. They failed and were arrested at customs.

Walter Strauss told his story: "From La Hille castle we had traveled via Toulouse, Lyons and Annemasse to St.-Cergues-les-Voirons. From there we wanted to get to Switzerland. But after we had crossed the frontier, a Swiss border guard saw us and stopped us; he directed us back to the French check-point. Four of us were sentenced on the spot to two weeks' imprisonment at Annemasse jail. After our release, they deported Adele Hochberger and Manfred Vos, while Inge Joseph and I were allowed to return to La Hille. Inge Helft, however, was allowed to pass by the Swiss border guard and thus she was able to hide somewhere in Switzerland. After a while, however, she had to leave the country and was later arrested in Nice. Miraculously, she returned to La Hille castle. She attempted a third escape and the last one was successful. She made it to Switzerland again; this time she was able to stay for good and was saved."

In January 1943, Léon Balland had to leave the children's home. He had been summoned for obligatory work in Germany. While still in France, he escaped from the train.

After the departure of Léon Balland, Renée Farny continued to escort the refugee children to the border on her own. She always used the same ruse to fool the border guards. An outing to the frontier was organized for the convalescent French children. The runaways were among them. As soon as the patrols had passed, the youths slipped away across the border, and the children returned to the home.

Odile Manos wrote a seminar paper at the University of Grenoble (France) concerning the clandestine passage of refugees from St.-Cergues-les-Voirons into Switzerland. Renée Farny's escape procedure is described in detail. On one occasion, fifty children from "Les Feux Follets" were told to play and sing and run around in a park near the frontier. The games continued until the evening. At nightfall, the barbed wire fence was cut and the refugees were smuggled across the border. Of the eleven who attempted the flight; five were caught and arrested, but six succeeded in escaping.

On February 8, 1943, Hommel and Farny, together with Rösli Naef from La Hille, were instructed by Red Cross headquarters in Berne to abstain from any activities which could tarnish the reputation of the organization. Laws and regulations laid down by the French government were to be respected, even if this meant a moral conflict for the individual.

The two ladies at "Les Feux Follets" in St.-Cergues-les-Voirons, however, did not follow these instructions, and continued with their escape preparations. Unfortunately, some of the youths were picked up and arrested after they had slipped through the fence. Infuriated, the French customs and border guards complained to the Swiss minister and demanded that all preparations and assistance for refugees escaping from La

Hille castle and St.-Cergues-les-Voirons should be stopped immediately.

The ambassador passed on a report to the Red Cross headquarters. In it, Rösli Naef's help to over twenty Jewish children from La Hille, the overnight stay at "Les Feux Follets" and various other preparatory measure were described in meticulous detail. It was also mentioned that several runaways had been caught, and that the German occupying authorities in Lyon were well informed and annoyed about the situation.

The behavior of the two women was considered to be "politically unwise" and, in view of the wintry weather conditions, "humanly incomprehensible". Everyone agreed that the Red Cross children's assistance should dissociate itself from the two women. There were suspicions, too, about Maurice Dubois, director of all the children's homes in southern France. He was recalled to Switzerland, where he was questioned. The dismissal of Germaine Hommel, Renée Farny and Rösli Naef was ordered, and the Vichy regime was informed of the decisions.

Even though she and Renée Farny had to leave the children's home at "Les Feux Follets", Germaine Hommel continued her illegal activities as a "schlepper" along the Swiss border and worked for the Resistance during 1943–44 until she was caught and sent to a labor camp. After the war, Germaine Hommel was named an Officer of the Legion of Honor.

On Sunday October 4, 1992, a memorable ceremony took place at St.-Cergues-les-Voirons, on the esplanade in front of the former children's home. Renée Farny and Germaine Hommel were honored (both posthumously) as "Righteous Among the Nations", although no members of their families were there to receive the awards.

Ariel Kerem, the adjoint to Israel's representative at the European Office of the United Nations in Geneva, presented Léon Balland with his medal of honor—and Jacques Roth, whose life had been saved as a child, was there. A medal posthumously honoring Marthe Bouvard was presented to her niece. (Marthe Bouvard had been the linen maid at "Les Feux Follets" and had actively supported the rescue activities at the home.)

The mayors of various communities of the region attended the ceremony, together with the representative of Yad Vashem, Herbert Herz.

It was on this memorable occasion that Herbert Herz finally managed to persuade Rösli Naef, who was present in the audience, to accept in person the medal that had been waiting for her since 1989.

Gret Tobler

A Helping Hand to Freedom

Margareta (Gret) Tobler started work as a kindergarten teacher at the Swiss Red Cross children's home at La Hille castle in southern France on January 4, 1943.

Without the aid of any guide or "schlepper", Gret Tobler single-handedly helped two young Jewish girls staying at La Hille to escape across the border to Switzerland. Gret Tobler wrote her own account of their eventful journey, and the story is also documented by Anne-Marie Im Hof-Piguet in her book *"La Filière"*.

Toni Rosenblatt, aged 12 and Inge Bernard, aged 15, had been granted visas to go to Switzerland. Obtaining permission to leave occupied France legally was, however, out of the question.

Gret Tobler quietly resolved that she would flee to Switzerland and take the two girls with her while their entry visas were still valid.

They left La Hille at 2.30 in the morning on December 10, 1943. After walking for three hours, they reached the railway station of Saint-Jean-de-Verges. A train took them to Toulouse, where they changed to a local train for Carcasonne. The train services were in chaos. That evening, somehow they all managed to squeeze on to the night express train to Lyons. The train was so crowded that there was not even enough room for

Gret to put down her rucksack and sit on it! After a five-hour delay, they arrived in Lyons. Just in time to catch a direct connection to Annemasse—which had to be diverted, because the tracks had been blown up.

From Annemasse, they walked along the border to St.-Cergue-les-Voirons. They had wanted to cross the frontier under cover of darkness, but barbed wire had been put up in the meantime.

Arriving at the Red Cross children's home "Les Feux Follets", they were warmly welcomed. There was nowhere else they could safely have stayed the night—and anyone found outside after the seven o'clock curfew was liable to be summarily shot.

The next day, Gret and the two girls took a Sunday afternoon stroll along the border. They found a little brook flowing underneath the barbed wire near the border control point. This could be their opportunity to slip across. Toni tried, but it wasn't going to work. A German soldier suddenly appeared, but he seemed not to notice them.

Attempting to approach the border near Machilly, they were intercepted by two French border guards with their dogs, who interrogated them and searched their bags before sending them back. Fortunately the guards did not find the girls' Swiss visas or Gret's Swiss money.

After another night at "Les Feux Follets", Gret tried to take the girls across via a visit to a convent that straddled the border. But their hopes were soon dashed; the Germans had the convent heavily guarded.

Sending Inge and Toni back to the children's home, Gret continued to search until she found a place where a small section of the new second line of barbed wire was incomplete. A brook flowed underneath the first line. That night, Inge slipped under the first line of barbed wire, ran several meters to the next wire entanglement, clambered through the open section—and was safely on Swiss soil.

Gret and Toni made the crossing at dawn. The Swiss border guards were amazed that they had succeeded.

Sebastian Steiger

The Man Who was More Than a Teacher

Sebastian Steiger was a young teacher in Basle and dedicated his life to education and child care. He had studied pedagogy at the University of Zurich.

He had heard stories that, following the German occupation of France on November 11, 1942, twelve children had succeeded in fleeing to Switzerland, but also that six children had been arrested by German border guards and returned to France.

Sebastian learned about a refugee girl named Inge Helft who failed twice to cross the Swiss border. All in all, she had walked over a thousand kilometers (600 miles) to get to the frontier, only to be picked up again by a border patrol on her third attempt. One of the guards wanted to give the starving child a bowl of soup before sending her back. She refused the soup. The guard relented and let her pass. These stories stirred Sebastian's conscience.

Steiger decided to volunteer as a teacher with the Swiss Red Cross since he knew that they operated children's homes in France for youngsters who had suffered mentally and physically from the effects of the war. His mother had given him the address of one of their shelters and the name of its headmaster, August Bohny. Sebastian wrote him a letter and in the reply he was advised to contact Red Cross headquarters in Geneva.

Children walking out through the main gate on one of the many happy days they spent at La Hille castle. (Source: Sebastian Steiger)

There they suggested that he should travel to the south of France and apply for work as a teacher at La Hille castle.

Sebastian obtained a visa for France and, towards the end of August 1943, he traveled to La Hille via Montluel. On arrival, he encountered a strange and miserable situation.

He noticed that there seemed to be no children over the age of 16—they were all hiding somewhere. The younger ones appeared traumatized. They talked about imminent and repeated raids by the French gendarmes. And, indeed, the police came to the castle every so often, under orders they had received from the German occupying authorities to take the children away.

The constant danger, coupled with news about children who failed in their attempts to cross the border, caused depression and fear among the children at the castle. The young teacher tried to get through to them, but it took a while to win their trust. He tried to encourage them by staging plays, arranging sports activities and going on hikes.

Sebastian Steiger was not just an ordinary schoolteacher. He also saw himself as a children's nurse, and soon he was integrated into the rescue system of the shelter. He was responsible for hiding the children quickly in the onion loft the event of an

La Hille castle: tower and main building. (Source: Andreas C. Fischer archives)

La Hille castle: eastern side portal, main building behind. (Source: Andreas C. Fischer archives)

alert so that the gendarmes would not find them. He also helped to organize escape routes to Spain and Switzerland.

In a book he later wrote, entitled *"Die Kinder von Schloss La Hille"* (*"The Children of La Hille Castle"*), Steiger describes the eerie situation he was faced with: "We could not understand why the Swiss government ruthlessly sent refugees back to France, among them children from La Hille castle, after they had been picked up somewhere at the border. Did Switzerland merit the name of a "safe haven" after behaving like this? It was a scandal. Perhaps the government did not know about the extermination camps in Germany, but that excuse had to be excluded as a possible explanation, since we all knew what was happening at Dachau as early as 1943."

In October of that same year, a woman named Emmi Ott was appointed as warden at La Hille. She tried to comply with the instructions from the Red Cross directors in Geneva. In view of the critical situation, though, she had to turn a blind eye to activities that seemed to be illegal.

SEVERE WINTER, CONSTANT THREAT OF RAIDS

A severe winter followed, creating new difficulties and causing greater hardship. The castle could not be heated properly and it turned into a giant refrigerator. Only one of the classrooms had a stove. The children caught cold and got sick. In addition to the cuts and bruises children normally have, they contracted boils and scabies, and some of them came down with fever, suffering from hypothermia. Sebastian's talents as a children's nurse were heavily in demand.

The room with a stove was turned into a clinic. Although Steiger had had the presence of mind to bring a small pharmacy kit along with him from Switzerland, it was soon depleted. He had to travel to Toulouse frequently to replenish his supplies of medicine, and also to buy educational material for the pupils.

Moulin Neuf, where Sebastian Steiger regularly took the children swimming. (Source: Andreas C. Fischer archives)

"In Toulouse I scoured the shops for articles we needed," Steiger wrote in his book. "It was crazy. At each street corner there were German soldiers who looked very menacing with their machine guns. Some of the uniformed men wore black caps with the Death's Head insignia. While I was looking for pencils and paper, I was very nervous and expected to be stopped and asked what I was doing. I reached for my passport in my pocket. My search became less and less hopeful, as there was nothing left in the shops."

As the raids by the gendarmes became more frequent, the onion loft was constantly in use and often filled to capacity. Therefore, it was decided to build a hut in the woods of nearby Moulin Neuf where the older children who could not be accommodated at neighboring farms could hide. The place they chose was in a dense forest, situated on a hill with a steep incline. The hut accommodated eight youngsters who got there under cover of darkness, since there were patrols roaming the area. Steiger's responsibility was to provide them with food and to maintain contact with them. At night he would secretly climb the hill to look after the children.

In spite of the tension, occasional panic and impending raids, Steiger did everything he could to cheer up the teenagers. On December 6, he dressed up as Santa Claus, and on Christmas Eve he organized a celebration complete with Christmas tree and carol singing.

But the situation continued to deteriorate. Their inability to find the older youths infuriated the gendarmes and their superiors. They knew that the children were still somewhere in the area—but where? Finally, they summoned the children by name to present themselves at the Gestapo headquarters in Toulouse and threatened all the residents of La Hille castle with severe sanctions if they failed to comply. At the castle, Steiger insisted that none of them should ever go to Toulouse.

A few days later, the shocking news reached them that the gendarmes had searched one of the farms where one of the youths, Walter Kamlet, was being accommodated. Fortunately, Walter had been working in the fields when the farmhouse was raided and was able to flee when he heard the trucks approaching. But the incident caused great concern.

Walter Kamlet and Edith Moser decided that they would now attempt an escape to the Swiss border. Steiger furnished them with the necessary identification documents and accompanied them part of the way. After an eventful journey, they reached the frontier and were met by Victoria Cordier. As she had done for others before, Victoria smuggled them across the border and brought them safely to the house of Anne-Marie Piguet's father, who readily received them.

One of the girls, Ilse Bruenell, was accommodated at the house of Madame Autier in the small town of Foix, after Madame Autier had approached Warden Ott on her own initiative, volunteering to provide shelter for youngsters in her own home. When Frau Ott found out, however, that Madame

Autier held a high post in the local police force, she had second thoughts, suspecting that this might be a trap. Sebastian was asked to find another solution for Ilse.

Rosa Goldmark, another child from Vienna, received news that her parents had been arrested and deported. She fell into a state of deep depression. Every two weeks she ran away from La Hille, with no particular destination in mind. They always went to look for her but sometimes the search took a very long time. Frau Ott decided to send Rosa to the psychiatric clinic at Lannemezan.

Sebastian Steiger had tried to help Rosa. He was not happy with her being sent to an insane asylum. He made up his mind to visit her. The trip to Lannemezan was an adventure in itself. He found Rosa in a hysterical condition, but lucid enough to ask to be taken back to La Hille.

This was easier said than done. When he left the clinic he was stopped by a French gendarme who wanted to see his papers and was about to arrest him, as he was not allowed to leave the area of La Hille. The gendarme even threatened to put him in prison for two weeks. Steiger explained that he was Swiss and a teacher at the Swiss children's home where he was looking after French children traumatized by the war. The gendarme let him go, but advised him that his case would be investigated and that he could expect to be summoned by the police.

Steiger was in no way intimidated by this incident or the threat. After a few days he visited Rosa again and saw that her mental condition had deteriorated. A few weeks later he got a message from the clinic saying that she had passed away.

MORE RESPONSIBILITIES FALL HIS WAY

After Gret Tobler, the kindergarten teacher, had fled to Switzerland, taking two young Jewish girls with her to safety, Steiger was given the responsibility of looking after the smaller children. As the gendarmes had promised, he was duly summoned for questioning by the Gestapo at Toulouse.

Because he took his duties seriously, he ignored the summons, knowing full well that this in itself would have been reason enough to arrest him.

Some of the older and middle children tried to flee to Switzerland or Spain. While many made it, others were picked up at the border and sent back to France. Some were arrested and deported. A few managed to evade the police again and made it back to La Hille castle, only to attempt yet another escape.

The invasion by the Allied troops and the news of the Russian advance on the eastern front led everyone to expect that the end of the war was near. That hope was mingled with fears, however, because none of the children knew whether their parents or other relatives were still alive. Rumors were rife.

Sometime during the summer of 1944 the raids stopped. The latent danger for the children grew smaller and a cautious feeling of security began to develop. Steiger organized excursions again. He encouraged the children to play and even took them swimming in the brook near Moulin Neuf.

Many of the Swiss Red Cross employees who had served at La Hille castle wanted to return to Switzerland. All of a sudden this caused unexpected difficulties, because the French authorities insisted on exit visas for all foreigners wanting to leave the country. The issuing of these visas took quite some time.

One day at the end of October 1944, the hour of departure had come for Sebastian Steiger and most of his Swiss colleagues. The scene could not have been more dramatic when he said goodbye to the children he had cared for during such a long and arduous time. The little ones sobbed and cried loudly; even the few older children who had not been abducted by the gendarmes or had not left of their own accord had tears in their eyes.

Steiger wrote in his book: "At four o'clock in the morning we left the castle and set out while it was still dark. When I reached the Lèze brook, I looked back one final time: there it was, its ramparts dark and somber, its silhouette sharp and majestic against the dark sky. With a sudden sadness in my heart I took my leave of La Hille castle and the children, and stepped into the vast emptiness..."

The journey to the border was arduous and stressful. Most of the trains were not running. Many bridges had been blown up. Under these circumstances, it took Steiger and his friends six days and nights to reach Nice.

From there they traveled on to Annecy in the Savoy region, south of Geneva. At the Red Cross office there, they learned that the border with Switzerland had been sealed, and that leaving France without a visa would be utterly impossible. Steiger and his friends had no choice other than to stay and to take up work locally with a Red Cross relief column near the border.

In the middle of the winter, on February 4, 1945, Steiger decided to cross the border into his native country. His attempt was successful although, while on his way to Geneva, he was picked up by a border patrol who explained that anybody who illegally crossed the border—even if Swiss nationals—would be regarded as a refugee. As he had no visa, they took him along to the Claparède refugee camp in Geneva. After being questioned, he was released.

A few months after Steiger and his group had departed, Emmi Ott left La Hille castle, and the Swiss children's shelter was closed. Children whose relatives could be traced were sent to them. The others were distributed among the various Red Cross columns.

Sadly, the La Hille children met a tragic fate. Twelve were deported; eleven did not survive. After the reckless attack of August 26, 1942, 21 children attempted to flee to Switzerland or Spain. Five were picked up at the Franco-Swiss border, and four of them had to return to France. The four children who were headed for Spain were caught when they tried to cross the frontier. One of the children, Rosa Goldmark, ended up in the psychiatric hospital at Lannemezan where she died of a broken heart.

In the spring of 1944, four children found refuge at an orphanage of the Franciscan sisters in Pamiers. Three reached the convent of Lévignac near Toulouse in the summer of the same year. Egon Berlin, a youngster who had joined the French "Maquis" guerilla organization, was killed in action on July 9, 1944.

Six children reached Palestine via Spain with the help of an American-Jewish refugee organization. Two went to the United States.

BECAME TIRELESS SUPPORTER OF ISRAEL

Steiger described his years at La Hille castle as the most fateful time of his life. He could not forget them after his return to Switzerland. He dedicated himself totally to the cause of Israel and the Jewish people. He organized a "Day of the Jewish Children" in 1958, in memory of the 1.5 million Jewish children who were murdered under the Nazi regime.

He visited Israel many times. Back in Switzerland, he gave lectures promoting Israel. He worked in the Christian-Jewish Community, was a member of the board of the Switzerland-Israel Association and also of the committee of the Children's Village Kirjat Yearim Society in Israel. Wherever he could, he supported the cause of Israel.

Sebastian Steiger considered a meeting at the Lehawot Habashan Kibbutz in Israel in 1985 a "major event" in his life. Two of the La Hille children organized a reunion of survivors who still could be traced, 41 years after their fateful years together at the castle.

On March 14, 1990 Marianne Bolga from Basle wrote a letter to Israel's ambassador to Switzerland in Berne, Raphael Gvir, asking whether it had ever been recognized that Sebastian Steiger had saved many Jewish children from certain death during the war. Raphael Gvir himself, when he was child, had crossed the border illegally from France to Switzerland near

Geneva during the night of October 3–4, 1942.

On August 29, 1993, a celebration was held in Basle. Ambassador Gvir made the following speech: "Sebastian Steiger volunteered for the Red Cross in 1943 to care for children who had suffered in the aftermath of the war. At La Hille castle in southern France there were many children who were traumatized, and most of them were also in constant danger of being caught, deported and murdered. Steiger taught the children and fought for them. He nursed them when they were sick and found the most adventurous and sometimes dangerous ways to teach them, entertain them and to provide them with the basic necessities of life.

"None of them was safe at the shelter; all of their names were registered with the police. Sooner or later they would get them. The Red Cross—alas!—felt bound by the conditions established by the regime and did little to ensure the safety of the children. Sebastian Steiger never hesitated when the well-being of his children was at stake. He acted contrary to the instructions of his superiors when their lives were in jeopardy.

"Food was scarce at the children's home. All were suffering from malnutrition and lack of vitamins. Steiger himself contracted jaundice and nearly died. He never thought of returning to Switzerland but rather helped his children to flee. He gave away his own identity card to a child who could flee to Switzerland. He forged papers, although he knew that he could face a life sentence for doing so. Anyone picked up without papers could be shot dead on the spot."

With these words Ambassador Gvir presented the Yad Vashem "Righteous Among the Nations" medal of honor to Sebastian Steiger.

Southwestern Switzerland and the region around the border with France, including Mont Risoux (Mont Risoud), the forest and the Jura mountains. This breathtakingly beautiful area was the setting for many of the dramatic events described in this book.

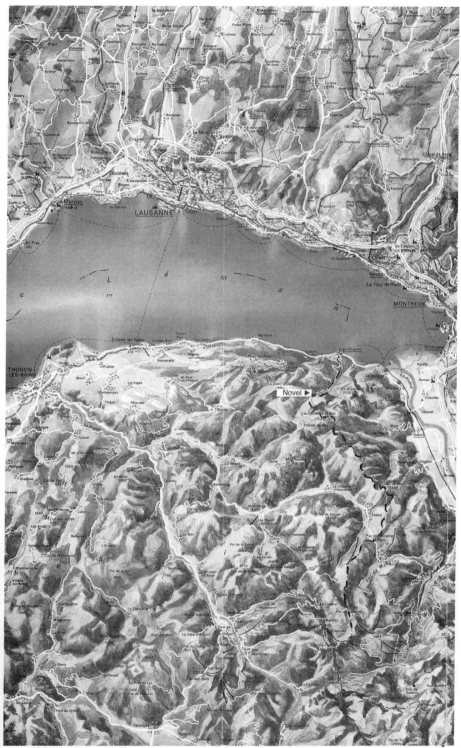

(Extract from a map published and printed by Kümmerly+Frey, CH-3000 Berne, copyright: Editor Photo-Ciné Service, Ch-8280 Kreuzlingen)

Anne-Marie Im Hof-Piguet

Over the Border Against the Law

In April 1943, Rösli Naef, warden of the children's home at La Hille castle in southern France, asked for an assistant or relief worker.

Anne-Marie Piguet lived in Le Sentier (in the French-speaking part of Switzerland). The daughter of a local forest inspector, she studied literature and pedagogy. In mid-June 1942, when she was about twenty-four years of age, she volunteered for service with the Swiss Red Cross and was assigned to the children's home operated by the Swiss at Montluel castle, about fifteen miles to the east of Lyons. She expected to find French boys and girls suffering from the effects of the war, but was surprised to find Spanish children and their parents living in the home. The Spanish Civil War, which had come to an end with the victory of Franco in 1939, had forced a large number of Republicans out of the country. They had crossed over the Pyrenees into France.

At Montluel castle, Anne-Marie had her first confrontation with the terror of the Vichy regime, and also her first contact with Jewish refugee children. In a book she wrote later entitled *La Filière* (German title: *Fluchtweg durch die Hintertür* —"Escape by the Back Door"), she wrote:

"Here I experienced true drama: for the first time in my life

100

Some of the Red Cross personnel working at La Hille castle. From left: Miss Ott, Sebastian Steiger, Annelies & Henri Kägi (on their wedding day) and Anne-Marie Piguet and, standing near Miss Piguet, Eugen Lyrer, a teacher at La Hille. (Source: Sebastian Steiger)

I saw what happened when people were deported. All we could do was to take care of the remnants of the human catastrophe—to look after children facing a highly uncertain future." Indeed, she had to fetch five small children from the camp at Rivesaltes; their parents were about to be deported.

Anne-Marie Piguet arrived at La Hille castle on May 6, 1943, one day before the former warden, Rösli Naef, had to leave. The new warden, Margrit Tännler, did her best to continue the assistance and rescue activities of Rösli Naef.

It was with a heavy heart that Rösli left La Hille. She knew only too well the dramatic events that had occurred at the castle, in Vichy and in Berne. But Anne-Marie still had to learn the cruel story. She spoke many times with the young boys and girls still living in the house, and slowly she began to understand. Later, back in Switzerland, Rösli Naef would add other details.

A Red Cross truck, used for relief food deliveries from Switzerland and the occasional outing for the children of La Hille castle, pictured in front of the castle in October 1944. (Source: Sebastian Steiger)

Anne-Marie was involved in the story of the castle from the day she arrived. Because of the increasingly frequent raids of the French gendarmes, acting on the orders of the German occupying forces, constant fear reigned at La Hille. Anne-Marie tried everything she could to calm the children. She also went out to the farms, where a number of the older youths were hiding. Far from being completely secure, they were also in jeopardy. At any time they could be detected, arrested, and deported to a concentration camp in the East—which would have meant certain death.

Anne-Marie Piguet knew the instructions of the Swiss Red Cross headquarters: not to offend against neutrality, because they did not want to unnecessarily antagonize the Vichy regime. Before coming to La Hille, she had been told repeatedly to obey all orders from the French gendarmerie. Her conscience told her to act differently.

She wrote in her book concerning this decision: "To me, my conscience was more important than the law. I saw Jewish children whose parents were in jeopardy, or missing, or had already been deported. I saw poor innocent creatures who had been 'thrown' into the dustbin of history by 'the malice of the times.' In a shattering way I realized the consequences of French anti-Semitism and so-called Swiss 'neutrality' which was probably nothing but a cool and calculating waiting game for things to change. In the face of the dreadful persecution of the Jews and the deportation of Jewish children to the German extermination camps, I did what I had to do."

SLIPPING PAST THE "BUTCHER OF LYONS"

Anne-Marie Piguet decided to take the future of "her children" into her own hands. The French gendarmes were still looking for the older children, who they knew were hiding somewhere. They would not give up.

She tried to think of a new way to escape. It was no longer possible to cross the border to Geneva, because the Swiss soldiers had orders to send everyone back to France. As a child, she had often gone walking with her father in the Risoud, a wide forest of fir trees. She knew very well the old stone wall that formed the border between France and Switzerland. It would certainly be possible to jump over that wall to safety.

During the summer, Anne-Marie had some holiday time, and she decided to try making the trip together with another member of the Red Cross, Hedwig Kündig. She was well aware of the dangers such a journey involved, but she also had great confidence in her Swiss passport. They crossed safely into Switzerland in the Vallée de Joux, the home of Anne-Marie's parents. While they were there, something really miraculous happened. "At a friend's house, I met Victoria Cordier, who was immediately ready to help. Victoria, her two sisters, Madeleine and Marie-Aimée, and her mother, had dedicated themselves to helping endangered people across the border.

The family was humble, but devoutly Catholic and deeply patriotic. Their little house was very near the border—this was really good fortune."

Victoria herself was working for the Resistance and the intelligence service. She was strong and fearless. Without Victoria, her sisters, and their mother's small house adjoining the wall of rock near the border, the rescue of twelve boys and girls without mishap would not have been possible.

In the first few days of September 1943, after Anne-Marie had returned to La Hille, there was renewed cause for alarm: the French gendarmes were back! They hid in the neighborhood, watching the castle day and night. The youngsters knew exactly the purpose of this determined police operation. Some of them were able to hide in the "onion loft," a secret room in the castle. But there was very little space in there! Making a noise or even having candle light was dangerous. After three days of confinement, they were all so nervous that they had to flee. Some tried their chances in France, but Addy Nussbaum, whose sister was already in Switzerland, definitely wanted to try the new escape route. So Anne-Marie decided to take Addy across the border. Since he had no identification papers, she had to provide him with documents, even if it meant forging them.

On September 12, 1943, they set out together for Switzerland. Addy was the first child to cross the border in the Risoud safely.

In the winter of 1943–44, ten to twelve other boys and girls took the same route, among them Inge Joseph, Edith Moser, Manfred Kamlet, Edith Goldapper, Inge Schragenheim, Walter Kamlet, and Paul Schlesinger and his mother. Even if the route was always the same, each new escape was a dramatic, risk-filled adventure in its own right.

Anne-Marie describes the escape route in her book: "We took the train to Lyons, to Lons-le Saunier at the foot of the French Jura mountains. A bus took us further to Champagnoles. There we met the sisters Victoria and

Madeleine Cordier. They knew every tree, nook, and cranny, and they guided the refugees through the woods. Not far from the Swiss border, the path gets very steep. We had to climb and cling on to small trees in order not to fall. We did not talk. We listened carefully to every strange noise."

It is not possible to recount all the incidents they had or the emotions they experienced on these missions. Preoccupied with the daily task of feeding the eighty inhabitants of the home and protecting the youngsters from immediate harm, Anne-Marie and the others at La Hille did not learn until later of another particular danger they faced: at that time, eastern France was the territory of notorious SS officer Klaus Barbie, also known as the Butcher of Lyons!

Anne-Marie's account continues: "We reached the extended ridge of Mont Risoud and, after climbing the steep rocks, we crossed into Switzerland. From there I knew the way—this was my father's territory where he was a forest inspector. But the danger of being picked up by a Swiss border patrol was always imminent. Within a zone spanning twenty-five kilometers, they had orders to send back to France every refugee they met. The fear of being caught at the last moment and being extradited to the Germans was always present."

These crossings—each one a different dramatic story—were exhausting physically, mentally, and emotionally. Each time Anne-Marie reached her home in Le Sentier, she was worn-out and thankful.

Anne-Marie and the Cordier sisters worked very well together, but their work differed from that of a *schlepper* operation in two important respects. A *schlepper* does not know personally the people who are being smuggled across the border; he is just helping for a short time, and he expects some payment for his work. The situation with the children of La Hille was quite different. Anne-Marie Piguet knew exactly the personality, the intelligence, the gifts, and the sufferings of each of the young people she tried to aid. She bore the responsibility from start to finish. Victoria and Madeleine were working in the same spirit. The story of Edith Goldapper and Inge Schragenheim demonstrates their approach.

Edith and Inge left the castle in November 1943 to meet the Cordier sisters at Champagnoles. But Anne-Marie was warned that the border guards had been reinforced and weather conditions were treacherous, with snow in the Jura. Attempting to cross the border at the time would have been fatal. What was the response of the Cordier sisters? They kept the girls at their house until the spring of 1944, even though food was scarce at the time. The Cordier family later had to endure the false accusations of jealous villagers, who alleged that they had profited financially from helping people across the border.

Anne-Marie's last trip took place in May 1944. The small group attempting the escape nearly met with disaster. They had already reached Swiss territory when a Swiss border guard appeared as if out of nowhere and stopped them. He wanted the refugees to turn back. This would have meant arrest on French territory and immediate deportation. Madeleine used all her powers of persuasion and, in the end, managed to convince the guard not to send them back but to allow them to enter Switzerland. Anne-Marie was disappointed that this group could not come to her home in Le Sentier. Instead they had to go directly to a Swiss camp for refugees. But the main thing was that they had been saved.

IMPELLED BY HUMANITARIAN SPIRIT

All the border crossings Anne-Marie Piguet organized to Switzerland took exactly the same route through the Risoud to the border deep in the forest. In her book she wrote: "I was present many times when Jewish parents were separated from their children, and I witnessed many deportations. I was fully aware of my duties and what the authorities expected of me— namely to maintain cool neutrality as a representative of the Swiss Red Cross in France, which had obviously been intimi-

Anne-Marie Im Hof-Piguet together with the author of this book, Meir Wagner. (June 2000) (Source: Meir Wagner photo)

dated by the Nazis. But, together with friends and colleagues, we sought ways and means to take the children in our care to a place of safety. Danger loomed especially for all youngsters aged sixteen or above. Because the Swiss had closed their borders and crossing at the official checkpoints was not possible, we had to resort to the old smugglers' adventurous contraband routes through the Jura mountains in the forest of Mont Risoud.

"I still carry with me the memories of those two years 1942 to 1944. These seem to be the longest years of my life because they were filled with constant tension, combined with experiencing indescribable atrocities. But they were very rich in quiet courage and the joy of helping."

After the war, Anne-Marie Piguet married historian Ulrich Im Hof. She has two daughters. She never gave up her humanitarian commitment and work. After the end of colonialism, when Europe and the United States were realizing the major problems of the Third World, Anne-Marie resolved to put her all energies into an institution called Swisscontact, which set up schools for vocational training around the world.

When Israel's ambassador to Switzerland, Raphael Gvir, presented the Yad Vashem "Righteous Among the Nations" medal of honor to Anne-Marie Piguet on November 28, 1991, he declared that she had done everything for humanitarian reasons, and that she had saved the lives of many youths and children during the Second World War in spite of fear. She did what she had to do despite the clear and constant peril to her own life.

Ambassador Gvir also presented medals to the Cordier sisters (Madame Victoria Ritz and Sister Madeleine Cordier) who had come to Berne specially from the French Jura for the occasion.

Fred and Lilette Reymond

A Tireless Team on the Freedom Trail

Watchmaker Fred Reymond was in the Swiss Militia Army from the age of 20 like any other able-bodied Swiss man. He held the post of intelligence officer. In 1940 he was commissioned to observe the activities of the German occupying forces in the eastern French provinces adjoining Switzerland. For this purpose he worked together with French agents–male and female–and crossed the frontier frequently.

Fred Reymond was born on Christmas Day, December 25,1907 in the small rural town of Le Sentier in western Switzerland. He lived there most of his life. He was a keen sportsman, and in his youth he was a champion wrestler. Fred and his wife Lilette had a little house up on Mont Risoud (also known geographically as "Mont Risoux") between Le Sentier and the border. The mountain road stops there. Fred knew the secret paths in the woods on both sides of the ridge like no one else.

One of his agents was Victoria Cordier who lived on the other side, close to the divide, in France. Fred met many people in the course of his surveillance activities, particularly those who were being persecuted by the Vichy regime and the German occupying forces. Among them were many Jews. Fred Reymond could not help but have compassion for them when he saw their anguish and misery. He decided to find a way to help.

Since he was active on both sides of the Franco-Swiss border, he was ideally placed to engineer the rescue of refugees, escaped prisoners of war, and marked members of the Resistance. Occasionally, British paratroopers, or French youths who had been drafted to work in German factories, appeared as well.

In most cases, Reymond's French agents escorted the escapees to a secret meeting place at the border. For quite some time there was a little gate, unguarded by the Swiss border patrols, where Fred smuggled them through. Along the way he expertly circumvented the heavily patrolled areas.

The danger of being discovered and sent back was much greater for the refugees if they moved during the daytime. Fred and Lilette therefore took them to their house on the ridge to hide them for up to 36 hours. They fed them and protected them, but it was also necessary to procure train tickets and other papers for them. When they departed, Fred usually gave them some money for the onward journey.

Most of Fred's frequent crossings into occupied France were by bicycle. Fred risked being stopped by German patrols. But he always managed to evade them, sometimes by the skin of his teeth. His frequent clandestine border crossings caused him some difficulties with the Swiss customs officials. They thought he was a smuggling goods across the border, and he was fined more than once. But being a "smuggler" was his cover for acting as a secret agent.

Some fifty years later, a Swiss newspaper picked up the unusual story of Fred Reymond and his rescue missions. He had kept them secret all that time. But a journalist who had heard of him invited him to tell a Swiss television audience how he and his wife had hidden refugees in their home in the years 1942 to 1944, and how they had arranged for their flights into Switzerland.

One of his agents was Bernard Bouveret from Foncine-le-Haut. He told of his collaboration with Fred Reymond as a courier, and how Fred had repeatedly risked his life to help hunted Jewish refugees find an escape route from occupied France into free Switzerland.

Another of Fred's contacts was Achille Griffon from Besançon, who had started to work for Swiss intelligence as early as 1939. He was in constant contact with Fred Reymond until 1945. He explained that Fred's house was open to the frightened refugees day and night. He told the story of the small unguarded gate up on the ridge and how Fred would stop at nothing when he had to help a person in need. "He was a man with guts and a good heart," said agent Griffon.

François Blondeau had a very personal experience: "My father Joseph Blondeau and my older brother were members of a Resistance unit that was responsible for helping refugees on the run. Fred Reymond often pedaled through the dangerous territory and craftily outflanked the guards and the guard dogs. He knew every nook and cranny of the land and the forest at the border. Nobody knows how many kilometers he pedaled his bike in order to save lives."

But Victoria Cordier from Chapelle-des-Bois knew how many times Fred Reymond had crossed the border clandestinely during the German occupation of France. She recalled how Fred, whom she had known from the outbreak of the war, came to look for and escort the refugees, by bringing them over the Mont Risoud ridge to Switzerland. "We escorted them together many times. Fred was particularly active at night. He and his agents did everything to track down hidden Jewish refugees before the border guards did, to avoid the risk of their being sent back." She also remembers the open house and how Fred Reymond and his wife fed and clothed the poor people before sending them on to liberty and safety.

Lilette, in particular, was a paragon of virtue, dedication and self-sacrifice. Nobody knows how she obtained provisions for the refugees, as all food was strictly rationed. She showed no sign of fatigue, although she worked day and night. She always found some words of encouragement and hope for the poor souls.

Anne-Marie Piguet was also in contact with Fred Reymond. "I do not know how he succeeded in dodging the German guards, but he did it–dozens of times. It was not only his thorough knowledge of the places, but also his intelligence and his discretion, combined with sheer intuition, that must have cut him out for this important role."

Fred and Lilette Reymond never asked about the identity of the refugees in their care. To

Fred Reymond, shortly before his death, during a walk in his beloved Jura Forest. (Source: Françoise Reymond)

them, every human being who was in danger or persecuted had the same rights. Together, they became a critical link along the frequently used freedom trail into Switzerland.

As early as 1940, in absentia, the Germans had sentenced Fred Reymond to death, to be shot on sight. In spite of this looming danger Fred never gave up and continued his rescue mission and intelligence work.

Herbert Herz, the Yad Vashem representative in Geneva, was particularly pleased to be able to announce to Fred Reymond on December 25, 1997–his 90th birthday–that he had been nominated as one of the "Righteous Among the Nations". The medal was presented in Berne on April 27, 1998 by the Ambassador of Israel.

Subsequently, at a champagne reception, Fred's local municipality awarded him its "Bourgeoisie d'Honneur". Herbert Herz, Sister Victoria Cordier and Anne-Marie Im Hof-Piguet were there, celebrating the happy occasion.

Fred Reymond passed away peacefully on August 18, 1999 at the age of 92. He is sorely missed by all who knew him, and fondly remembered for his uprightness, courage, discretion and modesty. His beloved wife Lilette died on September 9, 2000.

Marcel Junod

The Third Combatant

Initially a reluctant volunteer, Marcel Junod went on to become one of the most successful and illustrious delegates in the history of the Red Cross. A native of Switzerland, he had been in his final year of training as a surgeon at a hospital in Mulhouse in France when an urgent call from Geneva recruited him for temporary duty in Ethiopia.

About the time that news of the Spanish Civil War reached Geneva, Dr Marcel Junod returned from his nine-month tour of duty. He had hardly completed his report on Ethiopia when Red Cross President Max Huber asked him if he could go to Spain. The estimated three-week reconnaissance mission lasted three years. He flew to Barcelona in August 1936, with the intention of establishing contact with the legal government of Spain rather than the rebel Nationalist forces of General Franco.

Junod repeatedly encountered resistance from both sides in the civil war to the idea of humane treatment of prisoners. He also found that written agreements tended to be respected on an ad hoc basis.

After the defeat of the Loyalist government, Dr Junod returned to Switzerland, where he was called up for military service. When World War II began, he was again recruited by the Red Cross. He spent an illustrious period in Europe and the Far East.

Marcel Junod was posted to Berlin at his own request on September 16, 1939. At that time, he was the sole Red Cross delegate in the whole of Germany and the occupied territories. He moved into a room at the Hotel Adlon, and lost no time in making contact with the Ministry of Foreign Affairs, the German Red Cross, and the armed forces. His first objective was to be able to inspect the camps where many hundreds of foreigners had been interned at the beginning of the war, purely because of their nationality.

Prompted by reports that German civilians had been murdered by retreating Poles in the newly conquered areas of Posen and Bromberg in western Poland, the German authorities asked Junod to visit the area to document these atrocities. Geneva agreed to this request, but stipulated that none of Junod's evidence should be published in the press or used in official documents, and that Junod should be allowed to visit Polish prisoners, both civil and military.

Junod was furious to discover that, despite assurances of confidentiality, his name appeared prominently in the German press. But at least he was able to make his first visit to a German prisoner-of-war camp on September 27, 1939.

The Germans kept Junod under surveillance. Two "minders" (he called them ironically his "guardian angels") were assigned to watch his every move. If Junod stayed in a hotel, they would occupy the rooms on either side.

Junod's tenacity and commitment earned him the grudging respect of German Wehrmacht officers. His role in the "exchange" of some Luftwaffe officers during his time working with refugees in Spain also earned some goodwill.

While based in Berlin working on behalf of Allied prisoners, Marcel Junod carried out a second assignment for the Red Cross in November 1939. This involved visiting Warsaw. His "guardian angels" protested that this would be very difficult, but they backed down when Junod pointed out that the transport of the Wehrmacht has no difficulty in getting wherever it wants.

En route, to the astonishment of his guards, Junod insisted on stopping the car in the open countryside. He wanted to talk to a Polish prisoner "plowing a furrow through the sandy earth pitted with craters." Despite the obstacles and personal dangers, Junod was determined to find out for himself what was really going on.

In his book *Le Troisième Combattant* (English title: "Warrior Without Weapons"), Marcel Junod wrote: "Gradually I learned to divine what the Germans did not show me, to understand the double sense of words, to perceive the distress conveyed in the silence of a prisoner in the presence of his forbidding guard."

In Warsaw, Junod reported, "the air was foul with a horrible smell of decomposition. . . . The side streets had often been so devastated that they were now little more than paths. Out of eighteen thousand houses no less than eight thousand had been completely destroyed. Amidst these terrible ruins wandered crowds of miserable, trembling, and hungry people."

After being escorted to the Hotel Europeiski (where the German staff was installed), Junod actually managed to slip away from his guards and explore the streets of Warsaw unaccompanied. A passer-by introduced himself. "Prince Lipkovsky at your service. I also belong to the Red Cross." As the Prince gave his first-hand account of the horrors of the eight-day siege and the ensuing events, Junod marveled: "It seemed as though this man had been sent there just at this moment to guide me through the town and tell me about its terrifying ordeal."

They reached the edge of the ghetto, surrounded by barbed wire and guarded day and night. Prince Lipkovsky explained: "No one is allowed to enter or leave. There are three hundred-thousand Jews there, and heaven knows how they're existing. Perhaps a boat or two brings them food over the Vistula, because one of the limits of the quarter is marked by the river.

Their situation is dreadful. Typhus is reported to be raging there to such an extent that there is no longer anywhere the sick can be taken to. The Germans are searching for the Chief Rabbi everywhere, but they won't find him."

This was the kind of information Junod's Nazi minders were trying to keep from him at all costs. But, as on other occasions, his resourcefulness and determination helped him to discover the truth.

After Junod's third mission in the spring of 1940, and after putting up substantial resistance, the German authorities finally grudgingly agreed to the establishment of a permanent Red Cross delegation in Berlin. The courage and pioneering work of Marcel Junod had paved the way.

On a visit to Germany at the end of 1941, carrying diplomatic mail for the Swiss Legation in Berlin at the request of the Political Department, Marcel Junod's journey was interrupted at Stuttgart by the Gestapo. Somehow he managed to persuade his guards to take him to the Hotel Eden, where Dr Roland Marti (head of the Red Cross delegation) was staying—and he even managed to alert Marti to his predicament. The Gestapo interrogated Junod about some correspondence they had intercepted, mentioning a conversation with Junod, which they were attempting to use to "prove" that he was acting as an enemy agent! After cautioning Junod about the danger of seemingly "harmless" conversations after missions in Germany, they let him go. The warning did not go unheeded, and the Gestapo never bothered him again.

Returning to the Hotel Eden, Junod's priorities were clear. He told Roland Marti, Pierre Descoeudres, Jean-Maurice Rübli, and Robert Schirmer: "Let's get to work now." There was plenty of work to be done. As Junod later wrote: ". . . the five of us . . . were poring over an immense map of Germany and the occupied areas. Little red crosses marked the spot where the Oflags and Stalags we were entitled to visit were situated. But there were other camps which were always in our minds: the camps where the Russians were held, certain Polish camps which had been withdrawn from our list on the pretext that they were now voluntary labor camps, and, above all, those cursed places surrounded in mystery and secrecy where we knew that human beings were suffering anguish of mind and body: the concentration camps."

Only in 1946 was Junod able to return to his medical career.

In 1952 he was elected to the International Committee of the Red Cross and went on to become a Vice President of the ICRC. He died in 1961 at the age of fifty-seven.

August Bohny

Rallying a Town to Stand Up
to the Oppressor

July 26, 1986 was a day of celebration for the people of Le
Chambon-sur-Lignon in the French department of Haute Loire.

Men and women had come from the four corners of the
globe to this small rural town south of St. Etienne. They came
to commemorate the survival of hundreds of Jewish children
who, at the height of the Second World War, had been hidden
in this region, and had later escaped to Switzerland along
secret paths. Many of them had found refuge on local farms or
stayed at the sanctuaries of the Swiss children's homes. In spite
of the many raids by the French gendarmes, they were able to
spend their childhood relatively peacefully there.

Rudi had been deported from Germany to south-west
France with his entire family as early as 1940. Forty-six years
later, he returned alone to organize this commemorative event
and invited all the survivors he still could locate. They were living in many different parts of the world, and most of them
were now 60 years of age or older.

August Bohny and Friedel Bohny-Reiter were among the
guests. The former warden and his wife knew many of the children from the Rivesaltes internment camp. Also present were

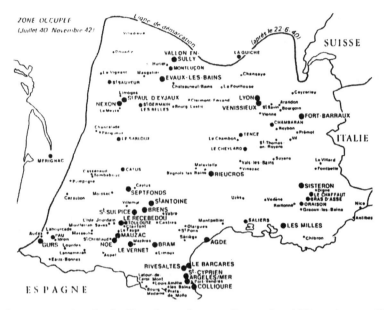

Internment sites in the French south zone, September 1939 to August 1944 (not shown is the Milles camp). (Source: Carte Monique Morales)

the many inhabitants of Le Chambon-sur-Lignon who had helped to hide the youths and children while the gendarmes were searching for them. The town's pastor from that time, André Trocmé, had passed away, but his widow, Magda, came to the ceremony. She was accompanied by chiefs of the Resistance—the French underground organization that was instrumental many times in helping youths set off for a safe country.

Le Chambon-sur-Lignon is an old Huguenot town, situated about 120 kilometers southwest of Lyons on a plain at an altitude of about 3,000 feet above sea level. In the 1940s it had about 3,000 inhabitants. It had become a center for sick and convalescent children who found refuge here.

Also attending the celebration was Los Angeles film producer Pierre Sauvage, who was born in Le Chambon in 1944.

His mother was a Jewess displaced from Poland; his father was French. Le Chambon was a safe haven for the young family. Sauvage was planning a documentary on the Resistance and its role during these years. It was a good opportunity to conduct interviews with many survivors and eye witnesses.

Memories–good and bad–were refreshed during the celebration. Many unforgettable experiences were recounted, as well as stories of what had become of the refugee children. The participants visited the Resistance Museum and saw photos and documents that reminded them of those difficult times. But they all agreed that the courage and the dedication of those members of the Swiss Children's Assistance was outstanding, unparalleled and unforgettable.

The Swiss Children's Assistance came into being after the defeat of France and the German occupation of northern France. Many children were suffering from the effects of the war and these victims were looked after by Swiss volunteers.

Men and women had joined the civil service for reasons of conscience. Pastor André Trocmé supported the project and got in touch with Rodolfo Olgiati, to work together with the French Protestant support organization CIMADE and to establish a shelter for the Jewish refugee children at Le Chambon-sur-Lignon.

The first children arrived on May 16, 1941. They came from the concentration camp at Gurs. By the end of October 1942, a second home had to be opened for children suffering from malnutrition and starvation. Thirty-five children from all over France were able to recuperate over a period of about six months. Of course, the demand for more shelters was growing constantly, and the Swiss Red Cross pitched in together with the Swiss Children's Assistance. They were further helped by the American Quakers, whose financial support was of great assistance. This meant that more children could be given shelter.

FRUSTRATING THE RAIDS BY THE VICHY POLICE

Bohny recalled that by mid-summer 1942 the heavy raids by the French gendarmerie had started. Early in the morning of August 26, four trucks carrying 50 gendarmes drove up to Le Chambon. They declared that they wanted to check the identity and papers of 72 inmates whose names were on their lists. As expected, there were children whose names were not on the roll, in this case, ten. They would have been taken away. Bohny protested vehemently. He argued that the opportunity for about 10,000 French children to rest and recuperate at various homes operated by the Swiss Red Cross in the north of France could be jeopardized. The threat worked. The commanding officer decided to leave without the extra children. After the gendarmes departed, Bohny wanted to telephone the departmental authorities in Le Puy immediately, but he could not reach anyone before eight o'clock.

"Nevertheless, we had gained some time," Bohny recounted. "The wanted children had breakfast and we alerted the inhabitants of Le Chambon. Without losing any time, the farmers took the children along and hid them on their farms. When the commanding officer returned at about nine in order to arrest the illegal residents, they were gone. He was furious and threatened reprisals. About a week later, I and two priests in the village received letters signed by the police and the mayor. They gave us an ultimatum to extradite the 72 children within 48 hours, or we would be arrested ourselves.

"We called an emergency meeting. It was decided that the children would not be left in the hands of the police or anybody else. It was necessary, however, to take precautions, and we allowed for every eventuality. Fortunately, it was only an attempt to intimidate us. The fifty gendarmes continued searching the houses and farms for the missing children, but they could not find any of them. After three weeks, they gave up and left."

This experience seemed to create a bond between the population of Le Chambon and the director of the children's homes. Several children at the Rivesaltes camp who were practically doomed to be deported were smuggled out and given refuge in the village. Although the inhabitants were risking their own safety if they had been found illegally hiding a child, they all helped. They also assisted in preparing an escape route to the Swiss border about 200 miles away. Several hideouts were set up along the way, and many children successfully escaped to safety in Switzerland.

As the need increased, two more children's homes were opened at Le Chambon in 1942. Here furniture and toys were manufactured. The nefarious raids by the Vichy police continued. In February 1943, two youths from one of the homes were arrested and dispatched to the concentration camp at Gurs. When Bohny heard about this, he protested vigorously. He persisted until he had succeeded in liberating the two boys and bringing them back to Le Chambon. After the war he said: "With a certain measure of justified pride, we dare say that we succeeded in looking after and protecting the young people who had been entrusted to us."

In spring 1943 August Bohny rented two neighboring farms, where he opened an agricultural college for the youths.

Between 1941 and 1943, about 800 children and youths stayed at the children's shelters in Le Chambon, the majority of them Jewish refugees. They were looked after by 35 employees, some of them refugees themselves, but eight of them were volunteers from Switzerland. The homes also had the help of two Swiss priests.

Dr. Lucien Lazare recommended August Bohny to Yad Vashem for the "Righteous Among the Nations" medal of honor and mentioned that he had "actively saved four members of the Schwarzschild family and a lot more Jewish refugees. As acting director of the Swiss children's homes at Le Chambon-sur-Lignon, he received many refugees from the concentration camps and looked after them with fervor and dignity. When the French police raided the homes, he actively arranged for the children to be hidden, and it was thanks to him and his efforts that the population of Le Chambon was ready to cooperate and receive the endangered children."

Pierre Sauvage presented his film *"Les Armes de l'Esprit"* *("Weapons of the Spirit")* at a colloquium held at Le Chambon in October 1990, when the Israeli Ambassador to France, Ovadia Sofer, presented the Yad Vashem "Righteous Among the Nations" medal to some twenty local residents, as well as a special presentation to the Mayor for the town of Le Chambon itself–an exceptional honor, in acknowledgment of the solidarity the local residents had shown.

Friedel Bohny-Reiter

The Ingenious "Milk Churn" Rescue Operation

Friedel Reiter was born in Vienna, Austria in 1912. Her father was killed in action as a soldier in the First World War when Friedel was just two years of age. After the war, she was able to emigrate to Switzerland as a child traumatized by war and was fostered by a family in Zurich. At the age of 20, she became a Swiss citizen.

Friedel trained as a children's nurse and worked as an assistant at a center for war-traumatized children. In November 1941, she was sent to the Rivesaltes internment camp, an outpost where the Vichy regime had first interned gypsies and stateless people before turning it into a concentration camp for Jews displaced from Germany, Austria and Belgium. When Friedel Reiter arrived, there were already about 14,000 men, women and children of all ages and backgrounds.

August 25, 1942 was a day that Friedel Reiter would never forget. Hundreds of new Jewish refugees had been herded up and driven to the camp by the gendarmes. Men, women and children had to line up for a roll call, and Friedel noticed several young women with babies in their arms. It was a pitiful sight.

A long train was waiting on the other side of the square and already groups of people were being directed towards the cattle wagons by the uniformed guards. There was an occasional cry for help. The eyes of these people were full of despair. Friedel Reiter knew where they were headed: to the east–to certain death.

A few days earlier, Friedel Reiter had witnessed the abuse of men and women by the French gendarmes and their German overlords. She had seen them withhold food from the refugees and she heard that they were giving them injections. Friedel obtained food for the hungry and for the mothers with babies as every day they came to her to ask for what they could not get otherwise. She felt impelled to act.

When she saw the condemned internees waiting, she grabbed some food from her depot and sneaked it to them while the guards were not looking or not around. She took the babies from some mothers who knew they could not save their children, and hid them in her hut. She also ran to the train and led out small children, craftily taking advantage of the general chaos and the inattention of the guards.

On that hot summer's day she did not succeed in leading many children away from the square or the death train. But she did have an idea how to save more children from their fate.

As Friedel had a special pass, she had access to any section of the Rivesaltes camp, including the area where food was delivered. There was a daily supply of milk in large churns. She knew that these churns, once empty, had to be taken away again. Friedel got acquainted with the truck drivers and accompanied them several times on their rounds.

Friedel Reiter was looking for a way to smuggle the very little children out of the camp inside these milk churns. She knew that this was a dangerous undertaking, but she relied on her special pass. She also had to find a safe place where the children could be taken; she found it at Elne, a home for mothers and babies, about ten miles away on the other side of Perpignan. When returning to the camp, she always brought back food that she had obtained from other Swiss Red Cross children's homes. The children that Friedel smuggled out of Rivesaltes inside the milk churns were able to hide at these homes. Some of them were later taken across the boundary to Switzerland and survived the Holocaust and the war.

LAST-MINUTE REPRIEVES FROM THE DEATH TRAINS

Rudi was a refugee child in 1941 when he arrived at Rivesaltes. He remembers how Friedel Reiter fetched him off the train just before it left the camp, deporting thousands. He was hidden at the food depot of the hut with the Swiss cross painted on the wall, together with other children who had been led back from the train by Friedel. Later they were all smuggled out in the milk churns. Friedel gave special care to those children who had lost their parents.

Friedel Reiter's help increased to about 1,500 food rations a day. She got support and financial aid from Swiss Children's Support and other charities, among them the American Quaker organization.

In 1942, trains carrying 600–1,000 internees were departing almost daily, carrying men, women and children on a journey of no return. First to Drancy in the occupied zone, then on to Auschwitz (although the name of the death camp was not generally known at that time).

Friedel Reiter asked the director of the Swiss Red Cross Children's Assistance, Maurice Dubois, to appeal to the Vichy regime to halt the deportations, but to no avail. She also collected names and addresses from the inmates at the camp and details of their relatives abroad, if they had any, so that she could let them know about the hideous fate of the poor victims.

As a child, Margot Wicki-Schwarzschild was taken to the Rivesaltes camp, where she was rescued by Friedel Reiter. Today she lives in Reinach, Switzerland. This is her story: "My family was from Kaiserslautern in Germany. My father Richard, my mother Louise, my little sister Hannelore and I were deported to southern France in 1941 together with a lot of other Jewish people from Rheinland-Pfalz. We arrived towards the end of the year at Rivesaltes camp. My sister and I were taken to the children's hut. I was suffering from malnutrition and an open wound on my knee. My mother wanted to see us, so Friedel took her in and gave her work. My father was forced to work at a nearby mine. He even managed to rent an apartment in a nearby village.

"We were able to leave the Rivesaltes camp and move in with him. But our happiness lasted only a few months. In August 1943, the French gendarmes came to get us, together with three other Jewish families, and took us back to the Rivesaltes camp. Marshal Pétain's regime fully implemented the Jewish laws of the Nazi occupying power.

"Daily they dispatched trains carrying off thousands of Jews to Auschwitz after assembling them in the square. We expected our turn to come at any time, but shortly before it happened, Friedel Reiter intervened. She knew my mother, who was non-Jewish, from her work at the Swiss children's hut. She went to the commanding officer of the camp and explained to him that we were a baptized family. She persisted until the man said: 'All right, take the woman and the children and hide them somewhere until the war is over, but the man, the Jew, has to go.' What a terrible blow for us. We cried and hugged him when he was due to leave. Of course, we all hoped to see him again sometime and agreed to meet at the Swiss Red Cross in Berne, once it was all over.

"My father was deported to Auschwitz and murdered in 1943. But we were saved, thanks to Friedel Reiter."

Like Margot, Hilde Kriser, who was born in 1924 in Cologne, found herself back at Rivesaltes camp in 1942. She, her parents and smaller sister had been expelled from Germany in May 1941 together with thousands of other Jewish refugees. "In November of that year," she says, "we were told to go to Pringy in the Savoy region near Annecy. I had to work at the Swiss Children's Support home and my sister had to go to school.

"But then, by mid-August 1942, my sister and I had to return to Rivesaltes on the instructions of the French gendarmerie. My mother was extremely worried about this development and accompanied us. She took us to see Friedel Reiter, the warden at the children's hut, and explained to her what had happened. We knew her from our earlier time at this site. Friedel tried to call Maurice Dubois in Toulouse but could not reach him. The next day the guards assembled us in the square, where we waited the whole day. In the evening we were directed towards the cattle train, when suddenly Friedel Reiter appeared together with a couple of gendarmes. She pointed in our direction and signaled to us that we should step back when the gendarmes were not looking. We could not even say goodbye to our mother as we ran towards Friedel. It all happened so very quickly.

"She took us into the children's hut under cover of darkness and hid us between sacks and barrels. She told us not to make any noise while she went back to the cattle train which was still being loaded with people. She kept us hidden until the train had left. The only thing she could do was tell our mother that we were safe."

During the many rescue missions to get children from the Rivesaltes camp to the children's home at Le Chambon-sur-Lignon she got to know the warden, August Bohny. They became friends and got married. Many of the children who were smuggled out of Rivesaltes by Friedel were placed on the farms in the region by August Bohny, who later also helped to prepare their escape to Switzerland. So many were saved thanks to the combined efforts of August and Friedel.

The story of Friedel Bohny-Reiter's rescue work at Rivesaltes was later made into a film by Swiss cinematographer Jacqueline Veuve.

Jeanne Berchmans (Marie Meienhofer)

The Quick-thinking Nun of Sacré-Coeur Convent

In Thonon-les-Bains, a town situated on the southern shores of Lake Geneva in the French Chablais region (Haute-Savoie), Sister Jeanne Berchmans was a nun at the Sacré-Coeur (Sacred Heart) convent. One day she heard the noise of heavy vehicles approaching. She recognized them as being German Wehrmacht trucks. Sister Jeanne had to act quickly. Hiding at the convent were three Jewish refugees, Taube Wittels, her daughter Renée and her son Bruno. Sister Jeanne took them upstairs to an unused room on the third floor, locked the door and put up a sign:

"QUARANTINE: SCARLET FEVER".

After entering the convent, the German soldiers marched from door to door, accompanied by Sister Jeanne. When they came to the door on the third floor, she quickly explained to the soldiers that there were contagious patients in the room. Being a native of central Switzerland, she spoke to the soldiers in perfect German. There was a moment of silence and hesitation. Then the soldiers turned around and marched off. It could have spelled death not only for the refugees but also for Sister Jeanne

Sister Jeanne Berchmans, née Marie Meienhofer, the day she was presented with the Yad Vashem medal at the retirement home at Givisiez, December 9, 1991. (Source: Herbert Herz archives, Yad Vashem, Geneva)

if they had decided to search the room. The three refugees owed their lives to the noble nun of Sacré-Coeur.

Sister Jeanne was born in November 1897 at Bremgarten, Switzerland. She was christened Marie Meienhofer, and at an early age she decided to dedicate her life to loving and caring for her fellow human beings. In 1924, she entered the Catholic order of the Sacré-Coeur.

Thonon-les-Bains, on the southern shore of Lake Geneva, was in the "free zone" of occupied France and Sister Jeanne worked at the convent as a teacher of French, German, shorthand and typing. About 400 girls attended the college. The classrooms were located in various cloister buildings. But by the time Germans raided the buildings, the pupils had already been moved to another schoolhouse. There were orchards and vegetable gardens, vineyards and a small farm in the convent grounds. Several small houses were reserved for elderly ladies. If it had not been for the stark danger looming, the setting would have been idyllic.

The Wittels family had fled their native Austria immediately after the "Anschluss" (annexation to the Third Reich) in 1938. Their escape route took them from Vienna via Czechoslovakia and Switzerland to France, and they stopped en route at Paris, Marseilles, Nice and St. Jean-de-Luz. They needed new identification papers and finally, against payment

Main entrance to the Sacré-Coeur convent at Thonon-les-Bains, where Sister Jeanne hid the Wittels family. (Photo taken between 1930 and 1940.) (Source: Herbert Herz archives, Yad Vashem, Geneva)

Main entrance to the Sacré-Coeur convent at Thonon-les-Bains that housed a kindergarten, a primary school and a college. (Photo taken in November 1999.) (Source: Andreas C. Fischer archives)

Side façade of the Sacré-Coeur convent at Thonon-les-Bains. Still today the gunshot marks can be seen from the attacks mounted by the Resistance against the Gestapo command post situated in these buildings up to 1944. The bullet holes serve as a remembrance for the brave. (Source: Andreas C. Fischer archives)

of a ransom, a "schlepper" led them to their final destination, Thonon-les-Bains.

It was an unlucky move. The police picked them up and questioned them. But they were fortunate in that the prosecuting attorney happened to be on vacation. An attorney from Chambéry was his temporary relief. This man, apparently a practicing Catholic, had compassion for the refugees when he heard of their odyssey. It did not take him long to get in touch with the nuns of the Sacré-Coeur at Thonon where Sister Jeanne was able to communicate with the Wittels easily in German. Based on their bogus identification papers, they passed as coming from Alsace-Lorraine, and they were entitled to stay at the convent.

Renée Leder, née Wittels, described the events in a report to Yad Vashem: "After entering the convent, we spent several years within its walls. None of us had ever imagined our lives would take such a turn. At the nunnery we were not only given food but real refuge. We lived by ourselves but we were never alone. After some weeks the nuns brought us shoes and fresh clothes, and I was even able to attend a home economics class. My mother tried to lend a hand, while my little brother went to

the convent kindergarten. Sister Jeanne grew particularly fond
of Bruno. She saw to it that he would get the same care and
upbringing as the other boys and, when he was a bit older, she
moved him to an orphanage nearby.

"The political conditions in 'free' Thonon got worse. The
French 'Maquis' (underground army) became more active in
the region as the advancing German forces drew nearer. The
inevitable happened: the convent was requisitioned and the
nuns had to leave. At this moment they 'crowned' their selflessness with an extraordinary humanitarian act: although they
lost everything and had to move to various locations, they took
us refugees along with them! We were treated like sisters in the
faith, but their religious rituals were never forced on us.

"Then, in 1944, liberation finally came! We had survived,
and we parted, happy that it was all over. But when Sister
Jeanne turned 79, my brother Bruno went to see her, and after
that reunion they engaged in a lively correspondence.

"Beyond any shadow of a doubt, when the Germans requisitioned the convent, it was the nuns' decision to take us along
that saved our lives."

Sister Anne Marguerite, née Odile Broche, recalled the first
time she met Sister Jeanne. They were both around 21 years of
age at the time, and they would later spend the years of the
Second World War together at the Sacré-Coeur convent. She
confirmed Wittel's story and described how magnanimous
Sister Jeanne had been to the persecuted Jewish refugees. She
had offered them sanctuary at the convent, and continued to
look after them in their hideout.

Sister Jeanne felt like a close relative of the Wittels. After the
liberation, the time came to say goodbye. The farewell scenes
could not have been more emotional or dramatic. Sister Jeanne
suffered from the pain of parting for a long time. She got over
it by accepting that "her" family, the Wittels, was now truly out
of danger and that nothing could harm them anymore. There
was no longer any need to keep them confined behind the thick
walls of the convent.

Sister Jeanne Berchmans had hidden another Jewish refugee child for a short period at Sacré-Coeur. She never accepted any money but acted because her heart and her deep faith told her to do what she had to do.

On December 8, 1991, Israel's ambassador to Switzerland, Raphael Gvir (who had himself been a refugee in Switzerland as a child), presented the Yad Vashem "Righteous Among the Nations" medal of honor to Sister Jeanne Berchmans in a ceremony at the retirement home of the sisters of "Sainte-Jeanne-Antide" at Givisiez near the city of Fribourg in Switzerland. Renée Leder-Wittels traveled from Vienna to be present for the occasion.

Scarcely able to contain her emotion, Sister Jeanne said: "Thank you very much for honoring me, but I really did very little..." Her actions and her courage, she said, were dictated by the love of God and her fellow human beings: "It cannot be said that I was courageous; it was the grace of God that put me there."

To conclude the ceremony, the Mother Superior of the home quoted these words of St François de Sales as a fitting description of the work of Sister Jeanne:

"Noise does no good; The good makes no noise"

Sister Jeanne Berchmans passed away two years later.

Sister Jeanne Berchmans (née Marie Meienhofer) during the ceremony. (Source: Renée Leder-Wittels, Vienna)

René Burkhardt

Persona Non Grata

As the Swiss Red Cross delegate-adjunct in Salonica, Dr René Burkhardt witnessed first hand the racist policy there, starting in the summer of 1942, and the arrival six months later of Wisliceny, one of Eichmann's adjutants. Without delay, he diligently informed Geneva of the concentration, segregation, and deportation measures that were being set in motion.

He also voiced his protest. When the first trains were leaving for Auschwitz on March 13, 1943, he passed the text for a telegram, to be sent to Geneva via the German Red Cross, to a trusted contact, the head of the German supply administration in Macedonia. The telegram was meant to be confidential, of course. Burkhardt's trust was betrayed, however, and the contents of his telegram were brought to the attention of the Reich plenipotentiary for Greece, Ambassador Altenburg.

The fateful telegram read as follows:

> Request telegraph International Committee metropolis Geneva, start deportation 45,000 Salonican Jews almost decided, examine urgently with governments concerned, deportation [sic] women and children to Palestine indispensable.

The German authorities demanded, then insisted, that René Burkhardt be recalled to Geneva.

136

Hans Schaffert

The Protestant Pastor who Protected the "Property of God"

Hans Schaffert had studied under the renowned professor of theology, Karl Barth at Basle University. Shortly after his graduation, he was sent out as a young Protestant pastor by the Swiss Children's Assistance organization, CIMADE, to the concentration camp at Gurs in southern France. His mission was expected to last about six months.

At the Gurs camp he had his first contact with displaced persons and Jewish refugees. Among them were a number of baptized Jewish Christians who had formed a religious community in Germany before being expelled.

In 1942, the mass deportations began from Gurs to the mustering camp of Drancy. This compound was heavily guarded from the outside by armed police. From time to time, these guards were called in to conduct a search of the huts in order to find all persons of Jewish descent. Whenever they found one, the prisoner was quick-marched to the square. Those who could not keep up the pace were brutally beaten. From the square they were directed to a freight train and transported away, never to be seen again.

Hans Schaffert personally witnessed these atrocious events. He saw the anguish and despair of the condemned. He went up

137

to Commander-in-chief Kaiser, asking him to stop the deportations or at least to slow them down. His request was curtly turned down.

Frustrated, he decided to collect food and distribute it to the prisoners awaiting deportation. He would stay with the prisoners until the train pulled out of the camp.

In a letter to Marc Boegner, pastor in Nîmes, he wrote of his traumatic experiences and warned about further action that the camp commander was planning. He appealed to the Protestant church to intervene urgently. "This tragedy was the most devastating experience of my life," Schaffert said later. "I resolved henceforth to devote all my resources and strength to rescuing persecuted Jews."

Schaffert successfully arranged the escape of many Jews to Spain or Switzerland. He gave them money—some in the local currency, some in the currency of their country of destination. After a while, the French authorities became suspicious of him and asked him to leave and return to Switzerland.

During his time at the Gurs concentration camp, Pastor Schaffert had, however, built up a strong and lasting relationship with the Jewish people. After returning to his native country, he was actively involved in pastoring and promoting the spiritual welfare of refugees, a charity of the Evangelical Church of Switzerland. Was it coincidence or fate that he now found himself caring for some of the very refugees he had helped to escape from Gurs and who were now safe in Switzerland?

His superior, Dr. Paul Vogt, reported: "Pastor Schaffert actively cared for the persecuted Jews. He organized kosher food so that Jewish people could practice their faith and rituals while being guests of a Christian church. He was conscientious in everything he did, showing courage, dedication and selflessness. For him it was of paramount importance that the displaced persons, the stateless and those deprived of their rights should find love, compassion and respect instead of the devastating hatred and disdain that the Jews had to experience during the war years. Hans Schaffert actively demonstrated his outgoing concern for his fellow human beings. He had a warm heart, and the plight of the Jewish people caused him extreme pangs of conscience. The courage of this dedicated Christian has served as a signal to many a young person interested in refugee relief and support work."

In his struggle for the rights of those deprived of them, Schaffert attacked the rigid refugee policies of the Swiss police. In his sermons he read reports of Jews suffering racial discrimination, persecution, expulsion and deportation to their deaths in the concentration camps. He often visited the Swiss camps for refugees and offered his help.

When the full-scale mass deportations of the Hungarian Jews commenced in 1944, Schaffert joined an underground organization, whose aim was to disseminate information about the Auschwitz extermination camp. His deliberate intention was to arouse the Swiss people and their government. He worked with the Hungarian Refugee Relief and Rescue organization in Zurich. His task was to smuggle passports and visas into Hungary at the height of the Second World War.

Dr. Gertrud Kurz of the Refugee Section of the Christian Peace Corps worked alongside Pastor Schaffert. She could not praise his courage and engagement for the cause of the persecuted Jews highly enough.

After the war was over, Schaffert worked with Marcel Pasche as a clergyman in Lille, northern France. Together with Jules Isaac, he helped to establish a Christian-Jewish friendship league. He was later sent to Leopoldville in the Congo as a representative of the Protestant Church Council.

One of Schaffert's strongest desires was to visit the land of Israel. In January 1967 he was invited to the Nachshonim Kibbutz. He wrote that he looked forward to getting to know the people and to experiencing life on a kibbutz in the Holy Land. He was convinced that a strong solidarity existed between Israel and the Church. "Since the days of my theological studies at Basle University, I have felt closely related to the

Jewish people. I manifested this relationship during the months I was at the Gurs concentration camp 1942. Unfortunately, I could only help a few of the persecuted Jews to flee to Spain or Switzerland."

When the Yad Vashem "Righteous Among the Nations" medal of honor was presented to Pastor Hans Schaffert in 1967, he said he was not worthy of it. He still had a sense of utter inadequacy in the face of the atrocities and the persecution. "I acted out of my deep theological conviction that whoever does wrong to the Jewish people does wrong to the property of God and to God himself." Those were his words.

Albert Gross

"Children, Thank the Almighty, You Are Saved!"

The Bishop of Fribourg and the President of Caritas in Switzerland decided to send Father Albert Gross to Gurs in southern France in 1942. His mission was to bring spiritual comfort to the inmates of the French concentration camp there.

Refugees from many different countries were concentrated and interned there, but most of those held were Jews deported from Germany by the Nazis. Once at the camp, Father Gross learned that the refugees needed more than spiritual support from him.

On November 11, 1942 the hitherto "free" part of France was taken over by the German occupying power, and the reign of terror engulfed all areas, including the concentration camp at Gurs.

Father Gross, born May 11, 1904, had his first experience of raids on Jews here. He witnessed Jews being arrested and carted off in cattle cars to Drancy, an even larger concentration camp in the Paris area, and he knew that they would be taken from there to eastern Europe.

He also knew that such atrocities were not compatible with his Christian upbringing, his faith, or his humanitarian world

Plaque commemorating the fate of 558 Jews, among them 45 children, who were handed over to the Nazis by the Vichy government to be taken away to the extermination camp of Auschwitz. (Source: Andreas C. Fischer archives)

view. He wanted to do something about it. He traveled to the Franco-Swiss border where, as a Swiss citizen, he had no difficulty in making contact with the Swiss border guards. After much soul-searching, he decided to take action without consulting his superiors, simply following the dictates of his own conscience.

Jewish inmates of the camps, among them Simone Weil (who later became minister of health in the French government and served as president of the European Parliament in Strasbourg), as well as Ruth Lambert, Alice Riche, and Simon Warzberg, reported after their escape that they would not have survived had it not been for the help of Father Gross. He had repeatedly risked his own life to save refugees.

A Danish deportee named Syemstvedt was working at the concentration camp and knew that many Jews were due to be deported to the East. In their despair they came to the Sunday morning mass held by Father Gross. Some of them asked to be baptized in the vain hope that, as Christians they would be spared. Father Gross, seeing their desperation, spoke to them and told them they were welcome to attend the religious services if they wanted to. But he said: "You become a Christian by conviction, not by necessity. I advise you to postpone such a weighty decision until the end of the war. In the meantime, I shall do everything in my power to save you from being deported."

This type of cattle car was used to deport internees from the various camps in the French south zone—first to the central camp of Drancy (near Paris), then to Auschwitz, Poland. (Source: Andreas C. Fischer archives)

Other inmates who were rescued by Father Gross reported that he was not only a true and magnanimous Christian but an excellent diplomat as well. Thanks to the good relations he had built up with the Swiss border guards, he was able to arrange the escape of many Jews to Switzerland.

On several occasions he had personally accompanied Jewish refugees across the border. Once in Switzerland, he looked after them, to ensure that they were well received.

One of the inmates was Rabbi George Vadnai. After the war he became the rabbi of Lausanne in Switzerland. He told his story: "I shall never forget July 20, 1943 at the concentration camp. The second deportation train had just left, and I lay down, fully dressed, on the plank bed at around ten in the evening. Shortly after dozing off to sleep, I felt a hand touching my shoulder. A flashlight lit up the hut. It was directed at me. I saw a uniformed French gendarme. He asked me brusquely if

I was George Vadnai. I replied in the affirmative, and he compared my face with the photograph he had on a list. In a most unfriendly manner, he ordered me to get up and follow him.

"The gendarme took me to a larger hut where I was brought before a commission. They were seated around a table and asked me where I was from. I explained that I was from Hungary, and they ordered me to stand on one side of the room. I knew that this meant deportation to Drancy, a large transit station.

"Suddenly, my eyes fell on Father Gross. Without thinking twice and summoning all my courage. I addressed him. 'Father,' I said, 'I am a rabbi. I belong to a different religion, but I hope you don't mind . . .' I did not get any further. Father Gross looked at me and, without saying a word, he got up and left the hut. I did not know what to expect.

"After a few minutes, however, he returned, accompanied by a tall man who said: 'Vadnai, take your belongings and don't join the group for the next train.' I followed them out. We walked through the darkness until we reached another hut. Inside, Father Gross took me aside and whispered: 'Don't get your hopes up too soon. The French have to transport a minimum of 750 Jews. If they reach this figure, you can stay. If not, you will have to go, too. For the moment we are moving you to the "reserve."'" With that, he left.

"There were about forty people in the hut. I knew a few of them. Some of them had been at my hut and had been arrested by the same gendarme. A few of them had been there for hours, feeling the danger getting clearer and closer. No wonder panic had set in and many were nervously moving around the room. Some started to pray. Suddenly, Father Gross was back. He gave them his blessings and said: 'Children, thank the Almighty, you are saved!'

"I know that Father Gross had saved my life and the lives of many others by moving us to the 'reserve.' This action, however, meant that he risked being arrested and deported himself."

Yet no danger ever caused Father Gross to give up. He continued his rescue work with relentless determination. He smuggled hundreds of Jewish refugees across the border to Switzerland, where they survived the war and the Nazi regime. After the war he returned to Switzerland, where he lived until his death in 1975.

Martha Schmidt

Tata, the Toddlers' Guardian Angel

Martha Schmidt was a middle-aged woman when she took a job as a children's nurse with the Cohen family in southern France.

Liliane Atlan, née Cohen, recounts the story: "I was born on January 14, 1932, at Montpellier. I have three sisters, Rachel, Josette and Danielle Denise. Martha Schmidt, the Swiss nurse, came to us after my sister Josette was born. Our family was well-to-do and we lived a peaceful life until 1942. My sisters and I, not knowing how to pronounce her name properly, called Martha 'Tata', a nickname that stuck.

"Our situation changed dramatically when German troops marched into Montpellier in November 1942 and when the whole of the south of France was occupied. My father was receiving threatening letters. He feared being arrested sooner or later. Because he did not want his family to be separated, he decided to move to the principality of Monaco, which was under Italian occupation but seemed to be a safe haven for Jewish refugees fleeing from the omnipresent Nazi persecution.

"My parents suggested that Martha not come with us in order not to risk her own life and safety unnecessarily. Martha, however, did want to comply. She considered herself a practicing Christian who should not only attend mass on Sunday

146

mornings, but who also wanted to share the life and fate of 'her' family. Little did we know that one day 'Tata' would be mother and father to all of us.

"The German troops followed the small trek of Jewish refugees to Monaco. SS units replaced Italian troops in the principality. The Gestapo went from house to house, searching for Jews in hiding. A difficult and extremely uncertain time began for us. We did not dare to go into the streets for fear of being arrested. My sister Rachel in particular (who looked very 'Jewish') had to be kept inside all the time because she risked not only being picked up by the SS squads but also betraying our hiding place. We were all in danger of being deported.

"Martha–Tata, our nurse–did everything she could to help. She was our guardian angel. She went shopping, did the household chores, cooked and taught us children the three Rs. She played with us and kept our the spirits up, even when danger loomed. She comforted us and actively lived her faith.

"As the danger grew more and more imminent, my father decided that the family should split up and that we should try to escape by different routes. He and mother would try to flee by one route, while we children should go with Martha, wherever she took us. Martha had volunteered to take care of us.

"We first traveled up to the Savoy region to a small town near the lake of Aiguebelette called Lépin-le-Lac. We registered at a local inn and Martha changed our family name to Chauvin. We were not aware of the fact that Lépin was a center of the French Resistance and therefore under constant surveillance by the SS.

"But when Martha found out, she immediately switched plans and made arrangements to take us to the Auvergne region in central France. She found a small house to rent and looked after us like a mother. A bond of love and devotion developed between us. Tata, as we called her, gave us that much-needed feeling of safety in a time of danger and insecurity. She took every precaution so that we would not be discovered as fleeing Jews.

"My sister Danielle Denise was born in 1944, during my parents' flight. They had stayed in contact with Martha and, after having weaned Danielle, my mother brought her to Martha. Tata agreed to look after the baby, too. This intensified the danger. But we were lucky. On one occasion, German troops were getting closer to the area where we lived. We heard them coming. We were desperate! Martha kept her composure and encouraged us to stay calm. Miraculously, the approaching troops changed their direction and disappeared. We were saved.

"Tata did not leave us when our family was reunited after the war. She stayed with us for another twenty years. She was the calming influence in our family and her faith in God complemented the kindness of her soul.

"After she had retired at the age of 65, Martha maintained her ties with our family. She even attended the Bar Mitzvah of one of my own children in Paris. On that occasion, I asked her a question I had been wanting to ask for a long time: 'Tata, why did you risk your life for us?' And she answered: 'Your father was a good man, and I knew that God would not allow anything bad to happen to his children...'.

"Martha Schmidt never married and did not have any children of her own. But my children think of her as their granny."

Josette Leopold, Liliane's sister, recalls: "After I was born, my parents engaged Martha as children's nurse. I only know that my sisters and I owe our lives to her. For four long years she not only skillfully hid us during our flight through France, she looked after us with love and dedication. My youngest sister was only ten months old when Martha took her in. In that most dangerous time between 1943 and 1945, she did everything to protect us. It took a lot of courage and self sacrifice."

Danielle Denise de Pignol, née Cohen, has no recollection of these events, as she was too young to comprehend what was going on. However, she loved Tata just as her older sisters did.

Martha Schmidt, born in Zurich on May 24, 1900, was presented with the Yad Vashem "Righteous Among the Nations"

medal of honor at the ripe old age of 93. Ambassador Gvir offi-
ciated at the presentation, held at a retirement home in Zurich
on February 21, 1994. The other residents of the home joined in
the celebrations, together with members of the Cohen family.

Roland and Jacqueline de Pury

The Pastor and His Wife Who Never Said No to Refugees

One Sunday morning in 1943, the German Gestapo burst into a church in Lyons while pastor Roland de Pury was conducting the service. They arrested him and took him away.

The Gestapo accused Pastor de Pury of having hidden and given support to Jewish refugees, opening his house to them and helping them across the border to Switzerland. He was held in custody for five months at the fortress of Montluc in Lyons. His life was spared when the Swiss authorities negotiated an exchange of prisoners with the Germans.

De Pury was born in Geneva on November 15, 1907. He studied theology at Bonn University under Karl Barth and graduated in 1933. Shortly after that he assumed a pastorate in Neuchâtel, Switzerland. During the Second World War, he pastored a church in Lyons, France, le Temple de la rue Lanterne.

In the Rhone valley he personally witnessed the persecution of the Jews, because many Jewish textile traders were established in the region. With the Vichy regime and the Germans wreaking havoc among the Jewish population, de Pury decided to dedicate his life to rescuing Jews, saving them from deportation and murder. His house became a sanctuary for Jewish refugees from all over France and Europe.

Pastor de Pury and his wife, Jacqueline, hid the persecuted refugees and cared for them in every way possible. Risking their own lives, the couple searched out secret paths to lead the refugees into Switzerland. Claudine Seligman from Paris described the rescue operations mounted by the de Purys:

"I knew the de Pury family, and I saw how they offered a shelter to Jews from Germany, Austria, Hungary, and Holland. Some stayed at their house for months. They provided them with food and lodging without asking for anything and without getting any financial support.

"The de Purys risked their lives to help countless Jewish refugees and saved them from being deported. It meant sacrificing their strength and wealth. There is no telling how many men, women, and children they saved.

"Whenever somebody was threatened with arrest by the Gestapo, Pastor de Pury arranged for secret passage over the border to Switzerland. The sculptor Hanna Orloff and her son were among those who were saved. Roland and Jacqueline de Pury even made sure they took some of her works of art with them. In Switzerland, too, de Pury arranged for the support of the refugees. The Gestapo must have kept him under surveillance; they knew of his activities."

Anny Latour from Paris adds her own description of de Pury's rescue activities. "My best friend, Rella Gottlieb, worked in an organization called General Israelite Union of France. She was in the "Foreign Jews" section. This organization assisted Jews who had lost everything, and obviously, it was under observation by the Germans. My friend had signed up because she wanted to rescue the children of Jewish refugees.

"Rella was in touch with Pastor de Pury. She sent the endangered Jewish children to him, knowing that he would look after them. The de Purys cared for the children at their own house, fed them, and later on guided them to the Swiss border. The pastor's dedication and courage were admirable.

He never said no when the safety or well-being of the refugees was at stake. Through him, dozens, if not hundreds, of Jews were rescued.

"On February 9, 1943 the Gestapo also came to Rella's office. They had discovered her double role—her official work and her clandestine activities. They arrested eighty-six people, employees and visitors to the center. They were first deported to Drancy, the concentration camp in central France, and later deported to Auschwitz. Only one survived."

Germaine Divuar now lives in Paris. She worked alongside de Pury, and proudly recalls that Pastor de Pury could always be relied on. He was not afraid to risk his life on these missions.

Then, the Gestapo arrested Pastor de Pury. Anny Latour recalls: "I was in Lyons when they arrested him and took him to the fortress of Montluc. It was as if the refugee community had lost their last hope when he was taken in. However, there was never any doubt about his loyalty."

Jean Marie Soutou, who was the head of an organization named Amitié Chrétienne ("Christian Friendship") and was later appointed French ambassador to Algeria, officially reported that from 1942 onwards, when massive persecution of Jews set in all over France, Swiss Pastor de Pury made an all-out effort to rescue the Jewish refugees.

Throughout these years, de Pury was actively supported by his wife, Jacqueline, née de Montmolin. She too came from Neuchâtel in Switzerland. This background helped her when she was helping to find shelters for the refugees she was hiding before escorting them to Switzerland.

Jacqueline died before she could be officially honored. However, in 1976 the Israeli ambassador in Paris decorated her posthumously, together with her valiant husband, with the Yad Vashem "Righteous Among the Nations" medal of honor. Pastor Roland de Pury visited Israel in 1978. While there, he planted a tree in memory of his late wife at Yad Vashem.

Karl Kolb and Vladimir von Steiger

Navigating in Treacherous Waters

In November 1943, at the age of fifty-eight, Karl Kolb, a businessman of Thurgovian origin and an expert on navigation, was sent to Bucharest, Romania, as the second Red Cross delegate to work with Vladimir von Steiger. Kolb was no stranger to the country. He had previously worked in Romania for ten years with a local petroleum company.

Vladimir von Steiger had been sent to Romania in 1942 by the combined committee on a purchasing mission. He had instructions to find out what aid would be necessary and possible in Transnistria and to investigate the prospects for emigration.

It took Karl Kolb several months to obtain the necessary visas to enable him to go to Bucharest and support the efforts of the delegate and the Swiss minister René de Weck, as well as to maintain contact with Jean de Bavier in Budapest and Gilbert Simond in Ankara, Turkey.

Kolb was a man of determination, not easily deterred from his goals.

His government contact was the vice president of the council of ministers and Minister for Foreign Affairs, Mihaï Antonescu. The Minister had allowed the Red Cross to distribute aid to Jewish internees in Transnistria. He also promised to allow 150 Jewish children, orphaned and abandoned in Transnistria, to be repatriated to Palestine each week if the Red Cross could organize their passage by boat.

Kolb issued Romanian Jews with special certificates which stated that the holder (named) appeared on the list of people authorized to emigrate to Palestine and that this emigration had been approved in principle by the royal Romanian government.

He found himself being solicited by rival Jewish organizations to favor emigrants of their choosing or at least to validate their choice. He was advised by Johannes Schwarzenberg at Geneva headquarters to remain neutral, and was cautioned that he was going beyond his role. A memo from Geneva stated: "None of the international conventions relating to the Red Cross mentions Jews among the people in favor of whom the International Committee may intervene. . . on the purely humanitarian level on which it is positioned, the International Committee does not make any distinction between Jews and non-Jews. . . . we note that your intervention in relation to special permits for the evacuation of Bucharest for Jews and foreigners is a measure outside the competence of the International Committee and which furthermore could be regarded as having a political character." They asked him to act with a certain prudence in the future on questions relating to Jews and to stay within his remit.

Kolb replied that he knew that his actions had not been based on these conventions. Everything he had been doing was based on an agreement he had made with Antonescu, who had asked him to investigate the situation of Romanian Jews deported to Transnistria and to give him some specific suggestions. He also stated that Antonescu had often referred to him as the representative of Geneva for minority questions. Kolb said he had always been careful to help advance the reputation of the Red Cross.

The special case where he had referred specifically to Jews had come about in the aftermath of the anti-Semitic law introduced in Romania, in reaction to which Swiss minister René de Weck had taken action to ensure the exemption of all Swiss Jews, as Switzerland would not agree to differentiate among its nationals on the basis of race and religion. De Weck had also managed to extend this exemption to all Jews belonging to those countries for which Switzerland was serving as the protecting power. Similar exemptions had been secured for foreign Jews under the protection of Sweden and Spain. This left only the Jews of Romanian nationality unprotected, hence in need of special assistance from the Red Cross.

Kolb and von Steiger stayed in Romania through the coup of August 23, 1944, the arrival of the Soviets, and the armistice in September.

The Bible-Coded Letters
That Slipped Past the Censors

Near the town of Le Chambon in the mountainous region of southern France is a rural village by the name of Fay-sur-Lignon. Its small church sheltered many refugees during the years from 1942 to 1944. Swiss-born pastor Daniel Curtet first welcomed the displaced and fleeing people into his home, and then moved them to the houses of the members of the Protestant community of Le Chambon. Thus he saved many from arrest or, worse still, from deportation.

Daniel Curtet was twenty-five when he first learned of the fate of the Jewish people when France was occupied by the forces of the German Wehrmacht. For the members of his community, too, it was the first time they had any significant contact with people of a different religion. When the first Jewish refugees came to his church, Pastor Curtet thought it would be possible to use his house but the influx became so great that soon he had to ask for help from the congregation. It took a little convincing before everyone was ready to take in, look after, and protect entire Jewish families.

Pastor Daniel Curtet never left the inhabitants of Fay and Le Chambon in ignorance of the risks they were taking. If discovered by the French and German authorities, they would have to face the consequences. But he spoke about the tragedy of the persecuted and recalled that the Protestants too had been victims of religious persecution not too long ago and that their ancestors had to endure violence and torture for their faith. He appealed to their tradition of tolerance and resistance.

Pastor Curtet's father, Charles, was the pastor of a church in the mountain village of Château d'Oex near Lausanne, Switzerland. Daniel wrote over seventy letters and fifteen postcards to him in which he described the plight and suffering of the Jewish refugees. He also talked about the help and assistance the members of his parish voluntarily were giving them. These letters were coded to circumvent the censorship of the French and German authorities. The letters have been preserved and many of them still have an official stamp "approved" or "passed by the censor".

The crafty pastor had used scripture from the Old and New Testaments in order to describe the dramatic events taking place in his church, his house, and his village. The first letter to his father was written on January 27, 1943 and was filled with information about German and Austrian Jews who were being persecuted. Other letters followed and tell of the love and outgoing concern of the villagers for the poor souls, and how they took the Jewish refugees into their homes in order to protect them. Several letters contain first-hand reports from the refugees themselves about their displacement, their persecution, and their flight from all the countries which had been occupied by Germany. One describes the deportation to Drancy in detail.

Some of the coded letters that Daniel Curtet sent to his father were published after the war. They are masterpieces of misleading the censor by using biblical quotations. They show how the Bible contains scriptures which refer to persecution and captivity, intolerance and cruelty—in short, man's inhumanity to man.

The population assisted their pastor in saving the lives of many hundreds of Jewish refugees. On June 17, 1987, a memorial plaque was unveiled at Le Chambon. It commemorates the villagers' determination to resist the forces of evil and to do good by helping their fellow human beings. Pastor Daniel Curtet received the Yad Vashem "Righteous Among the Nations" medal of honor the same year.

Paul and May Calame-Rosset

"An Angel With a Flaming Sword"

Paul Calame-Rosset was born in Tavannes in western Switzerland on February 16, 1905. The most dramatic days of his life, however, were to occur in Belgium during the Second World War. An architect by profession, Paul had moved to Brussels and established himself there before the war. He and his wife May were living in one of the nicest and most spacious houses in the up-scale area of Uccle.

Paul and May opened their house to refugees during the years of 1942 to 1944. It became a sanctuary for persecuted Jews, British parachutists lost behind enemy lines and 71 members of the Belgian underground army. Above the entrance to their mansion they had put up a board reading "Property of Switzerland". Nobody questioned this claim.

It was by sheer coincidence that the rescue work of Paul and May Calame-Rosset came to light in 1997. The representative of Yad Vashem in Geneva, Herbert Herz, was visiting with Edward Fürst, a Jewish optician in Geneva. During their conversation, the shop owner began to talk about a customer of his from Thônex, a suburb of Geneva. He had heard that during the war this man had been living in Brussels, where he had apparently been instrumental in saving several Jews from arrest and deportation.

Herz arranged to visit with Monsieur Calame-Rosset of Thônex. Arriving at the house, he met an elderly gentleman, almost 94 years of age. The visit was a surprise for both men. The old man immediately waved his hand dismissively when he learned of the reason for the visit, and said emphatically that he did not seek to be honored for what he and his wife had done during the war. He maintained that he did it because of his strong Protestant faith and for humanitarian reasons. That was why he had never written anything about his activities in the Belgian underground or his rescue of persecuted and endangered persons.

"When you hear somebody knocking at your door at midnight and a voice outside begging for help, how can you keep your door shut, especially if you know that this person will be murdered if left outside?" Calame-Rosset asked. "If I had acted in such a hardhearted manner, I could not have gone on living in the face of such a depraved act and attitude. When Moses came down from Mount Sinai he carried the Torah, and the Torah says: Love your neighbor as yourself. I believe that I have a duty to make sure that my fellow human beings can live in safety." With these words the old man tried to dissuade the interviewer from pursuing his goals.

Herbert Herz was not going to give up that easily, however. He published ads in three Jewish newspapers in Brussels seeking witnesses to Calame-Rosset's activities.

A professor of medicine, Dr Marcel Franckson, wrote that he was a commander of the "Martial Hotton" network of the Belgian underground army from 1940 onwards. He confirmed that Paul Calame-Rosset had enrolled in the underground army at the beginning of 1942 and was active in the intelligence and communications service. His wartime code-name was "Ted". He had repeatedly hidden members of the underground who were wanted by the Germans. The Gestapo tried to search his house several times, yet Calame-Rosset refused to let them do so. Half jokingly, half seriously he said: "My house is guarded by an angel with a flaming sword."

Dr. Franckson further reported that in April 1943 he was on the Gestapo's wanted list himself and was desperately searching for a hideout. "Paul and his wife May spontaneously offered their house as a shelter. May looked after me and fed me for more than eight weeks, just as she did British Royal Air Force men whose airplanes had been shot down. I also remember a young Jewish chap, about 18 years of age, whose name was Robert."

"Ted became the central pillar of our logistics in Brussels," Dr Franckson recalled. His house served as a communications center for the underground. Robert took the messages and relayed them in Calame-Rosset's absence.

Young Robert was not the only Jew to be given shelter by the Calames. His sister, too, found refuge at the house after their parents had been betrayed and deported to an extermination camp, where they died. When there was an impending raid and the Gestapo was approaching the house, Calame-Rosset would sneak her out to a friend's house. Robert himself lived at the house until the end of the war, when he fell seriously ill and passed away.

During the winter of 1942 and spring of 1943, Paul and May gave refuge to three members of the Cywié family—Henoch, his wife Golda and their daughter Rosa. Marc Cywié wrote on January 29, 1998: "My mother Henriette often used to go up to a house on the Dieweg road. Her parents and sister Rosa had found a hiding place there during the war. She still remembered having met British soldiers and parachutists when she secretly visited her family at the house. Whenever there was a raid by the Gestapo, the Calames quickly moved the refugees to a nearby apartment in the same street, in order to reduce the danger of being discovered."

Another Jewish family by the name of Lemberg were given shelter by the Calames, too. And there was the particularly sad case of a young Jewish woman who had jumped out of the window of her house in desperation when she heard that the Gestapo was approaching, and whom Paul and May Calame-

Rosset had cared for. Her name could not be found and her fate is unknown.

Paul Calame-Rosset made no attempt to hide his deep aversion to the Nazis. His high moral values and courage were admirable. Although his home country, Switzerland, was constitutionally obliged to maintain political neutrality, Paul saw himself as being under no such obligation. To him, Nazism was the personification of evil, and everything possible had to be done to fight against it. He showed the courage of his convictions by actively participating in armed resistance and sabotage, and saving as many people in distress as he could. The value of his services to the underground was inestimable. After the war he was awarded the "Croix de Guerre Belge", a high honor, and the prestigious British honor, the King's Medal for Courage in the Cause of Freedom. He was held in such high esteem by his former colleagues in the Belgian underground that they elected him as Honorary President of their association.

On September 16, 1998, at a very moving ceremony at the Salle des Fêtes in Thônex, the Ambassador of Israel to Switzerland, Yitzhak Mayer, presented Paul Calame-Rosset with the "Righteous Among the Nations" medal of honor. Present at the ceremony were Marc Cywié and his mother Henriette, representing one of the Jewish families who had been saved, and also Paul's former commander in the Belgian Resistance, Dr Marcel Franckson. They had come from Brussels specially for the occasion. Local dignitaries and the Belgian Consul-General, Madame Fostier, were also in attendance.

In his speech, Dr Franckson reminded "Ted" of the evening in 1943 when he asked him: "Why are you, a Swiss, a citizen of a neutral country, risking your life in the Resistance?" He replied: "There is no neutrality in the face of crime."

René Nodot

The Social Worker—and Passionate Secret Resistance Fighter

Alex Rosenzweig was picked up by the gendarmerie on August 26, 1943. He and 45 other Jews were taken from Trévoux to nearby Bourg-en-Bresse, where they were interned at Bichat school.

The commanding officer informed them that they would be transported to Germany for forced labor in the "Todt" organization. Rosenzweig expected the worst. He had been a German citizen in his youth, but had relinquished his citizenship and volunteered to serve in the French Army.

While Rosenzweig was awaiting deportation to Germany, a man named René Nodot appeared at the schoolhouse. He claimed to be a social worker at the Swiss General Consulate in Lyons, taking care of the interests of foreign and displaced persons. Nodot went to negotiate with the gendarmerie, asking for postponement of the deportation of the arrested Jews. After a few days he returned, informing the prisoners that he had secured their release. Nobody–not even Alex, who had been at school with René–knew that he was an active member of the Resistance.

In 1964, Alex Rosenzweig, now living in New York, met Nodot again at a memorial ceremony of former *"Maquisards"* (underground soldiers) and members of the Resistance. Their reunion was dramatic, to say the least. It took place at the Jean Perrin school in Lyons. René Nodot, who was then secretary of the Association of former Maquis and Resistance fighters, was honored for his rescue of Jewish refugees.

Nodot's claim to be a social worker at the Swiss General Consulate was not unfounded. Swiss-born Nodot (who had dual French and Swiss nationality) had indeed worked for the consulate between 1940 and 1944. In his function he had many contacts with persecuted Jews and refugees. But secretly, he had also joined the French underground movement and become a liaison officer in the French department of Ain, the areas of Bourg-en-Bresse and Jura, near the Swiss border.

It can be demonstrated that Nodot saved many Jews from deportation to the extermination camps. He started out by warning them of impending arrest. He advised them to leave their homes before the gendarmes or troops could get to them, and to hide wherever they could. He helped many Jewish people, especially women and children, to cross the border into Switzerland.

Alex Rosenzweig also recalled that, some days before his own arrest, his pregnant wife and his four-year-old son were separated from him. Nodot saw to it that, after Alex's release, his family was reunited. Later, René helped him find a job. His new employer was also a member of the Resistance.

Nodot even secured the release from prison of captive Jews who would otherwise have been deported. He thought of schemes such as issuing a doctor's certificate stating that a person was suffering from a contagious disease and that quarantine internment was necessary. Many were rescued in this manner.

The fact that Nodot was employed as a social worker by the Swiss consulate is confirmed by Léon Froment from Lyons, who was René's superior between 1942 and 1945. Froment was aware that Nodot was helping Jews escape across the border into Switzerland. (Nodot had not only helped many Jews, but also endangered underground fighters and wanted deserters of the French Army.)

Another man who worked alongside René Nodot was underground fighter René Miolane from Lyons. He relates his experience: "I had a visit in March 1943 from Nodot. He asked me if I could help him to smuggle little 7-year old Eva Stein into Switzerland. She was alone, as her mother, sister, aunt and grandmother had all left France as long as eight months previously. She had stayed with her father at a refugee home, but in his desperation and distress he had committed suicide. Nodot had taken the little girl to a guesthouse, where she was able to stay for a few months.

"Nodot looked for an opportunity to bring little Eva to Switzerland, to reunite her with her mother and family. He was in contact with a border guard who belonged to a secret organization that specialized in smuggling women and children across the border. I had already heard that Nodot had taken several people in jeopardy to my uncle, Felix Petit, who was mayor of the town of St.-Julien-en-Genevois. So I decided to help, and crossed the border secretly with Nodot. He would never accept any money but used his own to cover the cost. I often stayed the night at my uncle's house.

"Nodot successfully smuggled little Eva out and across the Swiss border. I wanted to know how she was and exchanged some letters with her family in Switzerland. This was yet another case of Nodot saving the lives of Jewish refugees, as he had done so many times."

Gaston Joubert from Lyons was a commander in the French Resistance. He confirmed that, from July 1943 onward, Nodot was a member, too. He was active under the command of René Basset, mainly in the department of Ain. Nodot relayed many messages and a great deal of secret information which was helpful to the Resistance. He participated in many Resistance escape missions, involving the smuggling of women and children across the border into Switzerland. Nodot was also an expert at forging papers for escaped French and Allied prisoners of war.

Nodot's contacts included pastors Boegner and Déchans of the Reformed Church of France, who both collaborated with the Resistance. Through his many contacts and liaisons with various branches of the Resistance and the "Maquis", Nodot played an important role in liberating France from the German occupation. The celebrated Nazi hunter Simon Wiesenthal recognized this and wrote a letter to René Nodot, commending him for his activities during those difficult years.

Professor René Nodot was honored by the French government in October 1957. He was made a Chevalier de la Légion d'Honneur. Nodot also received a certificate making him a member of the "National Volunteers' League of Smugglers of Refugees", and he became secretary of the Federation of Former Resistance and Maquis Fighters. (He had been a member of the Christian Resistance, Protestant branch, which advocated non-violent resistance.) In 1970, René Nodot published a book about his wartime experiences, entitled *"Les enfants ne partiront pas!"*–"The children are not going to leave!".

Carl Lutz
Gertrude Lutz
Peter Zürcher

The Courageous Consul in Besieged Budapest

Budapest, November 1944: Chaos reigned in the besieged Hungarian capital as the Red Army tightened its grip around the city. Gangs of "Arrow Cross" Nazi sympathizers were terrorizing the streets. News reached the Swiss Legation that some of them had forced their way into the safe houses set up by Swiss diplomats in Budapest. Until this time, these homes had been respected as sanctuaries. But now the gangs were intruding and dragging out Jews to crowd them into the ghettos.

Swiss Vice-Consul Carl Lutz and his wife Gertrude decided to pay a visit to the safe houses. The Jewish refugees needed to be protected from the encroaching Arrow Cross, and freed—if at all possible.

Shelling from the Russian artillery continued as the couple drove through the heavily bombarded city. Men and women were running from one side of the street to the other, hoping to find a little food in some of the shops that were still open. Carl and Gertrude saw armed Arrow Cross gangs beating up Jews

Entrance to the former British Embassy in Budapest which later became Lutz's residence. Situated in the "Castle quarter", it displayed the Swiss flag during the entire time of the Nazi occupation of Budapest.

Portrait of Carl Lutz.

Refugees line up (1944) in front of the Swiss Legation. They all hope to receive a "Schutzbrief" (letter of protection) and free passes or transit visas.

(Source for all illustrations in this chapter: Archiv für Zeitgeschichte, ETH-UNI Zurich)

Carl Lutz looking out from the basement window of his residence (the former British Embassy) after a raid. The façade is heavily marked by gunshots and shrapnel. On the left is a defused bomb shell. Early 1945.

Carl Lutz in an office he used for the rescue work of the Swiss Legation at the former US Embassy in Budapest.

Vice Consul Carl Lutz (in light-colored overcoat) with two other individuals. The one in the middle is (presumably) Harald Feller.

"Schutzbrief" (letter of protection), dated October 23, 1944, for one person (LASZLO MIKLOS) to be included in a Swiss collective passport. It shows the letterhead and stamp of the Swiss Legation in Budapest, Department of Foreign Interests.

"Schutzbrief" (letter of protection) dated April 11, 1944, as posted on buildings in the evacuation quarters of Budapest. It shows the Swiss emblem and bears Carl Lutz's signature.

Gertrude Lutz looking out from a flower-dressed 1st floor window of the Swiss Legation building in Budapest.

Undated confirmation, signed by various Hungarian officials, stating that Carl Lutz is representing the interests of Great Britain, the United States of America and other nations.

they had rounded up earlier, using whips and clubs. People were just staring from the windows of their houses, unable or unwilling to intervene.

Lutz's car, with the Swiss ensign on its mudguard, was stopped at Szent István Park on the eastern bank of the River Danube by a roving gang of thugs proudly wearing the Arrow Cross uniform. (The Arrow Cross was the Hungarian version of the swastika, each "leg" in the form of an arrow.) Nearby, other gang members were driving on a number of Jews they had captured, beating them with their pistol grips. Lutz stepped out of the car, identified himself and started to protest at the senseless brutality taking place on the other side of the street.

Meanwhile, Gertrude comforted the Jews as they huddled together, fearful of their lives. Lutz shouted to one of the Hungarian policemen standing by, demanding that he step in to protect the Jews. He even threatened to inform the Hungarian Ministry of Foreign Affairs.

Some of the gang leaders turned around and pointed their weapons at Lutz and his wife. They ordered them to shut up, clear out and mind their own business. Lutz adamantly refused to leave unless the traumatized Jews were set free and allowed to return to the safe houses. The Arrow Cross leaders were about to attack Lutz, but suddenly they changed their minds. They gave Lutz the opportunity to get in touch with the Hungarian Minister of Foreign Affairs, Baron Gábor von Kémény—a rather time-consuming affair in those days, as there was no properly-functioning telephone system in Hungary.

When he learned of the situation, Kémény intervened and ordered the thugs to stop. The leaders "apologized" and agreed to let Carl and Gertrude Lutz escort the Jews back to the safe houses.

FACE-TO-FACE WITH THE "FINAL SOLUTION"

Carl Lutz, a career diplomat in the service of the Swiss Confederation abroad, had been transferred to Budapest and appointed Vice Consul at the beginning of January, 1942. Within a short time he was promoted to head of the Department of Foreign Interests at the Swiss Legation.

As only a few countries still maintained diplomatic relations with Hungary at this stage of the conflict, Lutz had an important diplomatic and political task. By this time, the Swiss Mission in Budapest was representing the diplomatic and consular interests of the United States of America, Great Britain, Belgium, Yugoslavia, Egypt, Uruguay, Paraguay, Haiti, Venezuela, Honduras, El Salvador and Romania.

Lutz set up his office in the American Embassy building, situated at No. 18 Szabadság tér (or Liberty Square). Nearly twenty employees took care of the interests of about 600 Americans, 30 Britons and over 6,000 other foreign nationals still living in Hungary.

In Budapest, Lutz was squarely confronted with the unfolding tragedy of the Hungarian Jews. Shortly after the German occupation in March 1944, the "Sondereinsatzkommando", or special commando unit, arrived. It was headed by Adolf Eichmann, the "Obersturmbannführer" (SS officer with the rank of major) in Hungary. He was there to implement Adolf Hitler's "Endlösung", the "Final Solution" to the "Jewish Question". Within a short time, the persecution of Hungarian Jews reached its peak.

Lutz witnessed first-hand the general panic breaking out. Havoc reigned among the Jewish population because all the Jews were stripped of the most basic human rights. Soon, massive and barbarous detentions began. The Hungarian police readily helped to round up the Jews and confine them to the ghetto. Their methods were notoriously inhumane and brutal.

The mass deportations by train began exactly thirty days after the German Army had invaded Hungary. Ninety to 100 men and women were packed into each railway wagon, with no sanitary facilities. Children, infants and women in advanced pregnancy were all forced in. The myrmidon troops spared neither the hoary head nor the sick.

In the month between mid-April and mid-May 1944, about half a million Jews were formally arrested and rounded up in the provincial towns; between May 15 and July 9, 450,000 Jews were deported—mainly to the extermination camp at Auschwitz in occupied Poland.

In their anxiety and despair, many Jews contacted the Swiss Embassy, asking for help and protection. Lutz saw their utter misery and their desperate plight. He was stirred in his heart; pangs of conscience robbed him of his sleep.

Two Slovakian Jews had somehow managed to escape from the Auschwitz death camp. They reached Budapest around the time when Jews were being hunted more than ever before. From them Lutz learned the fate of those who had been deported, never to return. Lutz asked his superior, the Envoy Maximilian Jäger, to request instructions from Berne. As time was obviously running out, Lutz resolved to take action without waiting for orders from the Swiss Foreign Office.

At that time, a branch of the Jewish Agency (the "Palestine Office"), headed by Miklos Krausz, was active in Budapest. Krausz had obtained a number of "Palestine certificates" from the British. Great Britain was the mandatory power in Palestine. Such documents would obviously be of inestimable value to the persecuted Hungarian Jews. Anybody in possession of such a pass could envisage being able to emigrate to Palestine.

Lutz, whose embassy had been entrusted with British diplomatic interests in Hungary, was contacted by Krausz. When Lutz realized what he was being offered, he took an important and far-reaching decision. That decision was not in line with the instructions or the policy of his country but it was one that would subsequently save tens of thousands of Jews from the ovens of Auschwitz.

Because of his position and perhaps also his excellent relations with German officials, Carl Lutz was able to work out a plan to counteract the German mass deportations. First, Lutz contacted the German Ambassador in Budapest, Dr. Edmund Veesenmayer. He also got in touch with Adolf Eichmann who, along with his staff was residing at the Hotel Majestic on Svábhegy (the Swabian hill), one of the Buda hills to the west of the capital.

Both leaders received the Swiss Vice-Consul cordially. Lutz explained to Eichmann and the German ambassador that, as a representative of the interests of the British Empire, he was in possession of 7,800 Palestine certificates, permitting Jews from Hungary to emigrate to Palestine. Any person in possession of such a document, he emphasized, should automatically be placed under the protection of the Swiss Legation until it was possible to depart for Palestine.

Subsequent negotiations dragged on for months. In the meantime, Lutz "interpreted" the 7,800 certificates as "family documents", insisting that the passports of safe conduct should not only cover the bearers but also their dependants. All in all, this would mean placing over 50,000 people under the protection of the Swiss Legation.

Behind Lutz's apparent success lies a bit of personal history. He had worked as a consular officer in Tel Aviv in the late

1930s. With the outbreak of hostilities, Germans living in Palestine were considered as potential enemies and imprisoned by the British mandatory authorities. Lutz took some humanitarian action to relieve the fate of these German prisoners so that they were treated better by the British during their internment.

A letter written by Consul Dr. Otto Eckert of the German Foreign Office, dated May 16, 1941, confirms Carl Lutz's role in the fall of 1939 as a benefactor to the Germans interned abroad.

Maybe Berlin remembered that Carl Lutz had helped some 2,500 German nationals who had been interned. As a result of Lutz's earlier act of mercy towards German citizens, Berlin allowed him to place a large number of Jews in Hungary under Swiss protection.

There was a catch, however—one condition that still needed to be fulfilled and appeared virtually impossible. Besides the certificates, each and every one of the 50,000 Jews had to be in possession of an immigration pass for Palestine as well. Only then would the Germans countersign the letters of protection. This would be almost impossible to achieve.

Again, Lutz got in touch with the Swiss government in Berne. He pointed out the acute difficulties the Jews were in. He urged the officials to permit them to travel through Switzerland on their way to Palestine. The answer from Berne was disappointing. The Swiss government objected to such plans and declared that it was not in a position to open its borders to Hungarian Jews, even if they held Palestine certificates.

Envoy Maximilian Jäger was not even given permission to sign or approve the requests which could then have been submitted to the Hungarian and German officials.

Following this adverse decision, Lutz made up his mind to implement his plan to protect the Jews and rescue them from the threat of annihilation without Berne's consent or permission. He held that the humanitarian law of life was stronger and more important than the paragraphs of any legal code.

Thus, Carl Lutz became the first diplomat of a neutral country to issue "passports of safe conduct" (Schutzpässe) to Jews who were threatened with deportation to extermination camps. He insisted that all bearers of Palestine certificates should be regarded as British citizens who were therefore entitled to Swiss protection, since Switzerland was officially acting on behalf of the British Empire.

The impossible was beginning to happen!

The precedent of the Palestine document was followed by some of the other embassies. Lutz's success was also an inspiration and encouragement to Raoul Wallenberg, the Swedish diplomat, who met with Lutz a few days after arriving in Budapest.

Lutz had bargained successfully and courageously that all bearers of this document were regarded as British citizens. The Hungarian and German officials consistently respected the validity of the passport, and Switzerland could grant its protection until the refugees were ready and able to emigrate.

However, the difficulties of preparing the passports of safe conduct were enormous. More than 50,000 protective letters (Schutzbriefe) had to be issued, and neither the funds nor the manpower were available for this gigantic task. Fifty Jewish youths, however, volunteered to collect the personal information and, if necessary, take passport photographs of all the applicants. They accomplished the mammoth task within a very short time. Next, Lutz had to apply to the Hungarian government for permission to distribute the passports of safe conduct.

At this point, developments took yet another unexpected turn. Contrary to what had been previously agreed, the Hungarian police decided not to honor the protective letters. It took vociferous protesting against this capricious about-face before the Hungarian government instructed the police authorities to respect the papers like any other official documents. They finally complied. Only then was the protection of the 50,000 Jews guaranteed.

Carl Lutz had a high-ranking friend at the German Embassy. His name was Feine. From him, Lutz learned that "SS-Reichsführer" Heinrich Himmler had made a cynical offer to the Allies—to "trade" one million Jews in exchange for 10,000 heavy trucks ("able to withstand the winter, and not to be used on the Western front"), two million bars of soap and other army supplies. US President Franklin Delano Roosevelt had at least given this "deal" some consideration, but, unsurprisingly, it had been summarily rejected by the Soviets. (This plan was one of the few things that Adolf Eichmann was eager to claim some personal responsibility for in his memoirs, written from his prison cell in Haifa, Israel in 1961, and recently made public by the Israeli government.) Feine also passed on to Lutz a copy of a telegram addressed to Ambassador Veesenmayer. From this message, it was clear that the Eichmann "Sondereinsatzkommando" was a death squad. Veesenmayer himself was obviously a cynic and a murderer, too, although he had formally agreed to honor the passports of safe conduct.

Lutz was convinced that Veesenmayer and Eichmann had both blatantly lied to him, and that they intended to proceed with their dirty work, bringing the "Final Solution" to a conclusion. Just before the Germans started their mass deportations, the terrible plans also came to Carl Lutz's attention through Feine, and he passed the information on to Berne. There was no reaction, no clear plan of action from the Swiss government.

In October 1944, Soviet forces crossed into Hungary. On October 15, the Hungarian Regent Nicholas Horthy asked the Soviets for an armistice, whereupon the German SS, under Dr. Veesenmayer's orders, arrested him and carried him off to an unknown destination. They appointed Ferenc Szálasi, the leader of the fascist Arrow Cross, as Prime Minister.

The occupying forces decreed that the protective letters would no longer be accepted. The terror regime in Budapest swung into action. Jews were openly attacked by the Arrow

Cross gangs, dragged out of their homes or the safe houses and carried off. Many of them did not even make it to the concentration camps: they were either thrown into the River Danube or murdered in some other cruel manner. Those who were not killed right away were sentenced to forced labor, as decreed by the Szálasi regime.

Lutz contacted the diplomats of the other neutral nations still represented in Hungary. He protested vigorously against the new legislation and the renewed persecution of the Jews. He worded his protest note carefully and addressed it to Foreign Minister Baron von Kémény. In this diplomatic note, the neutral nations threatened to break off all contacts with the Szálasi regime unless it would recognize and accept the protective letters and stop its murderous actions against the Jews.

As an incentive, Lutz promised that he would use his leverage to have the Szálasi regime recognized by the nations he officially represented. The Hungarian government seemed to welcome the deal and agreed to accept the protective letters. Lutz, however, did not trust their promises and, with the number of Jews seeking asylum increasing every day, he stepped up the pace of his actions in order to save as many as he could. Still, he sensed that time was running out, and he feared that the fate of the Hungarian Jews had been sealed.

In his endeavors, Lutz contacted the Palestine Office, Dr Kastner's Jewish Rescue Committee and the Jewish underground organization Haganah. He took Miklos Krausz, the head of the Palestine Office and 150 of his coworkers into the Swiss Mission. Several Jews who were in immediate danger of deportation were also hidden in the Mission building. Since Lutz had negotiated extraterritorial status for the building with the Hungarian government, the Arrow Cross gangs did not dare come inside to arrest Jews.

Throughout this traumatic time, Carl's wife Gertrude assisted him wherever she could. She provided food to the hungry Jews and looked after them when they had health or other sanitary problems.

Members of the Jewish Pioneer Movement expertly forged protective letters for as many of the asylum seekers as possible. Lutz signed the bogus documents, making them official and legitimate. The number of fake protective letters reached approximately 120,000. With members of the Jewish Pioneer Movement working day and night, the false papers were distributed in the ghettos to thousands of Jews who were either menaced by the Hungarian government or threatened by the Germans.

Lutz felt impelled to do even more. He asked the Hungarian government for the use of twenty high-rise apartment buildings in Budapest. He needed these houses to provide shelter for 50,000 Jews prior to their departure for Palestine. The Swiss flag flew from the roofs of all these buildings. One of the buildings was situated in Wekerle Street, another in Vadász Street.

The pressure mounted as the Red Army drew closer to the Hungarian capital. Lutz needed to provide shelter for more and more Jewish refugees. While the tension in the city grew worse every day, Lutz and his helpers distributed an increasing number of protective letters.

As air raids became heavier, public order in Budapest disintegrated. The Arrow Cross gangs, now totally unrestrained, became more aggressive every day, brutally assaulting Jews in the streets. But the Swiss Vice-Consul was not intimidated. He appeared personally at many critical points, in particular at the places Jews were mustered prior to their deportation. Anyone who held a protective letter was taken out of the crowd and escorted by Lutz to one of the safe houses. Every time he witnessed a brutal raid by the Arrow Cross gangs, he protested vehemently to the Hungarian Ministry of Foreign Affairs.

One evening Lutz and his helpers appeared on the scene at a house in the ghetto where about 300 Jews were being held captive, the doors locked and bolted, the windows hermetically sealed by wooden boards. The people would have suffocated in misery had Lutz not intervened to save them.

Towards the end of 1944, the Hungarian government decreed that all Jews capable of physical work should be drafted into forced labor. This was one of the heaviest burdens Lutz endured in his tireless efforts, as many of these Jews held protective letters and were supposed to be under Swiss protection. All of this was done in blatant disregarded of the agreements.

Lutz was therefore obliged to intervene again and to request exemption from forced labor for all holders of protective letters. After much negotiation, he achieved his objective, but the Arrow Cross gangs did not always respect the deal. Lutz found himself having to intervene again and again.

By November 1944, the Red Army had reached the outskirts of Budapest. A sudden and dramatic shift occurred in the attitude of the Hungarian populace. The military declared that protective letters were of no value. The government gave the Swiss until November 15 to officially recognize the regime of Ferenc Szálasi, the Nazi-sympathizer Arrow Cross chief. Otherwise all protective letters would be rendered null and void—and they would all be confiscated. Hungary officially demanded that all Jews who were under Lutz's protection should immediately leave the country for Palestine.

On November 9 the Arrow Cross gangs raided the city, searching for Jews who had not reported for forced labor. The safe houses were not spared either. During this raid, many Jews were arrested and finally deported.

Another manhunt for Jews was initiated. Ten of thousands were taken from the ghetto to the Altofeuer brick factory of Obuda in the north west of Budapest, where they were held captive without food and in conditions of extreme cold.

As many of these Jews were in possession of protective letters, Carl and Gertrude Lutz drove to the brick factory several times in order to personally free Jews holding these documents. Gertrude stood in the freezing cold for many hours checking the papers, and demanding the rights that the holders were entitled to.

On one occasion, when Lutz visited the factory together
with Miklos Krausz, their automobile, bearing the Swiss
ensign, was stopped by the Arrow Cross gangs. Krausz was
manhandled and forcibly pulled out of the car. Lutz protested
loudly. He explained to the commanding officer that he and
those with him had official permission from the Hungarian
Foreign Minister, Baron von Kémény, to move freely within the
country wherever they wanted. The commander responded
angrily that Kémény would be held responsible for such freedom of movement, but in spite of their menacing hostility, they
finally released Krausz.

While Lutz and his wife were being threatened at gunpoint
by the Arrow Cross gangs near Szent István Park, the
Hungarian Government was carrying out the plans for a gigantic march of 27,000 able-bodied Jews from Hungary to
Germany. There they would be put to work in the arms industry. A second contingent of 40,000 was to follow, at the rate of
2,000 to 4,000 every day.

News reached Budapest that many had died, frozen, starving and exhausted, during the excruciating marches, even
before reaching the Austrian border. The representatives of the
Vatican, Switzerland, Sweden, Spain and Portugal protested
vigorously. They demanded that the German authorities and
the Szálasi regime stop these inhumane deportation marches
immediately.

Lutz gave orders to produce more and more protective letters.
He had received a large quantity of blank entry visas from the
representative of El Salvador. He filled in the names of Jews who
were already on the march to Germany. Carl and his wife drove
westward, catching up with the marchers. He signed the documents on the spot and distributed them together with the visas,
thus saving hundreds of Jews from misery and destruction.

The leader of the NS security forces (RSHA), Ernst
Kaltenbrunner, formally complained via the German Foreign
Office about Lutz's unacceptable interference. He reported that
Swiss representatives were following the marching columns of

Jews by car, distributing documents to them. As a result, a whole group of marchers had disappeared. For some reason, the Honved (Hungarian army) guards had respected the protective letters.

This is a letter signed by the chief of security police (SD), Kaltenbrunner, addressed to a high ranking officer in the SS, Wagner, at the Foreign Office, dated November 11, 1944. "As I am informed, during the deportation of Jews to the Reich special envoys from the Swiss Embassy drove after a column by automobile and distributed passports of safe conduct to the marching Jews in such great numbers that at the end of the marching day the majority of the column had disappeared, since the passports of safe conduct were respected by the accompanying Honved guards."

On one occasion, Carl Lutz, together with Friedrich Born of the Red Cross, joined forces with Swedish diplomats Raoul Wallenberg, Per Anger and Vilmos Langfelder and drove down the fateful road to Hegyeshalom, taking three truckloads of food and medical supplies with them. A drop in the bucket, in the face of such unspeakable human tragedy. Yet they still managed to save hundreds of lives.

As a consequence of the diplomatic protests, Szálasi stopped further death marches after November 20, 1944. He agreed, however, to carry on with the deportations of Jews after pressure from Ribbentrop, the German Foreign Minister. The last ever train, with thousands of deportees on board, left Budapest on December 3, 1944.

The closer the battle front got to Budapest, the more desperate the situation of the Jews in the city became. The German Ambassador Dr. Veesenmayer explained to Carl Lutz that the Budapest Jews were considered not only a plague, but also a real danger in the "hinterland" to the German "Lebensraum".

Terror now reigned in the streets of Budapest, and most of the time the Jews were the target. In response, Lutz allowed the Jewish Pioneers and the Haganah to operate from the safe houses. They had nothing to lose.

When the telephone line and the electricity supply were cut, the helpers organized fifty youths on bicycles. These youths dressed up as Arrow Cross gangs and gained entry to Jewish homes. From there they led out entire families to bring them to the safe houses. They helped to organize food for them, too.

The Russian siege of Budapest began at the end of 1944. The Arrow Cross gangs stepped up their vicious persecution of Jews still further. One of their raids was at the Vadász Street shelter. They broke into the home and started shooting into the crowd. A large number of the residents were wounded and many died as a result. Then there was another mass arrest of about 800 Jews, but they were released after energetic protests from Carl Lutz.

Because of the clear and present danger of the war situation, the Swiss Foreign Office ordered its diplomats to return to Switzerland without further delay. Envoy Jäger, who had repeatedly supported Lutz in his efforts to save the death-bound Jews, left Budapest together with the majority of his Swiss staff.

When bidding him farewell, his last words to Lutz were: "Just act according to the best of your knowledge and your conscience. But please do everything you can for the victims."

Lutz answered that he could not leave his post as he felt an inner calling to continue his work of salvation. He decided to stay on in Budapest. Some of the legation personnel remained in Buda, while others were relocated to a building in Pest, on the eastern side of the River Danube. All the bridges had now been destroyed by the German Wehrmacht. As a consequence, Carl Lutz entrusted Dr. Peter Zürcher with the distribution of the protective letters to the Jewish refugees in Pest. Zürcher was assisted by Ernst Von Rufs.

By mid-December the situation had become so dangerous that even the Hungarian government fled the capital. The two Swiss Legation buildings were completely cut off from each other, and Lutz, the official representative of Switzerland, could act only in a restricted extent from Buda.

The battle front moved from the hills around Budapest into the city. One day, by coincidence, Lutz and his wife got into the headquarters of the defense command in the middle of the city. Around the command post, heavy street battles were raging, and there were daily Russian air raids, mainly concentrating on the area where the Swiss Legation building was situated. One day a bomb hit the main tract. The staff only survived because they had taken refuge in the air raid shelter in the basement of the building. Most of Lutz's belongings went up in flames and smoke.

It was Gertrude who kept up the spirits of those present in those dire conditions in the basement. Soon they had run out of water, and the only water available was the ugly black liquid from the radiators of the central heating system.

When Gertrude occasionally stepped out to search for food, she exposed herself to even greater danger. On one occasion she nearly ran into a Russian tank brigade. But she kept up her efforts, especially protecting women and girls wherever she could; the danger of being raped by Russian soldiers was imminent and real.

When conditions got even worse at Buda, the few remaining staff moved to Pest by ferry. Anticipating that he would soon be confined to his residence in Buda, Carl Lutz appointed Peter Zürcher as his temporary representative in Pest. All this time, Carl maintained lines of communication with the Swiss and Hungarian governments in spite of growing difficulties.

He continued to have diplomatic immunity to the very end. His final work at the Swiss Legation consisted of plans for the aftermath of the war, cleaning the rubble and healing the wounds. This is what survivors, Jewish intellectuals who miraculously escaped and found refuge at the Swiss Embassy, later recorded. These reports have served historians as reliable documents.

But many Jews had survived by the skin of their teeth and were finally saved. More than 4,500 survivors were freed from the safe houses. Altogether, more than 17,000 had been protected during the Nazi terror at the shelters of Wekerle Street and Vadász Street. 250,000 Jews who had been crowded into the ghettos survived because they enjoyed the status of protected refugees thanks to Carl Lutz and his relentless diplomatic efforts.

Budapest finally fell to the Red Army forces on January 18, 1945. Shortly after the liberation of Budapest, the Soviet Governor ordered Lutz and his wife to leave the city immediately. Carl and Gertrude did not even have time to say goodbye to all their friends and colleagues. Even some of the legation staff were not able to bid them farewell, as the Russian military commanders had insisted that they depart within 24 hours.

A most adventurous journey took Carl and Gertrude Lutz from Budapest via Bucharest to Istanbul, and from there to Lisbon, Madrid and Barcelona, and then back to Berne in Switzerland.

It came as no surprise that Carl Lutz's health had suffered greatly. He was also depressed, due to the lack of official support from his government during these critical months. However, he knew that he and his wife had done everything they could to save as many Jews as possible.

After his return to his home country, Lutz faced disciplinary measures from the Swiss Foreign Office. In their opinion, he had repeatedly overstepped his authority and disregarded orders from Berne during his time as vice-consul and head of representation of the diplomatic interests of the warring nations. It was not until many years later that he was raised to the rank of Consul General.

In his own memoirs, Lutz wrote: "We all knew that the Germans exterminated millions of Jews they had deported to Auschwitz and other death camps (KZs). In various KZs they operated gas chambers, and news of this had reached the Swiss Legation as early as 1943. We had also heard of the heroic resistance fights at the Warsaw Ghetto. We knew that German tanks had rolled in and finished off the last 40,000 inhabitants. We maintained our silence. The governments of the neutral countries maintained their silence. The entire democratic world remained silent."

Lutz did not hold back either in his criticism of Swiss refugee policy. "Naturally, you may explain the attitude of the Swiss government during the war by the fact that the leaders were intimidated by the threats and menaces uttered in no uncertain terms by Hitler and Nazi Germany. My home country is a small country. During the war it was completely surrounded by German-occupied lands. Resistance against Germany would have been senseless right from the start. But if you look at the facts squarely and realistically, the arguments were beggarly and weak."

About the Germans, Lutz wrote: "The cynical attitude of the Germans which I witnessed during my negotiations with Ambassador Veesenmayer and 'SS-Obersturmbannführer' Eichmann, was aimed at misleading the negotiating partner. Veesenmayer and Eichmann always showed their best faces. They constantly expressed their understanding for my endeavors in the interest of the persecuted and the victims. At first, I believed them. With their help I hoped to be able to save all

Jews still alive in the summer of 1944. With hindsight and even from a distance, I cannot find an explanation for the hideous cruelty which ended in the extermination of millions of human beings, a tragedy unparalleled in history. How should one fathom and grasp why a certain clique could motivate an entire nation, yes, even several nations, to rob millions of men, to torture them and murder them under the pretense that the higher ranking and better race must eliminate the inferior like weeds?"

After the war, the political section of the Hungarian National Council ordered an inquiry into Swiss efforts to save the Jews in Hungary during the Second World War. A white paper was published. It said that the initiative was taken by the Swiss but that later the embassies of Sweden, Spain, Portugal and the Vatican also got involved.

Many years went by before the Swiss authorities fully recognized and appreciated Carl Lutz's heroic activities in Budapest during the war. The Swiss media cited him as a humanitarian whose antifascist convictions had caused him to take the side of the persecuted—a man for all seasons, so to speak. One commentator noted that Switzerland had been lucky to have a man like Lutz who, during this period of inhumanity, risked not only his career but also his life in order to help the victims.

The white paper also mentioned Peter Zürcher and Ernst Vonrufs as well as Harald Feller, the secretary at the Swiss Legation who, together with Lutz, had played an important and courageous role in liberating the Jews in January 1945.

Soon, the world recognized Carl Lutz and his work. He received numerous awards. During the Zionist congress in Basle, Switzerland in 1945, Carl Lutz received a long standing ovation from the assembled crowd. He was introduced by none other than Dr. Chaim Weizmann who was to become the first President of the State of Israel a few years later. On that occasion, Carl Lutz's name was written into the golden book of Keren Hakayemet. A street in Haifa, Israel, is named after him.

On May 24, 1948 the twelve states whose interests were represented by Lutz during 1944 expressed their special thanks to him for his good services on their behalf. He received honors and medals from the American and Hungarian governments. He was also decorated with the Cross of Honor, Order of Merit, by the Federal Republic of Germany. Carl Lutz was nominated three times for the Nobel Peace Prize.

Switzerland came around to recognizing the deeds of Carl Lutz, too. A sober official statement mentions that Vice-Consul Lutz distributed 7,800 passports of safe conduct to Jewish refugees and thus helped to save the lives of many tens of thousands of Jews who would otherwise have died miserably, and that he had informed the attachés of Sweden, Spain, Portugal and the Vatican, thus involving them in his saving work. It did not mention the fact that, unlike Carl Lutz, the Swedish diplomat Raoul Wallenberg had received full support from his government.

The official statement also notes that Lutz did everything in his power to save the Jews who had already embarked on a death march by distributing passports of safe conduct to them. (After all, there was a diplomatic note protesting about this event on file in Berne.)

In 1990, a year after the end of communism in Hungary, a monument in honor of Carl Lutz was created by the Hungarian sculptor Tamas Szabó. It was erected near the entrance to the former Jewish ghetto in Budapest. The sculpture depicts a man needing help and an angel coming to his aid.

Carl Lutz was born on April 30, 1895 in Walzenhausen in the mountains of the canton of Appenzell. He took a commercial apprenticeship in the border town of St. Margrethen, situated in the Rhine valley. In his youth he had learned from his mother that one should always be ready to help and assist one's fellow human beings without self interest. This leitmotiv stayed with him throughout his life.

In 1913, young Carl traveled to the United States of America, where he joined the Swiss consular corps about a year later. His first posting was to St. Louis, and in 1926 he worked as a consular employee in Philadelphia. In 1931 he met Gertrude Fankhauser who was working at the Swiss Consulate in St. Louis. During his mission in Philadelphia, Lutz was promoted to the position of consul. He returned to Switzerland in 1934, shortly after he and Gertrude had married.

A few months later, Lutz was sent on another tour of duty, this time to the Swiss Consulate at Tel Aviv, where he had his initial contacts with Zionism. He also became familiar with the idea of bringing Jews from all over the world back to their ancestral homeland where they would build up a modern state.

While he was in Palestine, bloody riots broke out between Jews and Arabs. Snipers and mines exacted a terrible toll. In 1939 Lutz was appointed the Vice Consul in Tel Aviv. He returned to Switzerland in 1941. Soon after that, he was posted to Berlin for a short period, before being given a special assignment in the legal department of the Swiss Foreign Office. He was posted to Budapest in January 1942.

After his return to Switzerland in 1945, he became the Swiss representative of German interests for eastern Switzerland in Zurich. He also served as a director of the World Council of Churches in Geneva. Gertrude Lutz, who had courageously and actively participated in her husband's salvation work during those ominous years in Hungary, became involved with "Spende", a charity for social welfare of the needy. Two years after their return from Budapest, Gertrude and Carl Lutz divorced.

Gertrude Lutz continued to be actively involved in UNICEF, working first in Brazil and later in Turkey. She held the office of vice president of the European Council of UNICEF.

Carl Lutz was called to lead negotiations with the Government of Israel concerning the status of the properties of the German Evangelical Church in Israel. Until August 2, 1953 he was responsible for the management of war reparations, another department of the Swiss Foreign Office.

In 1954 Lutz was sent to Bregenz, Austria, situated on the eastern shore of Lake Constance as Swiss Consul. He was promoted in 1960. His career as a diplomat in the service of Switzerland ended on June 30, 1961. His native village Walzenhausen awarded him the honor of freeman.

In 1964, the Yad Vashem Holocaust Memorial in Jerusalem presented Carl with the medal of honor, "Righteous Among the Nations". This decoration is conferred on those brave non-Jewish men and women who put their lives at risk to save Jews during the Shoah. Gertrude Lutz, who had valiantly stood by her husband during those crucial war years, planted a tree of remembrance for him at Yad Vashem.

Carl Lutz died peacefully in Berne at the age of 80 on February 13, 1975.

Dr Peter Zürcher was born in Zurich in 1914. He had business interests in Hungary in the early 1940s. In 1944 he joined the Department for Foreign Interests at the Swiss Legation in Budapest. From Christmas 1944 onwards, Pest as conditions worsened and Carl Lutz was unable to leave Buda, Zürcher served as interim head of the Department, based in Pest. Peter Zürcher followed in the footsteps of Carl Lutz and displayed tremendous courage in protecting the interests of Jews in the Hungarian capital against Arrow Cross aggression.

On one occasion, Peter Zürcher successfully thwarted an invasion of the Pest ghetto by the SS and Arrow Cross gangs, who were planning to massacre the inhabitants. He managed to intimidate the SS commandant with threats of future legal reprisals.

In January 1945, Zürcher learned of an Arrow Cross plan to evacuate most of the Jews from the houses under Swiss protection, and relocate them to ghetto, deport them or kill them. He immediately contacted Vajna, the Minister of the Interior, protesting in the strongest terms and demanding an end to Arrow Cross assaults on houses under the protection of the Swiss Legation. The planned evacuation was canceled.

One lady testified that Peter Zürcher allowed her to hide in his home while he arranged false papers for her, thus saving her life.

Peter Zürcher continued his work in Pest until the Soviet victory. He died in 1975, but his memory lives on. At a ceremony at the Amtshaus in Berne on September 6, 1999, Peter Zürcher was posthumously honored with the Yad Vashem medal "Righteous Among the Nations". The former First Secretary of the Swiss Legation, Harald Feller, was also honored at the ceremony. In a moving speech, Feller vividly recalled some of the heroic rescue efforts that saved thousands of lives.

Jean de Bavier

The Visionary Emissary of Hope

Jean de Bavier, brother of the Swiss chargé d'affaires in Athens, Greece, was sent to Budapest by the Red Cross in October 1943 at the age of fifty-one. The Committee was becoming increasingly concerned about the terrible events taking place in the capitals of Europe.

Before leaving Geneva, de Bavier had a meeting with Saly Mayer, the representative of the American Jewish Joint Distribution Committee.

On arrival in Budapest, de Bavier lost no time in establishing contact with the Swiss Legation, the local Red Cross, and the Hungarian authorities. He also met Samuel Stern, president of the Jewish community, and Dr. Kastner at the Palestine Agency, as well as Baroness Edith Weiss and other key figures.

With a view to arranging emigration of Jews to Palestine, he maintained close contact with Karl Kolb at the Red Cross delegation in Bucharest, Romania.

One of de Bavier's first projects was to prepare a report detailing the treatment of the Jews in Hungary. He visited internment camps where foreign civilians and soldiers were being held. The Red Cross instructed him not to visit camps where Hungarian citizens were interned, however, as that would have been tantamount to interference in Hungarian internal affairs.

De Bavier was gravely concerned about the plight of the Jews in Hungary and regularly wrote to Geneva, reporting and warning about the dangers he saw developing. The Swiss Legation in Budapest thought highly of Jean de Bavier and commented favorably about his work.

When the pro-Nazis seized power in Hungary, the Red Cross decided to strengthen its presence in central Europe by sending Georges Dunand to Bratislava. It also decided to increase the number of delegates in Budapest, although Jean de Bavier himself was recalled to Geneva. Friedrich Born was posted to Budapest in his place (on what was initially envisaged as a temporary assignment) in the spring of 1944.

Friedrich Born

The Red Cross Official Who Knew No Fear

On May 10, 1944, Friedrich Born arrived in Budapest as chief delegate of the International Committee of the Red Cross (ICRC). Deportation of Hungarian Jews to the death camp of Auschwitz was in full swing.

When Born first heard of the abductions and deportations, he alerted ICRC headquarters in Geneva. In his memorandum, dated May 26, 1944, he warned that, unless this development were halted immediately, not a single Hungarian Jew would be left. At the rate and speed it was progressing, it looked as if the extermination campaign would take no longer than two or three months.

Born received no answer from Geneva, so he repeated his warning message on June 10, 1944. He added that he could not remain idle in the face of such a terrible situation. He would do everything in his power to save the Jews from deportation, even without support from the Red Cross Geneva headquarters.

Born wrote: "The two months' occupation by the Wehrmacht had changed the face of the country, public life, and individual behavior in an extraordinary way. . . . Anyone who was familiar with the conditions of the country must soon

Copie conforme
ARCHIVES DU CICR

B e r i c h t

an das Internationale Komitee vom Roten Kreuz

erstattet von Friedrich Born

Delegierter für Ungarn

Juni 1945

INHALTSVERZEICHNIS.

Friedrich Born (Photo d'archives)

Digne des plus grands honneurs

En 1944, Friedrich Born, délégué du CICR basé à Budapest, en Hongrie, avait pris des initiatives personnelles pour sauver des Juifs. Le second volume de l'histoire du CICR, écrit par André Durand, relate entre autres les remarquables efforts de ce délégué pour tenter de protéger les innocents et les opprimés.

Le 5 juin 1987, à Jérusalem, le fils et la fille de Friedrich Born ont assisté à une cérémonie en l'honneur de leur père; à cette occasion, ils ont reçu, au nom de ce dernier, la plus haute distinction récompensant les personnes d'autres croyances ayant sauvé des Juifs au cours de la Deuxième Guerre mondiale.

Le CICR était représenté à cette cérémonie par son directeur général, M. Jacques Moreillon.

Report dated June 1945, written by Friedrich Born, delegate of the ICRC (International Committee of the Red Cross) in Hungary, describing his work from the start. The ICRC had started its assistance work just shortly after the occupation of Hungary by the German Wehrmacht in 1944. It describes the general living conditions of the population and the persecution of the Jews. It mentions prisoners of war of other nations, including US, British, French and Russian internees. (Archives of the ICRC, Geneva)

Friedrich Born in the plains of Hungary, standing next to the car he used for official missions. On the bumper of the car is the Red Cross emblem. (ETH-UNI Zurich and family archives of F. Born)

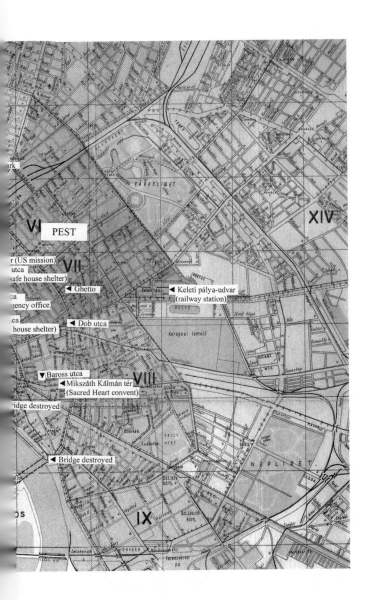

have realized what terrible things were being prepared and done. . . . Right after the beginning of the occupation, the measures against Hungarian Jews set in. The complete expropriation of Jewish businesses and the dispossession of individuals was decreed, and the elimination of all Jewish influence from all economic and academic areas was ordered" (Final Report to the ICRC HQ in Geneva by Friedrich Born, *ICRC Archives*, June 1945).

As a first step, Born approached the Hungarian government. He asked for permission to visit the camps at Kistarcsa and Szarvar, where Jews were gathered before being transported to Auschwitz. The two concentration camps were crowded with men, women, and children. There were practically no sanitary facilities, at least not sufficient for the large numbers of captives. Food and water were scarce, too.

Born asked Geneva to intervene immediately when he saw the circumstances in which these people were suffering. He demanded that the ICRC should protest officially against the persecution of the Jews and request that the harassment should cease without delay. Again, he received no reply. Born decided to take further action on his own initiative.

A native Hungarian, Peresz Rowas, was a member of the Hungarian resistance movement during the war. He survived, emigrated to Palestine, and became a member of Kibbutz Kfar Hamakkabi. He reported that "the Swiss Friedrich Born was one of those by whose help thousands of Hungarian Jews were saved from certain death."

How did this happen? Born organized and ran a special department at the ICRC office in Budapest with the aim of bringing together and protecting more than six thousand children from all over the country. His idea was that the Spanish Red Cross should take care of them and bring them to North Africa where they would be safe. However, this plan was never carried out. Nevertheless, the department became a center for the rescue of Jewish children. Safe houses, operating under the protection of the ICRC and Swiss diplomats, were set up.

Thousands of children and their Jewish nurses were saved.

Rowas wrote: "As one of the leaders of the Jewish underground movement in Hungary, I had a part in this rescue action. I selected the personnel for the shelters and I also organized the food supply." The offices at Mérleg Street and Baross Street were the centers of activities, supported by men and women of the Zionist movement and the Jewish Pioneers.

Born was aware of the clandestine work going on in the ICRC office, which should actually have been neutral and accountable to the Hungarian and Swiss governments. Although it is not recorded anywhere, Born must have given his consent to the illegal activities.

Rowas recorded that he "and Friedrich Born met several times. With his help I received a special identity card by which I was confirmed to be a Christian and a courier for the ICRC. Against all expectations, the card was recognized by the Hungarian authorities without any question. When the first card proved to be successful, Born issued others for several members of the Zionist movement and the Jewish Pioneers. Unhindered and officially approved, they could go about saving many Jews from being deported to Auschwitz."

RISKED HIS LIFE BY MAINTAINING ESSENTIAL CONTACTS

Friedrich Born openly carried out his activities contrary to the orders of his superiors in Geneva. He risked his life in his multiple contacts with the Hungarian government and the German occupying authorities; he would not be deterred. He exposed himself to further danger by establishing contacts with the Jewish Rescue Committee and the Zionist Pioneers.

Hansi Brandt, a key female employee at the Jewish Rescue Committee, wrote about Born: "Thanks to his activities we had the opportunity to find cover within the Red Cross for our rescue actions. Not only that, but Born gave us his full support and help."

Rafi Ben Shalom, a leader of the Zionist Pioneers, emigrated to Palestine after the war and settled in Kibbutz Haogen. "Friedrich Born," he remembers, "approved and helped to set up an International Committee of the Red Cross in occupied Budapest. It was headed by Dr. Otto Komolyi. After the seizure of power by the Arrow Cross on October 15, 1944 the committee helped to save many Jews, especially children. The committee employed a sizable staff of Jewish coworkers and set up over thirty children's homes which housed more than six thousand children. In all of this, Born was an important rescue institution. I also joined the committee, and my task was to establish contacts with the underground movement as well as to do intelligence work. The political information obtained would then be passed on to other key individuals."

Finally, in September 1944, the ICRC headquarters in Geneva decided to step in and do something about the situation of the Hungarian Jews, and to investigate the alleged deportations. Apparently, Born's repeated reports had alarmed them. But, at the same time, Geneva decided to curtail Born's activities as he had overstepped his authority.

This administrative limitation did not intimidate Born. He continued his rescue mission. When the Arrow Cross seized power, he warned Geneva about the impending risk of life for the Jews in Hungary. He addressed the German Ambassador, Dr. Edmund Veesenmayer, on his own initiative and also the Hungarian Foreign Minister, Baron Gábor von Kémény. He gave them an ultimatum to stop the persecution of the Jews. He took a particular stand on behalf of the Jewish children. On November 6, 1944 he received permission from the Hungarian government for representatives of the Red Cross to examine the situation in the ghettos and see the assembled Jews before their deportation to Auschwitz.

When Geneva headquarters informed Born that he should consider returning to Switzerland because the situation in Budapest was becoming too dangerous, he replied that he wanted to continue his rescue mission.

Part of that mission was to maintain a line to the Arrow Cross regime in order to ease the arduous lot of the Jews. Born asked for hospitals to be set up. Thousands of Jews were hospitalized there and thus saved from annihilation. Born also succeeded in increasing the number of Red Cross delegates in Hungary, further facilitating the rescue work.

When the German authorities ordered forced marches of tens of thousands of Jews to Austria and Germany in the latter part of 1944, Friedrich Born protested vigorously. He succeeded in saving thousands of Jews from taking part in the death marches by placing them under the protection of the Red Cross.

The doctoral thesis of Israeli lawyer Arieh Ben-Tov studies the part played by the Red Cross in the salvation of Hungarian Jews. Ben-Tov states that "Friedrich Born helped to save about six thousand Jewish children from deportation to Auschwitz. Most of his massive rescue actions were contrary to the express orders of the Red Cross Geneva headquarters. The management held the opinion that the Red Cross should not get involved in the internal affairs of the Hungarian state. In spite of this Born met repeatedly with the representatives of the Hungarian government, asking for a halt to the deportations. He knew no fear and did not shy away from visiting the German occupying authorities frequently in the name of the ICRC, demanding that they should change all their policies concerning the Jews. The Germans always replied that the ICRC had no right to interfere with what they regarded as internal affairs. The Red Cross wanted to remain neutral.

"Born did not give in. In some cases he successfully liberated Jews who were already destined to be deported and placed them under the protection of the ICRC. Since he also succeeded in obtaining extraterritorial status for the children's homes and hospitals, thousands of lives were saved. All of this he did by risking the position of the ICRC and his own life."

The Soviet forces captured Budapest on January 18, 1945. A few weeks later they declared Born persona non grata, as his rescue mission for the Jews had aroused their suspicions. Friedrich Born had to leave the city by the end of March. He later recalled that these were the heaviest moments of his life when he had to say good-bye to his friends in Budapest. He traveled via Ankara, Cairo, Athens, Naples, and Marseilles to Lyon, and finally arrived in Geneva on May 1, 1945.

Hildegard Gutzwiller

The Courageous Nun of the Sacred Heart Convent

On October 17, 1944 Agata Fried knocked at the doors of the Sophianum building of the Szent Sziv ("Sacred Heart") convent on Mikszath Kalman Square in Budapest asking for shelter, food, and help.

After the deportation of their parents to Auschwitz on May 16, 1944, Agata and her brother had fled Munkasz without means and arrived a few months later in Budapest. Her brother hid at the apartment of a Christian friend; she could not find a place to stay.

Agata witnessed Jews being arrested almost daily. She lived in constant fear of being picked up by the Germans or the Arrow Cross and then deported to the death camps.

She had kept a letter of recommendation given to her by the Catholic priest of Munkasz, Dr. Samu Ratkovsky. He had been the home tutor of the children of Count Pejachevich, the last Hungarian viceroy of Croatia. Agata remembered that the count's daughter, Countess Maria, was president of the Catholic charity organization Caritas in Budapest. She told Agata that there was only one hope for her, namely to seek refuge at the Sophianum, one of the buildings of the convent of the Sacred Heart order.

Countess Maria personally escorted Agata to the convent. Hildegard Gutzwiller, the Mother Superior, and her assistant welcomed Agata without asking too many questions. She remained hidden there until the end of the war. The convent became her home.

Decades later, in 1994, Agata Fried Eckstein wrote from Venezuela: "The Sophianum was paradise for thirty-six Jewish women at a time when Arrow Cross gangs roamed the streets of Budapest, wreaking havoc and killing many Jews. These women had just knocked at the doors of the convent and had been welcomed with open arms. At no time was any attempt made to convert the Jewish women. Mother Superior Hildegard Gutzwiller, who was a native Swiss, and her assistant Muller looked after us like after their own children. The nuns shared their meager morsels with us.

"When I told them that I thought my brother, who was hiding at the house of a Christian friend, was having difficulties, they decided to send him a hot meal every day.

"There was not even any question of compensation. Mother Superior and her assistant regarded themselves as responsible for the fate of the Jewish women they were hiding. Their motives were purely humanitarian and religious. They knew that any Jew who was arrested and deported would never come back. Deportation meant certain death.

"I was not the only one to find refuge in the convent. Shortly after I had been admitted, a friend of mine, Eva Weisz, also from Munkasz, came to the convent as well and was let in.

"We learned that another friend of ours, Agnes Klein, lived in the ghetto and was on a list of those to be deported to Auschwitz shortly. I told the Mother Superior and asked her for help. She decided to do something about it. Agnes was rescued and brought to the convent. Hildegard Gutzwiller even fetched Miklosz, the brother of Agnes Klein. She agreed to employ him as gardener at the children's home of the Sacred Heart order at No. 87 Budakeszi Street. There, between the

Unchanged main door of Szent Sziv (Sacred Heart) convent in Budapest, at Mikszath Kalman Square, through which Agata Fried from Munkasz entered in 1944, and found shelter and refuge along with Eva Weisz and Agnes Klein. (Photo taken in 1999.) (Source: Andreas C. Fischer archives)

densely forested Hárs hills, a Jewish man and his sixteen-year-old daughter were also hiding.

"I survived. Thanks to the help of Mother Superior Hildegard Gutzwiller I was not headed for the same destiny as my family. Only after the liberation did I learn about the tragic fate of my parents. My father, who had been a lawyer in Munkasz, died in the gas chambers of Auschwitz. My mother was transferred from Auschwitz to the Struthof-Natzweiler KZ in Alsace, but during the excruciating march she collapsed exhausted, her body affected by hypothermia. She died of typhoid fever in a German military hospital. My grandmother, four uncles, five aunts, and five cousins were deported to Auschwitz as well. Only four of them returned.

"After the war I married Hugo Eckstein and we now live in Caracas. I learned that after the capture of the city the communists had confiscated some of the buildings of the Sacred Heart in Budapest: the convent and the Philipineum at No. 21 Ajtósi Dürer Boulevard. The nuns were evacuated."

In a letter from Venezuela dated April 12, 1994, Agnes Klein, the other survivor and emigrée wrote: "In October 1944 I was admitted to the Sacred Heart convent in Budapest, where I found that more than thirty Jewish women, aged between eighteen and forty-two, had been received as well. During the following terrible time of persecution I found love and warmth, goodness, and safety in the convent. The nuns showed remarkable heroic courage in the hours of artillery fire and bombardment from the air. They gave us food when they were hungry themselves. They protected us."

GUARDED CONVENT AGAINST BREAK-INS

"They never tried to influence us in religious matters. They respected our faith. On several occasions the Hungarian Arrow Cross and German soldiers attempted to break into the convent at Mikszath Kalman Square, but Mother Superior Hildegard Gutzwiller resisted them with great courage. Many times she just stood in their way and explained that she would not allow the buildings to be searched. She succeeded every time and sent the troublemakers and intruders away."

The fact that members of the Hungarian Arrow Cross had tried to enter the convent on several occasions was also confirmed by Eva Weisz: "Every time, they pretended to be in possession of proof that the convent was hiding Jews. It was only thanks to the resistance of Mother Superior and her assistant that we were not discovered and deported.

"I had left Munkasz for Budapest on the very last train before Hungary was completely occupied by the German forces. When I arrived I was desperate. I had nobody to look for and nowhere to ask for shelter. Then, somebody suggested I should ask at the Sacred Heart convent for help. I was received, hidden and saved."

The three buildings of the Sacred Heart convent in Budapest gave shelter to eighty women, forty children, and ten men in these critical and dangerous times. The saved were able leave their refuge free and unscathed when the Hungarian capital was liberated by the Red Army.

Hildegard Gutzwiller was a native Swiss, born in Jegenstorf. At an early age she resolved to dedicate herself to love for her neighbor and helping the distressed. She joined the order of the Sacred Heart and was transferred to Budapest, where she was appointed Mother Superior. She remained faithful to her vows.

William and Laure Francken

The Good Samaritan's Summerhouse Refuge

They nicknamed him Wim in the Swiss village of Begnins, near Nyon, where he practiced medicine. Dr. William Francken, originally from Holland, had studied medicine and graduated from the University of Lausanne. At Gilly, he founded a hospital for patients with chronic lung diseases. He became a Swiss citizen and a popular country doctor. He kept a diary of his medical and private activities which he published in 1960; a second edition was printed in 1989.

Dr. Francken and his wife owned a chalet in the French village of Novel, high up in the Savoy Alps on the other side of Lake Geneva (Lac Léman in French). Although very close to the border, Novel was separated from Switzerland by two steep ravines. Wim and Laure spent most of their summer months there. Their small summerhouse, where their daughter and her husband live today, lies at an altitude of about 3,750 feet.

During 1942 and 1943, several groups of Jewish refugees arrived at the village. Men, women, and children, fleeing persecution by the German troops and the Vichy regime, were seeking a way to escape to Switzerland. Most of them had an

The Franckens' chalet above the village of Novel, France, where the doctor received many exhausted and wounded refugees before letting them depart clandestinely over the border to Switzerland. (Source: Andreas C. Fischer archives)

arduous journey behind them; they had traveled by bus, by train, in trucks, and on foot. They were exhausted.

At any point during their odyssey, they risked arrest. Hungry and in many cases sick, they arrived at Novel in small groups. Here, they had to hide until the right opportunity arose to slip across the border. Several needed medical attention and Dr. Francken looked after them. His wife Laure arranged a refuge for most of them at the summer house where they could hide and be fed.

Wim and Laure knew fully well what the consequences would be if their clandestine activities were discovered. Their hospitality, however, knew no bounds and they kept refugees hidden at their chalet until they were sufficiently strong and fit for the physical and mental stress of crossing the frontier.

Dr. Francken's activities did not stop at medical care; he got in touch with members of the Resistance and personally accompanied the refugees to the frontier. He helped them to get across when the border guards were not looking. Eyewitnesses confirm that he did this in thirty-seven cases. Most of the refugees who passed through the French Alps in this region had spent time at his summerhouse.

Also living in Novel at that time was Ernest Brouze. He and his cousin Germaine, natives of the French village, were friends of William and Laure Francken.

The hundreds of Jewish refugees who streamed into Novel between the years 1942 and 1944 wanted to use it as stepping stone to somehow cross over the border into Switzerland. The deep ravines that separate the two countries were, however, a formidable impasse. Nobody would make it to the other side unaided. Ernest and Germaine Brouze helped whenever they could, sometimes assisted by members of the Resistance and the Maquis, the underground forces.

At Ernest's house, too, the door was always open. Like the Franckens, he and his cousin fed and cared for the exhausted refugees. The fugitives were hidden at a barn near the Franckens' chalet. They took care of the children, especially when they were weak and sick after their arduous flight. They kept children hidden for days, if need be. Ernest had friends

Ernest Brouze's hay barn near the Franckens' chalet where "overflow" refugees temporarily lodged. (Source: Andreas C. Fischer archives)

among the local police and border guards, who would often turn a blind eye when he took part in an illegal crossing attempt.

Recalling the war years, Ernest Brouze said in May 1977: "I got to know Wim and Laure long before the war. I was the caretaker of their summerhouse, Le Clou at Novel, as I owned a barn very close to it. I can confirm that many Jewish refugees and members of the Maquis were given hospitality. As many of them were sick or wounded, he gave them professional care. Dr. Francken often accompanied groups to Lovenex, from where they got down to Vouvry in the canton of Valais in

Ernest Brouze's home in the village of Novel, where the emaciated refugees were fed and cared for before being hidden in the hay barn. (Source: Andreas C. Fischer archives)

The balcony of the Franckens' chalet above Novel, where hundreds of refugees found shelter after having fled from occupied southern France. (Source: Andreas C. Fischer archives)

Switzerland. Some of those trying to escape were picked up by the Swiss police and sent back to France. I admire the self-sacrifice and courage of Dr. Francken and his wife Laure. We kept in close contact with them even after the war."

Professor A. Bondi from Rehovot also wrote in 1977: "A friend of mine, Mrs. Trawes from Rehovot, has just returned from a visit to France and Switzerland. She brought back a booklet describing the rescue activities mounted for Jewish refugees along the Franco-Swiss border. The actions of Wim Francken and his wife figured prominently in the book. Mrs. Trawes still remembers the Franckens and was very impressed by their help for Jewish refugees."

René Bouvet, a former mayor of Novel, and now a local hotelier, said that he had "known the Franckens during the Second World War. I saw them helping the Jewish refugees who arrived at our village, from where they wanted to get over the border. We could call Wim a Good Samaritan. He and his wife were upright, courageous, and discreet people. Wim never charged the refugees or the villagers anything for medical services. I can honestly say that they merited being made honorary citizens of Novel in 1954.

"The situation in 1942 and 1943 was not easy; at first, the refugees hid in the surrounding forests until they thought the time was right to effect an escape to Switzerland. Dr. Francken soon mustered several helpers from the village to assist the refugees in crossing the border. The solidarity among the villagers was tremendous during this difficult time."

In his book *Mit Rückkehr der Erinnerung ("When Memory Comes")*, Professor Saul Friedländer wrote that his parents had sent him a letter during the war indicating the date and place where they had intended to cross the border clandestinely. Years later, he drove up to Novel and was told of the events that had taken place during that time.

He was given a brochure written by Laure Francken, commemorating the incidents, the rescue actions and the escape attempts that took place between September 27 and October 6, 1942. The letter from his parents was dated September 30, 1942.

In this booklet, Laure Francken had written: "We never heard anything more about the fate of a Jewish couple from Czechoslovakia who stayed at our chalet for a while. Perhaps they were arrested and sent back to France. Who knows? The Swiss border guards sometimes closed their eyes when elderly people or families with children and babies were passing over."

From this scanty evidence, Saul Friedländer concluded that this was a reference to his parents, who must have been caught and sent back to France. They were probably held at the camp of Rivesaltes or Drancy before being finally transported to Auschwitz, the death camp in occupied Poland.

An article in the local newspaper, *Journal de Nyon,* on September 27, 1964 reported a ceremony which had taken place the previous day at Novel, where a monument was unveiled in honor of Dr. Wim Francken. The president of the committee, Edmond Bassin, mentioned in his speech the generous and selfless help Dr. Francken had given the refugees and the entire population of Novel. His enthusiasm, his dedication and his magnanimity had made him a legend during his lifetime, Bassin said. Now, after this death, his former patients and everybody who had known him were happy to see this posthumous memorial to Dr. Francken. The article also noted that his wife had always been a tremendous help to him.

24 Heures, another Swiss newspaper, again took up the story on October 26, 1996, describing the help and assistance given by Dr. William Francken, a country doctor and true humanitarian, to all refugees who wanted to flee to Switzerland during the Second World War. It mentioned the hospitality of the doctor and his wife and conveyed the gratitude of many refugees who had survived as a direct result of their courageous efforts.

Israel's Ambassador to Switzerland, Yitzhak Mayer, presented the Yad Vashem "Righteous Among the Nations" medal of honor to Ernest Brouze on April 27, 1998. Since Germaine had fallen seriously ill, her daughter accepted the medal on her behalf. The President of the Swiss Confederation, Flavio Cotti, also attended the ceremony, which was held in Berne.

The citation stated that the activities of Ernest and his cousin Germaine had been forgotten for a long time, but that their efforts to guide Jewish refugees as well as freedom fighters to a safe place were exemplary. They were so modest about their war-time activities that they kept silent for years. Their courage and dedication, however, had served as an inspiration to many who knew them. It was René Bouvet who brought their honorable deeds to public attention. At the same ceremony, the Yad Vashem medal was also conferred posthumously on Dr. William Francken and his wife Laure.

 *Jean-Edouard Friedrich*

Roland Marti
Pierre Descoeudres
Robert Schirmer

In the Devil's Lair

Dr. Roland Marti, who had worked together with Dr Marcel Junod in Spain during the Spanish Civil War, was appointed as head of the new Red Cross delegation in Berlin in the spring of 1940. He continued in that capacity until the end of 1944. Dr Pierre Descoeudres was the first additional delegate to join him. Initially their only office was a room in the Hotel Eden.

Marti and Descoeudres began traveling all over Germany, visiting prisoner of war camps, labor camps and hospitals, averaging 150 kilometers per day.

The Berlin delegation was responsible for all the territories of the German Reich, including the occupied territories, notably Holland, Belgium and France. Its staff remained extremely small for most of the war; it was strengthened by the arrival of Robert Schirmer, Jean-Maurice Rübli and Emile Exchaquet before the end of 1941.

In their reports, the Berlin delegation provided Geneva with first-hand information about the living conditions of Jews in Berlin and the increasing constraints and difficulties they faced. They continued to do so throughout the war. Marti and his staff found it difficult to understand that there often seemed to be no immediate reaction to their reports.

Pierre Descoeudres and Roland Marti had managed to visit the Buchenwald concentration camp early in the summer of 1940, having been authorized by the Ministry of Foreign Affairs to visit 212 Dutch civilian inmates there. They took the opportunity to file a detailed report, which included the fact that they had seen some German Jews who were interned there. But that visit was a rare exception. In addition, the visit had been announced ahead of time, and it was evident that everything had been prepared down to the minutest detail.

In November 1941, the Berlin delegation witnessed, day by day, the deportation of Jews from the German capital. They kept Geneva informed of these frightening events. In one note, Dr Exchaquet documented a conversation with a Jewish doctor about the current situation of the Jews in Berlin. Although this matter was outside the remit of the activities of the Red Cross delegates in Germany, he thought that Geneva should be aware of it. He reported that Jews were obliged to wear a yellow star; that Jews were being systematically evacuated from Berlin in convoys of about 3,000 at a time.

In January 1942, Marti officially requested permission from the German authorities to inspect the camp at Mauthausen. Dr Sethe at the Ministry of Foreign Affairs (who had arranged for their earlier visit to Buchenwald) replied that such a visit would be absolutely impossible—even for one of Dr Sethe's own representatives. After that, Marti tried to establish contacts using less official channels.

In February 1942, the delegation moved to a large house on Ballenstederstrasse. That remained its headquarters until the autumn of 1943, when it relocated to premises at Am Grossen Wannsee 2–4. As Allied bombing raids intensified and the German government authorities became increasingly decentralized, the activities of the Red Cross delegation became even more difficult.

Operating as they were in a police state, and only grudgingly tolerated by the German authorities, Marti and his small staff worked hard to alleviate suffering where they could. In 1942 alone, the eight delegates and one secretary undertook a prodigious amount of work, visiting 502 camps and holding over 1,000 meetings with the German civil and military authorities. That year, each delegate traveled an average of 27,500 kilometers.

As they were unable to obtain general authorization to enter the concentration camps to investigate the conditions there, the Red Cross delegates in Berlin attempted to gain admittance to the camps on a case-by-case basis. But the closest they were able to get was establishing contact with the camp commandants. Although they had meetings with the commandants of Ravensbrück, Oranienburg, Dachau, Natzweiler, Buchenwald and Flossenberg, all they were able to discuss was the delivery of Red Cross parcels. Yet even pursuing this approach enabled them to glean some precious information: insisting that the camp inmates sign receipts for their parcels allowed the Red Cross to assemble information about the identity of thousands of detainees. Often, one receipt would come back signed by a number of inmates. In this way, the Red Cross learned the names and whereabouts of additional deportees—who would in future also be able to receive parcels.

At the end of January 1944, Roland Marti and Robert Schirmer decided to try a different way of making contact with the camp inmates. Instead of going through the Ministry of Foreign Affairs, they got in touch with the Gestapo! A meeting took place at the Gestapo headquarters at Albrechtstrasse 8, Berlin. They wanted authorization for the Red Cross to send collective Red Cross parcels to various detainees in concentration camps. They mentioned specifically some Norwegian students and some high-profile French prisoners in the Tyrol. Regrettably, the meeting achieved nothing at all. As Marti reported, the Gestapo cynically advised them to refer all their questions and concerns to the German Red Cross, and insisted that parcels could only be sent to prisoners whose names and addresses were known.

In the spring of 1944, the Berlin delegation informed the Ministry of Foreign Affairs that it intended to increase the number of delegates in the German capital to twelve. The authorities acquiesced.

Some indication of the extent to which living conditions were deteriorating within Germany is given by the fact that Marti asked Geneva to send cigarettes for use as "currency". "More and more personalities we have to deal with," he wrote, "ask us for Swiss tobacco or some basic item of necessity, whether they are in the Ministry of Foreign Affairs or the OKW, all the way from the chief of the OKW to the officers who accompany us. Such services greatly facilitate our relationships with the various authorities."

In May 1944, an air raid shelter was built in the garden of the building where the Berlin delegation was housed. A satellite office was opened at Uffing near Murnau in July 1944. Another in Vienna followed in December of the same year, to look after the interests of Hungarian Jews who had been deported to the area.

In January 1945, Johannes Schwarzenberg, who was responsible for Red Cross assistance to the concentration camps, urged the Red Cross to strengthen the delegation in Berlin. Roland Marti had reported that a staff of 12 was totally inadequate for the work they had to do. He also suggested that "specialists" should be trained for working with the concentration camps; the existing delegates had often been seconded by Geneva for special missions at short notice. Finally, by April 1945, the number of staff available to the Berlin delegation had risen to 40.

It was not only in Germany that Robert Schirmer saw active service for the Red Cross. In July 1944, Dr Schirmer (who was at that time deputy head of the Berlin delegation) left Berlin for

Hungary on a highly sensitive special mission—to deliver a letter from the Red Cross in Geneva to Regent Horthy, expressing grave concern about the treatment of Hungarian Jews.

While in Hungary, Schirmer visited the Jews in Budapest ghetto, as well as the camps at Kistarcsa and Szarvar. He sent a detailed report to Geneva by diplomatic mail, describing conditions and requesting food and clothing parcels for the internees.

Schirmer played an important role, alongside Friedrich Born, in protecting the interests of Jews in Budapest. He also tried to arrange for the Red Cross to visit camps near Vienna, where Jews from Hungary had been interned, communicating with Hans von Mauthner, a Hungarian Jew living in Vienna, who knew personally the head of the Vienna Gestapo.

On October 18, 1944, Schirmer and Born met the new Hungarian Minister of Foreign Affairs, Baron Gábor von Kémény, and demanded that the Geneva Convention be respected. The following day, the two men successfully appealed to the Minister of the Interior and managed to convince him that the Jewish senate was a necessary institution which should be protected.

Schirmer worked with Born in placing as many Jews as possible under the protection of the Red Cross. He left Budapest for Geneva on October 29, 1944, before returning to Berlin; his place was taken by Hans Weyermann. Back in Germany, Schirmer continued his work, tirelessly seeking new ways of gaining admittance for Red Cross personnel to the concentration camps.

Also attached to the Swiss Red Cross delegation in Berlin was Jean-Edouard Friedrich, who served there in 1943 and 1944.

In the words of André von Moos of the International Committee of the Red Cross: "Jean-Edouard Friedrich was not yet 30 when he was confronted with the persecution of the Jews in Germany and Holland, and during a mission in May 1943, he was filled with a deep feeling of revulsion. He set out to do everything in his power to help men, women and children in the Third Reich who were being persecuted because of the race they belonged to."

In her autobiography *"Über den grünen Hügel — Erinnerungen an Deutschland" ("Over the Green Hill — Memories of Germany"),* Lotte Strauss recounts how Jean-Edouard Friedrich helped her and her husband to enter Switzerland. He received them in his office and managed to send word to their relatives in Switzerland about the plight of the Strauss family. He used the special Red Cross mail service to escape the German censors. Having obtained papers for the couple, he personally accompanied them to a place where they were able to cross the border into Switzerland.

During a mission in Stuttgart, Friedrich escorted a young woman to Singen, near the Swiss border, where they met a "schlepper" who was going to smuggle her into Switzerland. When the German authorities spotted them, Friedrich diverted their attention to himself, giving the refugees time to escape. He was arrested and kept in prison overnight.

More than half a century later, at a ceremony at the Amtshaus in Berne on September 6, 1999, Jean-Edouard Friedrich was presented with the Yad Vashem "Righteous Among the Nations" medal of honor by Yitzhak Mayer, Ambassador of the State of Israel to Switzerland. Jean-Edouard Friedrich passed away a few months later.

Emile Barras

Triumphs and Tragedies
in the Life of a Schlepper

Emile Barras was born on May 30, 1921 at Avry-devant-Pont in the canton of Fribourg in western Switzerland. Of dual nationality (Swiss and French), he lived in France for most of his life. During World War II he was living in the French village of Viry near St.-Julien-en-Genevois, about ten kilometers from Geneva. He joined the AS (Armée Secrète) and worked for the Resistance together with his friend Joseph Fournier.

May 1944 was an especially traumatic month for Emile Barras. One evening, he was waiting on the platform of the small railway station at Viry for a train to arrive. This was a special train, with 30 Jewish children on board.

The previous day, Emile had received instructions from his friend Joseph Fournier, a fellow member of the Resistance, to go and wait for this train. There was no question in Emile's mind about what the children's destination would be. He knew all the secret paths and all the nooks and crannies of the border region around Viry, and he was going to have to take the children across the border clandestinely. On several previous occasions, he had taken Allied soldiers across the frontier, and

every now and then the Resistance asked him to bring somebody into France from Switzerland, too. These were mainly
illegal immigrants holding forged papers who wanted to join
the Allied forces advancing from the South.

This time it was different. It came as a surprise to see that
there were some German border guards and a number of soldiers on the platform also waiting for the train to arrive. The
station was normally deserted. In his mind, Emile ran through
what to do to avoid the children falling into the hands of the
Germans. Then came a loudspeaker announcement saying that
the train would be considerably delayed.

The Germans soldiers talked for a few minutes and then left
the station. After a while, the train arrived and the children got
off. With them was Marianne Cohn, a young Jewish woman,
originally from Germany, who had taken refuge in France and
was active in the Resistance. Emile and Marianne had worked
together before. Quickly, they all left the station.

At nightfall, Emile led them along winding paths to the border, carefully avoiding even getting near the German patrols.
The escape was successful and they reached Swiss territory
without any hindrance. Marianne accompanied the children
and, once she was on the other side, they met some Swiss border guards. Marianne asked one of them whether she could use
the telephone at the checkpoint office. She informed the organization in Geneva responsible for the reception of refugee children that another of her missions had been successfully accomplished.

Marianne returned to France. A few days later, she informed
Barras via Fournier that she would be coming again with
another group of Jewish refugee children. Barras advised her
against traveling by train, because he expected the German soldiers would be at the station. He could not imagine that the
incident had passed totally unnoticed; somebody must have
gotten wind of it. For this reason, and because they did not
want to risk anything, Marianne and Fournier decided to
arrange the transportation of the youngsters by truck.

THE PLAN SUDDENLY GOES TERRIBLY WRONG

At a hiding place near the village of Viry, Barras waited and waited. There was no sign of the truck—what had happened? In fact, the truck had set off from Annecy later than scheduled, with about 30 children and young people on board, accompanied by Marianne Cohn, and with Joseph Fournier at the wheel. Finally, as night was falling, they reached the outskirts of Viry, and Joseph stopped the truck beside a footpath.

The children started climbing out of the truck. But then, before Emile had time to make contact with his Resistance colleagues, an armored vehicle suddenly appeared on the scene. Emile's mind was racing and his heart was pounding. German soldiers, alerted by the presence of a group of children out in the countryside at such a late hour, had come to investigate. Emile hid behind a barn and managed to avoid being captured by the skin of his teeth.

Gunshots rang out through the night. Emile, horror-stricken, could only watch helplessly. He heard the little ones crying and the older children shouting for help, but he was unable to do anything to prevent them being forced back into the truck and driven off with an army escort.

As soon as it was safe to venture out, Emile immediately started to inquire about the fate of Marianne, Joseph and the children. He found out that the Wehrmacht had taken them to the Gestapo "Pax" prison (named after the Hotel Pax opposite, where the Gestapo had set up their headquarters). The thought of having lost two good friends at once almost drove Emile insane. The day before this disaster happened he had just turned 23.

Raoul Fournier, Joseph's brother, tells his story of the incident: "On May 31, 1944, I followed at a distance behind the truck that Joseph was driving. We had stopped just outside Viry when suddenly a Wehrmacht armored vehicle drove up. Armed soldiers jumped out, surrounded the truck and fired shots in the air. I found myself in the midst of these soldiers and one of them asked for my papers. He wanted to know why I was there. I had a doctor's prescription in my pocket and explained that I was on the way to a pharmacy. The soldier looked at me in disbelief and said that he suspected me of actually being a 'schlepper'. He ordered me to leave the vicinity immediately.

"I saw where Emile Barras was hiding but I went the other way in order not to place him in danger. Of course I knew that he and my brother were working together to smuggle people across the border into Switzerland.

"I found out that Joseph and Marianne were taken to 'Pax', the Gestapo prison in Annemasse. Joseph was kept there for about a week. While there, he was beaten and suffered torture and pain. After his release, he told me that a colleague in Viry had denounced him. The Germans wanted him to make a confession and betray his superiors. A week later, he was released, apparently after the police chief of St. Julien had intervened on his behalf.

"A few months later, Joseph died before reaching the age of forty. I believe that his maltreatment at the prison was one of the reasons for his early death."

Alice Portier-Lenz was among the children who were to have crossed the border into Switzerland on May 31, 1944. She remembered the dramatic twist the action took. "There were 32 of us children in a convoy, coming up from Limoges towards the Swiss border. The convoy had been organized by the OSE Jewish branch of the Resistance and Rabbi Deutsch from Limoges.

"Marianne Cohn met us at a public garden at the lakeside in Annecy. She was late and we were not able to leave at the scheduled time. The driver of our truck was Joseph Fournier. They explained to us that we would be taken to a place near Viry from where we were to attempt the crossing of the Swiss border, only 200 meters away. We were told that a 'schlepper' would guide us. We were all very nervous but Marianne told us to stay calm. She told us that she had taken this route several times already and that she knew our guide very well. He could be trusted.

"On the way, Marianne told us that just a few days ago a group of 20 children had crossed successfully. I was glad to hear that, because my 13-year old sister Grete was among them. After my parents had received confirmation from Geneva that Grete was safe, they decided to let me depart with the next children's group.

"But this time, things went terribly wrong. When we reached the meeting place, an armored vehicle drove up; soldiers jumped out and ran around. Some held fierce dogs on a leash. We panicked. It was around eight in the evening and a soldier asked Marianne what the children were doing here at this hour. I heard her say that we were on our way to a vacation at a nearby children's home.

"Some of the boys started to run. The soldiers fired shots into the air and unleashed the dogs to chase after them. When they had gathered us together, we were loaded back onto our truck. The officer said he wanted to accompany us to the home in person to find out whether Marianne's explanation was true. I asked her quietly where our 'schlepper' was, and she replied that hopefully he had escaped when he saw the German soldiers.

"When we got to the children's home, an elderly lady received us. She told the officer that she had not received any news about our arrival. 'You lied!' the officer shouted angrily at Marianne. 'You will pay dearly for that!'

"Then the Germans took us to the Annemasse terminal, a bus and train station. Here we were separated from Marianne and Joseph. They were taken to the Gestapo prison of Pax while we were accommodated in a large building before being imprisoned."

Marcel Katz from Dole said this about the worst day of his young life: "I was sitting in the truck facing backwards. Suddenly, I heard shouts: 'Get off, get off, jump!' I was one of the first, and I took a smaller boy by the hand to help him out.

"Shots were fired and cries for help rang out in the night.

The young boy was so scared that he was trembling. At that moment I saw the dogs coming toward us. But the soldiers quickly shoved us back into the truck.

"We were taken to Annemasse. We were all seriously affected by the dramatic turn of events. I felt really sick and was taken to hospital the next day. The Germans treated us nicely at first and wanted to know who was responsible for the convoy and who was going to take us across the border. I did not know their names. Only in 1995 did I find out that Emile Barras was the 'schlepper' whom we had waited for and who never appeared."

Sam Jacquet from Metz had a similar story: "Nobody saw the man who was to take us across the border; perhaps that was just as well. Although we did not think so at that time because from where we were we could see the Swiss flag flying. When we were stopped, four youths jumped off and started running. That's when the soldiers fired the shot."

The mayor of Annemasse, Jean Deffaugt, intervened with the authorities and managed to ensure that the prisoners were not maltreated. He also managed to secure the release of the children under 12 years of age, who were transferred to a nearby children's home. The older children and adolescents remained imprisoned, and so, too, did Marianne Cohn.

The Resistance devised a plan to enable Marianne Cohn to escape. It appeared to have every chance of success, but Marianne adamantly refused to be rescued, as she did not want to endanger the lives of her young fellow prisoners.

On July 8, Gestapo officers arrived from another region. They seized Marianne Cohn and other Resistance members from the "Pax" prison and took them off to an unknown destination. They were never seen again alive.

About seven young prisoners were still being held captive at the "Pax" prison. Once again, the mayor intervened. Already sensing the approach of the Liberation, the Germans began to fear that the Resistance in Haute-Savoie would block their retreat. Jean Deffaugt struck a deal with the Germans: "You will not touch the Jewish children in prison, and in exchange we will let you escape towards Switzerland". This verbal contract was honored on August 18, 1944, the day when Annemasse was liberated. All the children were saved.

After the Liberation, the bodies of six former members of the Resistance were found in a mass grave at Ville-la-Grand near Annemasse. Among them, terribly mutilated, was the body of a woman whose face was no longer recognizable. It was only by means of a shoe still attached to the corpse that the remains of 22-year-old Marianne Cohn could be identified. This heroic young woman, who had helped many children to escape to freedom, deserves to be remembered as a martyr of the Jewish Resistance.

On the fiftieth anniversary of the Liberation, on August 18, 1994, some of those who had been saved by the efforts of Marianne Cohn and Jean Deffaugt attended a special ceremony at Annemasse. They paid tribute to their former mayor, in whose honor a monument had been erected, as well as to Marianne Cohn, after whom a local school was named.

After a report of the fiftieth anniversary events appeared in a local newspaper, the representative of the "children" who had survived, Léon Herzberg of Nancy, was surprised to receive a telephone call from a former member of the Resistance who remembered having worked with Marianne Cohn. This was none other than Emile Barras. After the war, American President Dwight D. Eisenhower had written Barras a letter of commendation, thanking him on behalf of the American people for his support of the Allied Forces during the Invasion of Europe, but Barras had kept quiet all these years about his role in some of these other dramatic events.

Léon Herzberg in turn told his friend Herbert Herz, the Yad Vashem representative based in Geneva. Then it was Emile's turn to be surprised, when he received a visit from Herbert Herz. Although seriously weakened by illness, Emile Barras was alert and lucid. He provided many valuable details about the events surrounding these wartime arrests which had not been known before. He also introduced Herbert Herz to Raoul Fournier, brother of the late Joseph Fournier.

At a ceremony held at Viry on June 16, 1996, the Yad Vashem medal of "Righteous Among the Nations" was conferred on Joseph Fournier and Emile Barras—both posthumously, as Emile himself had passed away earlier the same year.

Ernest Wittwer

Six Weeks in Jail,
That Others Could Live Free

During the night of April 26–27, 1944, a young man was arrested at Porrentruy railway station in the Swiss Jura region. His name was Ernest Wittwer, a farmer from Vereaux, in the Haute-Saône region of France. When the police picked him up, there were two boys with him—René and Fredy Lévy, aged fifteen and thirteen years, from the Alsace region.

During questioning, the police learned that Wittwer and the boys had crossed the Swiss border illegally. They also learned that Wittwer, born on September 10, 1922, was Swiss. He had moved to France with his parents when he was fifteen. Ernest told the police that he had every right to be in Switzerland. He admitted that this was his first attempt to help anyone cross the border.

He had only done this, he said, because the two boys had lost their parents and were living with the Wyss family at Grey in France who were in great danger of being reported to the German authorities for giving shelter to Jewish refugees. Raids on Jews had been stepped up in the area, and Madame Wyss had asked Ernest to take the boys to Switzerland.

The Wittwer and Wyss families were friends. They helped each other a great deal in this time of need. When Ernest set out with the two boys, Madame Wyss gave him a sum of money, about three thousand French francs—not much by today's

231

standards, but enough to keep them going for a while. They all hoped the escape would be successful, that the boys would be delivered safely to their aunt's home in Basle, and that Ernest would be able to return safely to Vereaux.

The journey proved more arduous than they had thought. Traveling by train and bus took more than eleven hours. They marched across the border unchecked, but their success did not last long. During the night they were arrested by the police and taken to Neuchâtel.

Whenever asked why he had done it, Wittwer said he acted for humanitarian reasons because he knew that the two boys would otherwise end up at a concentration camp and possibly die. At the time they were arrested, he still had a little over half of the money; he gave it to Police Corporal Eberle, asking him to look after the children. They deducted a fine of ten francs from that sum and asked Wittwer to go back to France.

According to the police archives, Wittwer attempted a second crossing a few weeks later. Again he was unsuccessful and had to return. Ann Guedel, whose house had served as a base, later reported that Wittwer had attempted to cross the Swiss border at least five times.

The two boys who were saved by Ernest Wittwer were first taken to a refugee camp near Lausanne, but they were later freed and went to stay with their relatives, the Wahl family in Basle. Camille Wahl said that the boys' father, Lucien Levy, was a distant relative of their family, but she had no idea that the boys were on their way to them. Apparently Lucien had remembered their address and given it to his children before sending them on their way to safety. Camille had only heard from the authorities when the boys arrived in Lausanne. She was asked to take care of them.

On May 31, 1944, Ernest Wittwer was sentenced to forty-five days in jail for illegally crossing the border and for smuggling people from one country to another.

Ernest Wittwer was born in 1923 and died in 1976.

On September 9, 1999 at the City Hall in Berne, a ceremony

conducted by Prefect Sebastian Bentz took place. One of the survivors, Fredy Levy, attended. Israel's Ambassador to Switzerland, Yitzhak Mayer, presented the Yad Vashem "Righteous Among the Nations" medal of honor to Thierry Wittwer, Ernest's son. Before the presentation, Ambassador Mayer made a very moving speech. In it, he asked what had made it possible for the Shoah to have taken place and why—alas!—so few had had the courage to stand against the devilish machinery of destruction. Mayer himself had been a refugee in Switzerland during the war.

Also attending the ceremony were the Minister of Foreign Affairs of the Swiss Confederation, Joseph Deiss; the Ambassador of Hungary, Dr. Pal Schmitt; and the representative of Yad Vashem, Herbert Herz from Geneva.

Georges Dunand

Not Taking "No" for an Answer

"What can be done when the victims are outlaws? You have to fight...or use guile to aid them." Those were the words of Georges Dunand, writing about his wartime experiences in his book *"Ne perdez pas leur trace!" ("Don't lose track of them!")*. The fact that he chose to publish his memoirs is in itself an indication that Georges Dunand, the Red Cross delegate in Bratislava, was a man who knew how to think for himself. He was a force to be reckoned with.

When he was preparing to leave Switzerland for Slovakia, Dunand was told by Carl Burckhardt (then Vice-President of the International Committee of the Red Cross): "There is a lot to be attempted and probably very little to be achieved. We can hardly give you precise instructions apart from our immutable principles. Here is the watchword: 'Go straight ahead,' but be careful that the Committee doesn't have to disown you."

Prior to this appointment, Dunand had been an attaché at the Swiss Federal War Office with responsibility for industry and labor. He arrived in Bratislava at the end of October 1944. The Germans had begun their brutal intervention in Jewish affairs in Slovakia two months earlier.

Unlike the Red Cross delegates in other areas, Dunand did not have heavy responsibilities in respect of civilian internees or prisoners of war, as they did not exist in large numbers in

Slovakia at the time. This, together with the instructions he was given by Geneva, meant that he had the opportunity to become very heavily involved in trying helping the Jews in Slovakia—albeit in circumstances where achieving anything by official action was virtually impossible.

Before coming to Slovakia, Dunand had heard that Jews were being interned at the Szered camp in deplorable conditions. He soon learned that the situation was even worse than that: the objective seemed to be to exterminate all the Slovakian Jews; Szered was merely a transit camp. Deportation was being carried out on a weekly basis. Dunand repeatedly requested permission to visit Szered, but permission was always refused.

Early in 1945, after delivering a letter from the Red Cross President to the head of state, Mgr Tiso, Dunand approached the Ministry of Foreign Affairs. Could not at least women, children and the sick be exempted from deportation and placed under Red Cross protection? After referring to the German Embassy, the reply was negative. "Total liquidation of the Jewish problem" was the determined objective.

Some 164 Jews, who were in possession of documents apparently indicating that they were citizens of the US or South American countries, had taken refuge in a mansion at Marianka in mid-September 1944. The Germans soon came to investigate. All but three of the refugees were declared to have invalid papers and were taken to Szered awaiting deportation. Dunand was outraged at this scandalous behavior. He visited Marianka to offer financial assistance to the refugees who were still there. He witnessed first-hand their intimidation by the Germans and protested, both to the local authorities and the Ministry of Foreign Affairs. Dunand was a resourceful man and used every threat, argument and device he could think of—but all to no avail.

Some Jews had managed to obtain Palestine certificates, Swiss entry visas and other documents. But under no circumstances would the Germans permit emigration across occupied territory. Dunand thought of issuing letters of protection, as Friedrich Born had been doing in Hungary. He issued four such letters before Geneva advised him to exercise extreme prudence in this area. Dunand also referred repeatedly in his reports to the idea of "exchanging" Jews for goods or money as a desperate way of securing their release. But the fact remained that, officially, there was nothing at all that it was in Dunand's power to do.

Increasingly frustrated, Dunand decided that there was only one way he could do anything practical to help. The risks were enormous, though. To start with, the entire enterprise was illegal! The Jews would have to go into hiding—and keep changing their hiding-places. Money would be needed to pay for entry to the bunkers and for renting the necessary premises, which could be cellars or the remains of bombed houses.

Before taking up his posting to Bratislava, Dunand had met Saly Mayer who, in his capacity as representative of Joint (the American Jewish Joint Distribution Committee), had arranged substantial funding, as well as referring him to trusted contacts who would be able to help further. But the local Joint representatives had been apprehended by the Gestapo in the meantime. In the end, Joint agreed, exceptionally, to allow money to be distributed without having any direct control over its allocation. Desperate times called for desperate measures.

Dunand was fortunate to have a valuable ally in the Swiss Consul General in Bratislava, Max Grässli, and his staff. As Dunand would later write, Grässli interpreted "Swiss economic interests" very broadly indeed. Grässli and his wife would often hide Jews in their own residence.

Dunand maintained his frequent and vociferous protests to the Slovakian authorities. At the same time, throughout the winter of 1944–1945, the fearless Red Cross delegate devoted himself to the daily task of helping to hide the Jews, looking after their possessions, even their children sometimes, supporting and encouraging them, and providing food and other necessities.

Paul Dunant

Volunteering for Theresienstadt

In 1945, Frederic Siordet, head of the Red Cross delegations commission, and Paul Dunant stopped at the fortress town of Theresienstadt in the course of a tour of inspection that took them from southern Germany to Berlin, Prague, and Vienna. They were not able to penetrate the ghetto or the "small fortress" where thousands of prisoners were incarcerated, totally cut off from the outside world.

Paul Dunant set up his base in Prague, hoping to be able to negotiate with *Reichsprotektor* Hermann Franck to obtain authorization to visit the town (the Swiss legation had received authorization in principle in Berlin at the end of March). In the end, it was Otto Lehner who obtained permission in Berlin from Heinrich Müller, head of the Gestapo, and on April 6 the two delegates penetrated the ghetto, but not the small fortress, accompanied by Eberhard von Thadden, of the Ministry of Foreign Affairs.

After two fruitless attempts at the end of April, Paul Dunant finally managed to gain admittance and set himself up in Theresienstadt. He placed the ghetto under the protection of the Red Cross with the agreement of the Germans and the Council of Elders. In this capacity, he delivered the survivors, including almost five thousand prisoners finally liberated from the small fortress, to the new Czech authorities. The Red Cross played an important role in giving aid, protecting the population, and repatriating the deportees.

Louis Haefliger

The Legendary Liberator of Mauthausen

One of the most dramatic stories of all is that of the liberation of the concentration camp at Mauthausen, and the surrounding community in former Austria, as a result of the daring and resourcefulness of Red Cross delegate Louis Haefliger, a tall, bespectacled thirty-year-old Swiss former newspaperman.

The events related in his matter-of-fact "Report of the stay of a Red Cross delegate in Mauthausen up to the liberation of the camp from April 27 to May 8, 1945" are the stuff of which thriller novels are made.

In March 1945, Red Cross President Carl Burckhardt had unsuccessfully requested that the death camps be placed under Red Cross protection. SS General Ernst Kaltenbrunner had, however, agreed that Red Cross delegates could be allowed to enter the camps—but only on condition that they remain there until the end of the war. Haefliger was one of the volunteers.

Haefliger's first challenge was to persuade Camp Commandant Franz Zieris to admit him to the notorious camp of death—where new arrivals were customarily "welcomed" with the ominous greeting: "You will not be alive tomorrow!" Once inside, he was obliged to share a room in the prison barracks with a young SS trooper, *Obersturmführer* Reiner, whose confidence and cooperation he quickly managed to secure!

Portrait of Louis Haefliger (1951) (Source: Archiv für Zeitgeschichte, ETH-UNI Zurich)

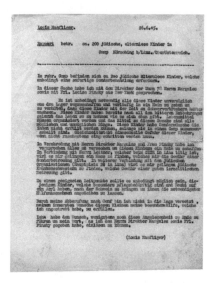

Report of June 26, 1945 (summary): "In the camp of Hörsching (near Linz, Austria) 200 Jewish orphan children are in urgent need of special treatment. The children must be taken out of this camp and transferred to a home immediately, otherwise they risk becoming delinquent, or being sexually abused. They need food and shelter, since they have had to go without the bare necessities of life for too long. Director Margules and Mrs. Pinsky have promised to take the children into a home with the help of Mr. Leitner from the Red Cross who will find a suitable building. I shall find Jewish nurses to ensure proper childcare. Children who need mental or physical care shall be taken to Switzerland. It is my deepest desire that these little ones must get the utmost special attention." (Source: Archiv für Zeitgeschichte, ETH-UNI Zurich)

Louis Haefliger (with glasses, r.) in conversation with a prisoner at the Mauthausen concentration camp, while another Red Cross aide takes notes. (Source: Archiv für Zeitgeschichte, ETH-UNI Zurich)

Through Reiner, he learned of a vengeful Nazi plan to use twenty-four tons of dynamite to blow up the Messerschmitt aircraft factory at Gusen, killing all its forty thousand slave workers, as well as to destroy the Mauthausen camp in an act of senseless destruction at the approach of the Allied troops.

Haefliger managed to persuade Commandant Zieris to countermand these orders!

He then secured the cooperation of the mayor of nearby St Georgen and drove out in his car (clandestinely repainted white for the occasion) to meet and negotiate with the oncoming American troops.

As he wrote in his journal: "The camps of Mauthausen and Gusen are liberated; the biggest Austrian aviation plant has not been blown up; extremely valuable machinery has been saved; the communities of St Georgen, Gusen, and Mauthausen have been spared by the war. The task I set myself has been completed: the camps have not been destroyed; sixty thousand human beings have been freed, although the Americans have not yet entered Linz and the battle is raging."

Harald Feller

The Secretary's Dual Role

After graduating from law school and before joining the Swiss diplomatic corps, Harald Feller was a clerk in the penal court of the department of justice of the canton of Berne. He spent the initial years of World War II working at the Swiss Foreign Office (then known as the Federal Political Department) before being posted to Budapest early in 1943.

At the time when the Jewish population of Hungary was suffering severe persecution and facing deportation by the Nazi occupying forces, Harald Feller was the First Secretary of the Swiss Legation headed by Envoy Maximilian Jäger. During those crucial years, he was an eyewitness to the terror regime of the Nazi occupying forces, the rage and atrocities of the Hungarian Arrow Cross gangs, and the rescue work of Carl Lutz and Raoul Wallenberg. He also lived through the Red Army siege that started on Christmas Day 1944 and lasted until February 12, 1945.

A REFUGE IN BUDA

Harald Feller, a bachelor, lived in a spacious mansion situated in the Buda part of the capital, on the western slope of the castle hill. The lady who owned the mansion had placed it at his disposal and asked him to look after it when she moved her family into the countryside right after the German invasion in

Harald Feller saved Jewish lives while acting as Legation head in Budapest. (Source: A. Kl. Isr. Wochenblatt)

the spring of 1944. After her departure, the stately house was left almost empty. Many of the servants' rooms were at the rear of the building, facing towards the garden, which was protected from unwelcome attention by a high wall. Harald regarded these circumstances as a tacit invitation— which he made use of in June 1944, when a Hungarian Jew he knew personally asked him for help. He made up his mind to invite this man, a writer, to live in hiding at the house, soon to be followed by his wife and child, and also his parents.

Harald remembers that the Arrow Cross regarded Swiss neutrality as being tantamount to espionage and sympathy with the Jews. Maybe that assessment was not so far wrong; Harald certainly pursued private rescue activities on his own initiative, taking advantage of the neutral status of Switzerland and the protection that the Swiss Legation granted its officers.

"But I had to keep the two areas of my activities quite strictly separate," Feller said. "As a diplomat, I had to officially represent Swiss interests; as a private citizen, however, I felt I had to stand up for human rights."

Budapest was now teeming with German Wehrmacht troops. Paramilitary, pro-Nazi Arrow Cross gangs, SS officers and Gestapo personnel were also roaming the streets. Moreover, due to bombing and shelling by the advancing Soviet forces, living in the city had become extremely dangerous.

SWISS PROTECTION EXTENDED

According to the Swiss federal laws in force at that time, Swiss women marrying nationals of other states would automatically lose their Swiss citizenship. One of the twenty guests at Harald's house was a Hungarian Jew who had married a Swiss Jewish woman. It would have been extremely dangerous for him to live at home, and his wife, too, constantly ran the risk of being arrested, put in the ghetto and deported to a death camp. In view of the impending danger, the Swiss government reinstated Swiss nationality for all the women concerned.

Some years prior to the War, another Hungarian Jew, Willi Rottenberg, had married a Swiss-born Jewess named Bertha. They used to travel to Switzerland to spend their summer vacations in St. Gallen where Bertha's mother lived. In 1938 and 1939 they took along their little daughter Eva. Bertha's mother could see the signs of war. Convinced that the Jewish population was in great danger, she urged Willi and Bertha not to return to Hungary. But Willi Rottenberg did not share her fears, and returned to his home country with his young family, shortly before the War broke out.

For three years things remained relatively quiet in Hungary. Then in March 1944 the Nazi troops invaded, and Willi was among the first to be arrested. In the summer of the same year he was sent to the labor camp of Komarom.

At the Legation's offices, Feller had heard that there were a number of Swiss women married to Hungarians living in Budapest. The head of the Swiss Legation, Envoy Maximilian Jäger, officially entrusted Feller with the task of looking after

Frontal view of the famous Hotel Métropole, downtown Vienna, before 1938. (Source: Direktion der Museen der Stadt Wien)

four Jewish mothers and their children. Among them was Willi Rottenberg's wife Bertha and her daughter Eva. Bertha was pregnant with her second child at the time.

Harald was acutely aware that his own life was in danger, as he ran the risk of being picked up every time he secretly drove out of the city to the country farms to buy food for the clandestine guests at his home. Sometimes he made official visits to the ghetto in the center of Pest. When he saw what the Nazis and their Hungarian collaborators were doing to these human beings, he made up his mind to help wherever he could. Although he took the utmost care not to contravene the rules of his employer in his private activities, he knew that the authorities—Hungarian and German—were scrutinizing his every move, just waiting for him to make the slightest mistake

The former Hotel Métropole was confiscated and transformed into the Gestapo headquarters of the Ostmark (annexed Austria) in March 1938. It was here that the seven Jewish fugitives were taken, to be accommodated and lodged by the Gestapo overnight during their flight from Budapest to Switzerland in October 1944. Note the embrasures at the ground-floor windows. (Source: Direktion der Museen der Stadt Wien, HM Nr. 79.000/16.931)

as an excuse to declare him *persona non grata* and ask the Swiss government to recall him to Berne.

In October 1944, Hungarian Regent Nicholas Horthy was arrested and Ferenc Szálasi, leader of the fascist Arrow Cross, was appointed as Prime Minister by the German SS. The Nazi terror intensified from that time onwards, but Feller also stepped up his secret rescue work.

As Secretary of the Swiss Legation, Feller had been charged with the task of finding a way to bring these women and chil-

Today, in place of the bombed and demolished Hotel Métropole (Gestapo headquarters) is a monument, inscribed "NEVER FORGET". The plaque reads: "In this place was the Gestapo building. It was hell for all confessing Austrians. It was the gateway to death for many. It now lies in ruins, just like the Reich. Austria however, and our dead ones, will rise again…" Beneath it is another plaque dedicated to the "VICTIMS OF FASCISM". (Source: Andreas C. Fischer archives)

dren out of Hungary and safely back to Switzerland. A major problem was the fact that, whatever route he chose, it would lead the travelers through occupied countries. The shortest one, via Vienna—now capital of the German "Ostmark"—was particularly dangerous. All the preparations for the journey were under a cloud, he felt, as he could not personally accompany the small group of wary travelers to ensure their safety.

Instead, Harald asked the counselor for Jewish affairs at the German Legation to help him to prepare the necessary travel documents. Although he had officially negotiated with the German Legation for a safe journey through "Ostmark", he was most concerned about the possibility of random arrest, which would have led to internment in a concentration camp. The German official promised Feller not to disclose the fact that the women were Jewish. He also guaranteed that he would not let any harm come to them en route to the Swiss border. As it turned out, Harald had picked the right man for the job.

DEPARTURE DELAYED

Feller had found a spacious apartment outside the ghetto and away from the streets where Jews were forced to live. There he accommodated the four women and their children. They were relatively safe there. In August 1944, Bertha Rottenberg, in an advanced stage of pregnancy, expected that she, her daughter and their companions would soon be boarding the train to Switzerland. One evening, as she was carefully removing all the yellow stars from their clothes, she suddenly felt her contractions beginning. The thought crossed her mind that this was about the most inappropriate moment imaginable.

The next day, a message reached Feller at the office that Bertha Rottenberg had gone into labor and was in hospital. The departure would have to be postponed. A few days later, during a heavy bombing raid, Bertha gave birth to her second daughter, Vera. Mother and baby returned to the apartment.

The shelling of Budapest continued, and every time the sirens sounded, the families had to seek shelter in the basement of the house. The area just opposite the Hungarian National Museum was thought to be safe, but one day the museum suffered a direct hit. It burned down.

"One night, when we were again seeking shelter in the basement of the house," Eva Koralnik-Rottenberg recalls, "a bomb hit the neighboring building. Everything shook and the wall crumbled. A large piece of brick fell onto Vera's cot. The women screamed, but when we went to look, we found that nothing had happened to the baby."

The danger was such that they would have to leave Budapest and get away from the war zone immediately. Harald Feller came by the house personally to see the Rottenberg family and their friends. He mentioned that an escape to Switzerland through Austria had been arranged. He was very apprehensive about what could happen to the travelers once they were out of his reach, on the long train journey through Nazi-occupied territories. Well aware of the dangers they faced, the small group of four women, two children and the baby set out, carrying with them a little food for the journey, a cot and a supply of diapers. The children were carefully instructed to say only: "Papa is at the front," if anybody asked them.

The train to Vienna left from Budapest's Keleti pálya-udvar railway station. The windows of the wagons were blacked out with thick curtains, and the compartments were lit only by blue bulbs to prevent detection by reconnaissance aircraft. The train stopped every so often as bombs were dropped on towns along the railway route. "It was horrifying," Eva Koralnik-Rottenberg remembers, "and we were all afraid of what could happen." But they reached Vienna safely.

JEWISH GUESTS INCOGNITO AT THE "GESTAPO HOTEL"

At Vienna Westbahnhof station, to their utter dismay, the travelers found out that they had missed their connection. The next westbound train did not leave until the next day. As if out of nowhere, two Gestapo men in black leather coats approached the group and greeted them politely. They asked whether this was the family that was traveling to Switzerland. The question shocked Bertha Rottenberg, but she kept calm and replied in the affirmative. The Gestapo men invited them to come along. This was too much and Bertha declined, politely but firmly. They would prefer to stay and wait at the station.

The Germans then said that it was against their rules to leave women, children (and even a baby!) unattended at a railway station. When Bertha again politely refused, the Gestapo officers urged them to come along as the car was already waiting. Suddenly, a man who had been standing nearby said rather impatiently in Swiss German: "Just get on and don't create a fuss!" They never found out who he was.

After a short ride through downtown streets, the frightened women arrived at the prestigious Métropole Hotel, which had been transformed into the Gestapo headquarters. Eva Koralnik still remembers the grand entrance hall and the impressive lobby: it was very elegant, with lots of marble and red carpets. When the Jewish ladies entered, several of the men gave them the customary Nazi salute—not knowing, of course, who they were. A German shepherd dog, almost as big as Eva, wagged its tail; a friendly sign of welcome, perhaps.

The women and their children were led to a suite. Their baggage was kept at reception. They did not dare to say a word.

Bertha Rottenberg was unable to hide her nervousness, although the kind blonde room-maid soon brought them a bite to eat and something to drink. All was nicely arranged and served on a silver platter. The children devoured the sandwiches; they were very hungry. Bertha could not stop herself pacing around the suite all night, anxiously watching her baby and waiting for morning to come. The luggage never came up, so they all stayed in their traveling clothes.

At daybreak, the concierge called them to the lobby. After breakfast, a black Mercedes limousine took the women and children back to the Westbahnhof. They boarded the train, and found their luggage already stored in the racks above their seats. They did not realize that Harald Feller had organized everything with the help of his discreet German friend.

After many hours, the steam train finally arrived at Feldkirch, the westernmost city before the Swiss border. Here the group had no choice but to stay overnight at the station, because they had missed the last train to Switzerland. The station clerks put together a few wooden tables so that the women could sleep on them and did not have to huddle on the cold floor. As a token of their appreciation, the women shared their last cake with the station clerks, who in turn had brewed some tea.

During the night, the tension was mounting and became almost unbearable. So close to the border, would they make it or be caught? They almost panicked. But on the morning of October 6, 1944, they crossed the border without problems and arrived at Buchs. Safe at last!

Under Swiss immigration laws, all travelers from the "east" had to undergo a medical check. The border guards wanted to put them into quarantine. But after checking them for lice and parasites, they decided that these were "civilized" travelers, and let them continue their journey. A passer-by gave them some Swiss money for the train tickets to St. Gallen, and some change for a phone call to their relatives.

Bertha Rottenberg's mother was completely unaware of what had been going on in Hungary. She had regularly visited the internment camp at the barracks, asking refugees from Hungary whether they had any news of her relatives. Not hearing a word, she started to fear the worst. When the phone rang that day in October 1944, she was speechless with joy and relief.

The whole family went down to the station—mother, grandmother and even two uncles came. Tears of joy ran down everybody's cheeks. A hazardous journey had ended safely. In retrospect, they all realized that without the help and careful planning of Harald Feller, much, if not everything, could have gone wrong.

Eva, who did not speak a word of German at that time, was put in school right away. She had already learned to read and

Harald Feller and Eva Koralnik together with Meir Wagner at Hotel Bellevue Palace in Berne, 1999. (Source: Meir Wagner photo)

write at school in Budapest, but this new language was totally alien to her. The uncertainty and the fear of war stayed with her for years, especially as her family did not receive Swiss identification papers and was regarded as stateless for a long time. Willi Rottenberg was only allowed to emigrate to Switzerland many years after the war.

After completing her schooling in St. Gallen, Eva studied at the University of Geneva, where she obtained the diploma of the International Interpreter School. Her translation into German of an anthology of Israeli short stories, *"Shalom"*, was published by Diogenes Verlag, with a preface by Nobel prize-winning author Heinrich Böll. Today, Eva Koralnik is a partner in an international literary agency based in Zurich. She recently received the "Friends of Jerusalem Award" for her work on behalf of Israeli literature abroad.

Eva's younger sister Vera, born in war-torn Budapest in 1944, also lives in Switzerland today. Dr. Vera Rottenberg-Liatowitsch is a Federal Court judge at the Federal Tribunal in Lausanne, the highest position a judge can hold in Switzerland. One of her traveling companions on her eventful wartime journey had given her a "pengö", a small Hungarian coin; it shows the year it was minted: 1944. Vera wears it as a talisman on her wrist as a reminder of her flight to freedom.

THE DRAMA CONTINUES

Harald remained in Budapest. After the Germans had installed Szalási in October 1944, Envoy Jäger was recalled to Berne. He did not return to his post in Hungary. Other officials, among them counselor Kilchmann, also returned to Switzerland, leaving Harald Feller and the chancellor of the Swiss Legation, Max Meier, on their own.

Once, at the end of 1944, Harald escaped by the skin of his teeth. On December 29, his car with the Swiss ensign on the mudguard was stopped downtown by an Arrow Cross gang. Stopping diplomats' vehicles seemed to be their favorite pastime. Harald was violently forced out of the car and taken to a commando post where he was questioned and tortured. As if by a miracle, he was released in the early hours of the morning. It was a scary experience, but even this level of intimidation did not deter the young Swiss diplomat.

Although he was the youngest diplomat there, Harald Feller was appointed as interim head of the Swiss Legation. He was obliged, however, to leave his mansion to come and live at the office. This meant he would no longer be able to look after his private guests, a humanitarian task he had taken very seriously.

A few weeks after the invasion of the Red Army on February 12, 1945, Harald Feller and Max Meier were taken to

Moscow, where they were interned. As there were no diplomatic relations between the Soviet Union and Switzerland, for a long time nobody knew what had happened to the Swiss diplomats. In January 1946 they were allowed to return home.

Some of Harald Feller's extraordinary humanitarian deeds in wartime Budapest—both his official duties and his private rescue work—were recalled on September 6, 1999, at a special ceremony in Berne. The octogenarian (he was born on January 15, 1913) gave a very emotional speech about the events of 1944 and 1945, paying tribute particularly to Carl Lutz's formidable rescue efforts which surpassed his own by far.

Also present at the ceremony were Eva Koralnik and her sister, Federal Court Judge Dr. Vera Rottenberg-Liatowitsch, whose survival had been due to Harald Feller's intervention and assistance.

Israel's ambassador to Switzerland, Yitzhak Mayer, presented Harald Feller with the Yad Vashem "Righteous Among the Nations" medal. Feller humbly accepted it, in his words: "...on behalf all those men and women who selflessly helped refugees and whose names will probably never be known".

Charles-Jean Bovet

The Painstaking Priest Who Made Escape-Planning an Art

A native of the canton of Fribourg, Charles-Jean Bovet was a Catholic priest in France during the Second World War. He served in the parish of Archamps (a short distance from Geneva) from 1942 until November 1944. The area was teeming with refugees, and it was widely known that Father Bovet was willing to risk his life to help them. He offered to find ways and means to enable them to escape to Switzerland. Many refugees were saved as a result of his efforts.

One of those who escaped was Bernhard Blumenkranz, who had fled from Austria to southern France as early as 1938. When the German occupation was extended to this part of the country as well, he was arrested and taken to the concentration camp at Gurs. The terror at this camp became so unbearable that Blumenkranz decided to flee. When he was planning his escape, someone mentioned the name of Father Bovet—a name he would remember for the rest of his life.

After escaping from the camp, Blumenkranz sought out Father Bovet, whom he found to be friendly and encouraging. Bovet accommodated Bernhard at his house, where he planned his escape to Switzerland. Bernhard Blumenkranz later learned that Father Bovet had helped many Jews in the same manner and along the same route.

Another sworn opponent of the Nazi regime was the Catholic Bishop of Annecy. He was on the Germans' wanted list. He recalled how he got to know Father Bovet. "It was early in the morning of September 22, 1942, when I was trying to flee to Switzerland because the Gestapo had threatened to arrest me. A farmer volunteered to help me and took me to his farm. But, once there, he started lecturing me about the fact that I was not the only one in danger, and that I should think of the millions of soldiers on the various fronts in Europe and elsewhere in this war.

"Suddenly, a priest appeared at the house. I explained my situation, but he was not from the region and did not know how to help me. However, he promised that he would talk to a colleague. Father Bovet welcomed me warmly and soon we were talking about an escape route. He even offered me several options, so that I could choose the one I preferred.

"We waited until nightfall. Father Bovet knew exactly when the border guards passed the square. He therefore knew when would be the best moment for our clandestine border crossing. He had everything planned down to the minutest detail. He even had Swiss coins ready in case we needed to take the tramway to reach the center of Geneva.

"Everything went well, and I was deeply grateful for having been rescued. I wrote a letter to Father Bovet right after my successful arrival in Switzerland, but before sending it I had second thoughts. I realized that such a letter—if intercepted by the censors—would have endangered further rescue missions and the refugees, as well as Father Bovet himself. Therefore I did not mail the letter.

Forty years later, I looked for this unfinished letter and found it among my papers. I wanted to send it to Father Bovet, the man to whom I owed so much. My belated thanks came too late, though. Father Bovet had died at Dijon on March 20, 1952."

Arthur and Jeanne Lavergnat

The Heroes of "No-Man's-Land"

To the south of Geneva, at the foot of Mont Salève, there was a house and farm that, although located on the Swiss side of the border between France and Switzerland, effectively formed a sort of "no-man's-land" during the German occupation of France in 1943 and 1944. Both sides of the property were lined with barbed wire fencing. The Germans patrolled the length of the road in front of the house, while the Swiss army protected the territory behind the farm. Arthur Lavergnat and his wife Jeanne, who were market gardeners, lived here. From the windows of their house they watched many a dramatic scene taking place on French soil.

Arthur and Jeanne maintained contact with members of the Resistance who tried to smuggle refugees across this strip of land into Switzerland. Arthur, born at Bossey in France and raised in nearby Troinex, knew the area very well. Every time the escorts brought refugees to the fence, he not only signaled to them when the moment was most propitious to cross, but he also prepared gaps in the barbed wire fences on both sides of the strip.

Because of the insecure and dangerous situation, the refugees–once out of France–had to be housed clandestinely by the Lavergnats before they could be led across the second

258

fence into Switzerland. But during their stay they were received like relatives at the lonely house.

The risk to which Arthur and Jeanne exposed themselves by these illegal activities was enormous. On the French side, the local police watched things very closely. The German troops patrolled regularly and often fired random gunshots at the house. Between patrols, slipping across the border was possible, but always extremely risky.

The danger was even more real for the Lavergnats than for the smugglers. The Swiss border guards could raid the house at any time, and had they found any refugees hidden, they would have arrested the couple on the spot. No doubt the border guards were suspicious, but miraculously, not one of the escapes was ever discovered. In more than 40 instances, Arthur and Jeanne helped refugees make their escape through the barbed wire fences into Switzerland.

Rolande Birgy from Paris, who was one of the escorts for refugees during the war, remembered her experiences with the Lavergnats and the house in "no-man's-land".

"I often accompanied endangered Jewish children and adults to the border fence and to the house in the strip between France and Switzerland. Lavergnat always told us when the 'coast was clear'. We all knew that the strip was being kept under surveillance by an officer from Bossey castle where the Germans had set up their local headquarters, yet Lavergnat was never afraid.

"When we came to the fence, we found the gap that Lavergnat had prepared. The refugees passed through without luggage, as we had left it hidden close to the border. Lavergnat promised that he would get it later and smuggle it across.

"I crossed the border about forty times, accompanying refugees. These activities went on from March 1943 to August 18, 1944, and only once did we run into a German officer. I greeted him and he saluted back. Apparently, he took me for one of the locals.

"Lavergnat risked his life many times with his rescue activities. The German, French and Swiss border guards had instructions to shoot on sight when they discovered illegal refugees on the run. The house was a target for random shots; they could have hit Arthur or Jeanne."

Gilbert Ceffa from Geneva reported: "From 1942 to 1944 I was assisting Marius Jolivet, the parish priest of Collonges-sous-Salève. We were looking after members in the Franco-Swiss border region. Father Jolivet worked together with the Lavergnats who had a house in the no-man's-land between France and Switzerland. I witnessed many times how Jolivet took refugees to their house where they were hidden until it was safe to take them across the border to Switzerland."

Father Jolivet was an active member of the Reistance, involved in communicating military information from France to the American OSS (Office of Strategic Services) in Geneva, as well as facilitating the passage of people and messages to and from France and Switzerland. He was also later honored by Yad Vashem for his work in saving Jewish children. Protestant volunteers, including René Nodot, would bring the children to Father Jolivet's parish. From there, the Lavergnats' farm was the next step on their path to freedom in Switzerland. On the French side, Father Jolivet would watch from a hilltop to determine the best time to make the crossing.

After a brief stay on the Lavergnats' farm (ranging from a few a hours to several days), Arthur would take care of helping the fugitives to cross the border clandestinely, individually or in groups, past the Swiss border guards. Some Jewish children were smuggled across the border in a cart, hidden under vegetables grown on the farm and destined for the market in Geveva.

After the war, Arthur Lavergnat became a Swiss citizen. He was honored by the US government for his contribution to the work of the Office of Strategic Services.

On April 27, 1998 at the Swiss Federal Palace in Berne, a ceremony conducted by National Councilor François Loeb took place. Israel's Ambassador to Switzerland, Yitzhak Mayer, presented the Yad Vashem "Righteous Among the Nations" medal of honor to Jeanne Lavergnat and posthumously to her husband Arthur. Yitzhak Mayer had himself been a refugee in Switzerland during the war.

Attending the ceremony were the President of the Swiss Confederation, Flavio Cotti, the President of the Swiss Senate, Ulrich Zimmerli, many members of the Swiss parliament, US Ambassador Madeleine Kunin and the representative of Yad Vashem, Herbert Herz from Geneva.

Herz had collected eyewitness reports from many who survived as a result of the rescue work of Arthur and Jeanne Lavergnat. President Cotti mentioned in his speech that "in a time of darkness over Europe", some Swiss 'Righteous Among the Nations' had given a testimony to the principles of humanity. "We are glad," he said, "to have heroes among us, men and women who followed only the voice of their consciences and whose actions have been truly humanitarian."

In 1998, fifty of the "Righteous Among the Nations" from

around the world were invited to come to Israel for the fiftieth anniversary of the creation of the State of Israel. On that unforgettable occasion, Jeanne Lavergnat was there. She had been chosen to represent "the Righteous of Switzerland".

Epilogue

The Unsung Heroes We Can Never Repay

The roll call of heroism is not yet over. In a sense, of course, it never will be. We will never know exactly how many "ordinary," unassuming men and women quietly but resolutely risked life and livelihood to help preserve the lives of other members of the human race when it was within their power to do so. Whether known and celebrated or forever shrouded in anonymity, humankind owes them all a collective debt of gratitude that can never be repaid.

Yet there remains something that we, their heirs, can do in their honor— something, indeed, that we must not fail to do if we claim to be serious about sharing the values they lived and died by.

While the memory of these ambassadors of hope and humanity threatens to fade with every passing day, the more "newsworthy" leitmotifs of recent history continue to hit the headlines with relentless regularity and increasing intensity. The Red Cross and the Red Crescent are "alive and well"—and the relief they offer is still, tragically, much in demand. Individually, as well as in larger groups, human beings continue to suffer needlessly every day. The term "genocide" has entered our vocabulary, although "ethnic cleansing" sounds more politically correct these days—an opinion not shared, however, by those on the receiving end of the latest incarnation of man's inhumanity to man. Meanwhile, advances in technology promise to transform the previously unthinkable into the easily achievable in ways that would make the hair of yesterday's arch-criminals stand on end and consign their "grand designs" to the sandbox. We may have the technology of the future—but have we learned the lessons of the past? Will our children and grandchildren learn from our experience?

Actions speak louder than words! That was manifestly the case in the lives of the men and women whose stories are recounted in this book. History will record whether or not the citizens of the twenty-first century were willing to rise to the challenge.

What must be done? Let us recall the words of Yitzhak Mayer, Ambassador of the State of Israel to Switzerland, and himself a refugee in Switzerland during the war:

> The children of the Shoah generation have an obligation to do everything to see that the unfathomable evil will not be forgotten. But we are also obliged to name the good, which might be disparagingly small in comparison to the evil, but yet is of immense moral stature. We must make a universal effort at education, which has not yet begun, in order to trade onward the heritage of those few Righteous who stood up against the man-made horror. . . .
>
> This is an anthology of the courage to stand up for one's convictions. Tell the stories in the classrooms, on the radio, in your television studios. Weave them into your literature and stage plays, your scripts and novels. Spread the optimism and trust in the human capacity to rise to unimaginable heights of moral perfection. These are the heroes—Swiss heroes because they are Swiss—universal heroes because they are humans.

Bibliography

Actio Nr. 14, August–September 1988, Bulletin Schweizer RK,

Interview with Maurice Dubois

Adolf Eichmann, Götzen ("Idols") – prison memoirs, Haifa, 1961

Alexander Grossmann, Nur das Gewissen, Carl Lutz und seine Budapester Aktion, Verlag im Waldgut, Frauenfeld, 1986

Alfred Häsler, The Lifeboat is Full, Funk and Wagnalls, New York, 1969

André Durand, History of the ICRC

Anne-Marie Im Hof-Piguet, Fluchtweg durch die Hintertür, Eine Rotkreuz-Helferin im besetzten Frankreich 1942–1944, Verlag im Waldgut, Frauenfeld, 1985

Anne-Marie Im Hof-Piguet, La Filière-En France occupée 1942–1944, Edition de la Thièle, 1985

Arieh Ben-Tov, Das Rote Kreuz kam zu spät, Zurich, 1990

Arieh Ben-Tov, Facing the Holocaust in Budapest, The International Committee of the Red Cross and the Jews in Hungary, 1943-1945, Henry Dunant Institute, Geneva, 1988

August Bohny, Le Secours Suisse au Chambon-sur-Lignon

Carl Lutz, Die Judenverfolgungen unter Hitler in Deutschland, Neue Zürcher Zeitung, 30.6.1961

Carlo Schmid, Erinnerungen, Scherz, Berne/Munich/Vienna, 1979

Claudine & Daniel Pierrejean, Les secrets de l'Affaire Raoul Wallenberg, L'Harmattan, 1998

Claus Gaedeman, Paul Grüninger, Retter der Verfolgten, Das Beste aus Readers Digest, 5.5.1973

Die Zeit, No. 52 21. December 1979, p. 9-10 "Carlo Schmid"

Drago Arsenijevic, Voluntary Hostages of the SS, Editions France-Empire, Paris, 1984

Friedel Bohny-Reiter, Camp Rivesaltes, Secours aux internés, 1990

Friedel Bohny-Reiter, Journal des Rivesaltes 1941–1942, Editions Zoé, Carouge-Geneva, 1992

Friedel Bohny-Reiter, Verlauf der Vernichtung, Editions Zoé, Carouge-Geneva, 1992

Henri Duprez, 1940-1945 Même combat dans l'ombre et dans la lumière, La Pensée Universelle, Paris

Imanuel Heyman, 1942 Les enfants juifs de France à la frontière suisse, P-M Favre, Lausanne, 1984

Imanuel Leuschner, Konsul Carl Lutz im Dienste der Menschlichkeit, Heft Judaica, 1.3.1985

Jacques Rachel, Les juifs en Savoie du Moyen Age à nos jours, Edition Atra, 1984

Jacques Roth, Yovel, Albin Michel Verlag, 1982

Jean-Claude Favez, Une mission impossible? Le CICR, les déportations et les camps de concentration nazis, Editions Payot Lausanne, 1988

Laure Francken, Erinnerungen an Rettung im Sommer und Herbst 1942

Le Nouveau Quotidien, Sauvetage des Juifs à Rivesaltes

Lucy S. Dawidowicz, The War against the Jews 1933-45, Penguin Books, 1990

Marc-André Charguéraud, L'Étoile jaune et la Croix-Rouge: Le Comité international de la Croix-Rouge et l'Holocauste, 1939-1945, Labor et Fides, Geneva / Les Editions du Cerf, Paris, 1999

Marcel Junod, Warrior without Weapons, ICRC, Geneva, 1982

Marcel Pasche, Années de guerre et de fraternité, Edit. Ouverture, Lausanne 1995, ISBN 2-88413-045-4

Micha Grin, William Francken, Médecin de Campagne, Cabédita, 1962

Marcel Pasche, Années de guerre et de fraternité, Edit. Ouverture, Lausanne 1995, ISBN 2-88413-045-4

Micha Grin, William Francken, Médecin de Campagne, Cabédita, 1962

Mordecai Paldiel, The Path of the Righteous, KTAV Publishing House, Inc. and JFCR/ADL, 1993, ISBN 0-88125-376-6

Petra Weber, Carlo Schmid 1896 – 1979, C.H. Beck

Ph. Bogner, Ici on aimait les Juifs

Ph. Hallie, Das Blut der Unschuldigen

Rencontre, Editions régionales de l'Arche, Revue du FSJU, June/July 1970

René Nodot, Les enfants ne partiront pas!, Imprimerie nouvelle lyonnaise, Lyons, 1970

René Nodot, Résistance non violente 1940–1944, Memoires, Lyon type CRDP, 1978

Richard Deming, Heroes of the International Red Cross, ICRC, Geneva 1982

Saul Friedländer, Mit Rückkehr der Erinnerung

Sebastian Steiger, Die Kinder von Schloss La Hille, 1943: Am Fuss der Pyrenäen, Brunnen-Verlag, Basle, 1992

Stefan Keller, Délit d'Humanité, L'Affaire Grüninger, Introduction by Ruth Dreifuss, Editions d'En Bas, Lausanne

Stefan Keller, Geschichte von Flucht und Hilfe, Grüningers Fall, Rotpunktverlag, Zurich, 1994

The Archives of the Swiss Consul General Charles Lutz, Yad Vashem Studies, Vol. XV, Jerusalem, 1958

Yad Vashem, Archives of the Yad Vashem Holocaust Memorial, Jerusalem

Yehuda Bauer, American Jewry and the Holocaust

About the Author

Meir Wagner was born in Czernowitz, Romania on June 18, 1934. When he was seven years old, his entire family was deported to the Ukraine and interned in a concentration camp until the end of the war. Following the takeover of the family sawmill business by the communist state, he emigrated to Israel.

After graduating from Bar Ilan University in Theology and Education, he worked as a high school teacher, and later spent four years as a visiting professor of Jewish Studies in Johannesburg, South Africa.

Meir is married to Swiss-born Else Ruth Kahn. They have three sons, and moved to Switzerland in 1970 to manage the family-owned Hotel Silberhorn at Grindelwald, a popular resort in the Swiss Alps. Meir was a member of the tourist board of the Jungfrau region of the Bernese Oberland and actively promoted the region internationally, quickly earning the title of "foreign minister" of Grindelwald. He also worked closely with Swiss members of parliament and was asked to lead a parliamentary information delegation to Israel. He was received at the White House by President Ronald Reagan and presented him with a special collection of Swiss souvenirs.

At a meeting with British Prime Minister Margaret Thatcher, Wagner extended an invitation for several hundred Gulf War pilots of the US, British, French and Canadian air forces to spend two weeks at Grindelwald for rest and recuperation as guests of the Bernese Oberland region. His humanitarian initiative was officially recognized and did much to enhance relations between Switzerland and the countries concerned.

Since the fall of the Iron Curtain, Meir Wagner has been instrumental in opening new air traffic routes, and promoting tourism and cultural exchanges. As an unofficial ambassador for Switzerland, dedicated to global understanding, he continues to play a key role in building bridges between nations and has been the guest of heads of state throughout Eastern and Northern Europe.

Invited to contribute to a "think tank" of Swiss members of parliament headed by National Councilor François Loeb, Meir Wagner suggested that the positive role played by Swiss citizens, diplomats and Red Cross representatives during the Second World War deserved to be brought to the attention of a wider public. His suggestion was warmly welcomed, and this book was the direct result.